Postcolonial No

ROUTLEDGE RESEARCH IN POSTCOLONIAL LITERATURES

Edited in collaboration with the Centre for Colonial and Postcolonial Studies, University of Kent at Canterbury, this series presents a wide range of research into postcolonial literatures by specialists in the field. Volumes will concentrate on writers and writing originating in previously (or presently) colonized areas, and will include material from non-anglophone as well as anglophone colonies and literatures. Series editors: Donna Landry and Caroline Rooney.

1. *Magical Realism in West African Fiction: Seeing with a Third Eye* by Brenda Cooper
2. *The Postcolonial Jane Austen* edited by You-Me Park and Rajeswari Sunder Rajan
3. *Contemporary Caribbean Women's Poetry: Making Style* by Denisede Caires Narain
4. *African Literature, Animism and Politics* by Caroline Rooney
5. *Caribbean-English Passages: Intertextuality in a Postcolonial Tradition* by Tobias Döring
6. *Islands in History and Representation* edited by Rod Edmond and Vanessa Smith
7. *Civility and Empire: Literature and Culture in British India, 1822–1922* by Anindyo Roy
8. *Women Writing the West Indies, 1804–1939: 'A Hot Place, Belonging To Us'* by Evelyn O'Callaghan
9. *Postcolonial Pacific Writing: Representations of the body* by Michelle Keown
10. *Writing Woman, Writing Place: Contemporary Australian and South African Fiction* by Sue Kossew
11. *Literary Radicalism in India: Gender, Nation and the Transition to Independence* by Priyamvada Gopal
12. *Postcolonial Conrad: Paradoxes of Empire* by Terry Collits
13. *American Pacificism: Oceania in the U.S. Imagination* by Paul Lyons
14. *Decolonizing Culture in the Pacific: Reading History and Trauma in Contemporary Fiction* by Susan Y. Najita
15. *Writing Sri Lanka: Literature, Resistance and the Politics of Place* by Minoli Salgado
16. *Literature of the Indian Diaspora: Theorizing the Diasporic Imaginary* by Vijay Mishra
17. *Secularism in the Postcolonial Indian Novel: National and Cosmopolitan Narratives in English* by Neelam Srivastava
18. *English Writing and India, 1600–1920: Colonizing Aesthetics* by Pramod K. Nayar
19. *Decolonising Gender: Literature, Enlightenment and the Feminine Real* by Caroline Rooney
20. *Postcolonial Theory and Autobiography* by David Huddart
21. *Contemporary Arab Women Writers* by Anastasia Valassopoulos
22. *Postcolonialism, Psychoanalysis and Burton: Power Play of Empire* by Ben Grant
23. *Transnationalism in Southern African Literature: Modernists, Realists, and the Inequality of Print Culture* by Stefan Helgesson
24. *Land and Nationalism in Fictions from Southern Africa* by James Graham
25. *Paradise Discourse, Imperialism, and Globalization: Exploiting Eden* by Sharae Deckard
26. *The Idea of the Antipodes: Place, People, and Voices* by Matthew Boyd Goldie
27. *Feminism, Literature and Rape Narratives: Violence and Violation* edited by Sorcha Gunne and Zoë Brigley Thompson
28. *Locating Transnational Ideals* edited by Walter Goebel and Saskia Schabio
29. *Transnational Negotiations in Caribbean Diasporic Literature: Remitting the Text* by Kezia Page
30. *Representing Mixed Race in Jamaica and England from the Abolition Era to the Present* by S. Salih
31. *Postcolonial Nostalgias: Writing, Representation and Memory* by Dennis Walder

Related Titles

Postcolonial Life-Writing: Culture, Politics, and Self-Representation by Bart Moore-Gilbert

Postcolonial Nostalgias

Writing, Representation, and Memory

Dennis Walder

Routledge
Taylor & Francis Group
NEW YORK AND LONDON

First published 2011
by Routledge 2 Park Square, Milton Park, Abingdon, OX144RN
Simultaneously published in the USA and Canada
by Routledge
711 Third Avenue, NewYork, NY 10017

Routledge is an imprint of the Taylor & Francis Group, an informa business

© 2011 Dennis Walder

First issued in paperback 2012

The right of Dennis Walder to be identified as author of this work has been asserted by him/her in accordance with sections 77 and 78 of the Copyright, Designs and Patents Act 1988.

Typeset in Baskerville by IBT Global

All rights reserved. No part of this book may be reprinted or reproduced or utilised in any form or by any electronic, mechanical, or other means, now know nor hereafter invented, including photocopying and recording, or in any information storage or retrieval system, without permission in writing from the publishers.

Library of Congress Cataloging-in-Publication Data
Walder, Dennis.
  Postcolonial nostalgias : writing, representation and memory / by Dennis Walder.
    p. cm. — (Routledge research in postcolonial literatures ; 31)
  Includes bibliographical references and index.
  1. Commonwealth fiction (English)–History and criticism. 2. English fiction–20th century–History and criticism. 3. Nostalgia in literature. 4. Postcolonialism in literature. I. Title.
  PR9084.W35 2011
  823'.91409353–dc22
                                           2010017580

ISBN13: 978-0-415-44533-7 (hbk)
ISBN13: 978-0-203-84038-2 (ebk)
ISBN13: 978-0-415-62829-7 (pbk)

For Mary, Anna, and Rohan

Contents

	Preface and Acknowledgements	ix
1	Introduction: The Persistence of Nostalgia	1
2	'How is it going, Mr. Naipaul?': Remembering Postcolonial Identites	24
3	'The Broken String': Remembering the Homeland	47
4	'Alone in a Landscape': Remembering Doris Lessing's Africa	72
5	Recalling the Hidden Ends of Empire: W. G. Sebald	94
6	Remembering 'Bitter Histories': From Achebe to Adichie	116
7	Nostalgia for the Present: J. G. Ballard's *Empire of the Sun*	139
8	Endnote	163
	Notes	169
	Bibliography	189
	Index	203

Preface and Acknowledgements

This book consists of a series of comparative reflections upon the representation in literary and, occasionally, related cultural forms of memory, and especially that aspect of memory that has a special resonance for migrants and others entangled by the long histories of colonialism—that is, nostalgia. I think of myself as a postcolonial, 'diasporic' subject; hence this book is motivated by a personal response to particular events, texts, and images. However, my aim has been to generalise my own and, at times, my family's colonial experiences so as to provide some purchase on the experiences of others—an obligation which, I argue, is often forgotten, even in the memory business.

I have had a long-term interest in representations of memory and identity, with Southern Africa a continuing thread, providing one instance of the degree to which, in societies with histories of exploiting difference to maintain inequalities of power, the sense of identity is not just a matter of negotiation, as some theorists put it, but a site of profound uncertainty and a struggle to remember and forgive as well as to forget. The ambiguities generated by this struggle suggest new possibilities for bringing value judgements into play in discussing a wider range of texts and their shifting interpretations than I can deal with here, and in that sense, this study is intended to be exemplary rather than comprehensive.

Earlier versions of parts of this book have appeared in *Journal of Commonwealth Studies*, *Textual Practice*, *Third World Quarterly,* and *Postcolonial Studies: Changing Perceptions*, Trento: Dip. di Studi Letterari, 2006. I am grateful to their editors. I wish to thank Bill Bell and Faith Pullin of Edinburgh University for inviting me to give the annual Blackwell Lecture for 2004, which began the trail completed in this book. I would also like to thank the following for advice, conversation, encouragement, and, in some cases, for inviting me to present further talks and papers from which the book has grown: Jenny Altschuler, Elleke Boehmer, Duncan Brown, Jeanne Colleran, Sara Rich Dorman, Kai Easton, Miki Flockemann, Tag Gronberg, Suman Gupta,

Abdulrazak Gurnah, Isabel Hofmeyr, Philip Holden, Glenn Hooper, Lyn Innes, David Johnson, Douglas Kerr, Premesh Lalu, Mary MacLeod, Bart Moore-Gilbert, Mpalive Msiska, Alastair Niven, Oriana Palusci, the late Paul Overy, Rajeev Patke, Caroline Rooney, Angela Smith, Lindy Stiebel, Dan Vukovich, William Watkin, Susan Watkins, Michael Wessels.

I would also like to thank the British Academy and the Open University Arts Faculty Research Committee for their financial support. The British Library and the Open University Library were invaluable resources. The Manuscripts and Archives Department at the University of Cape Town Library kindly allowed access to the unique Bleek/Lloyd Collection (see Chapter 3). Finally, I would like to thank Jonathan Price for expert help with the proofs and index.

1 Introduction
The Persistence of Nostalgia

> I see nothing in the future that tempts me; all that can charm me now is to recollect the past, and my recollections of the time of which I speak, as vivid as they are true, often let me live content in the midst of my misfortunes.
>
> Jean-Jacques Rousseau, *Confessions*, 1782–89[1]

> That is the land of lost content,
> I see it shining plain,
> The happy highways where I went
> And cannot come again.
>
> A. E. Housman, '*A Shropshire Lad*', 1896[2]

> ... the whole world is summed up in that sunlight on a palace in Venice which makes us determine on our journey.
>
> Marcel Proust, *By Way of Sainte-Beuve* [1908][3]

> Too strange the sudden change
> Of the times we buried when we left.
>
> Lenrie Peters, 'Home Coming', 1981[4]

Introduction: The Scope and Argument of this Book

Nostalgia in a curious way connects people across historical as well as national and personal boundaries. I call it curious because I cannot think of a better word for describing that strange, even uncanny mix of individual and social desires that prompts the search for remembered times and places that constitutes it, and which seems to become prominent at certain critical periods of human history, including our own. Nostalgia was first named in the mid seventeenth century, and first emerged widely during the rise of industrialisation in modern Europe, when the writings of the European Romantics challenged what was happening in the world by exploring—as

Rousseau and Goethe and Wordsworth explored—the restorative, nurturing potential of memory for the threatened individual. During the nineteenth century it was of central importance in writers and thinkers as far apart as Dickens and Turgenev or Ruskin and Nietzsche, an importance heightened in the early twentieth century by the works of Bergson, Freud, and Proust. Nearer our own time, the rise in migration and exile accompanying the ends of empire and the disasters of war explored by writers as varied as Doris Lessing and W. G. Sebald, Chinua Achebe and J. G. Ballard, has led to a representation of the present as a place marked by a trail of survivors searching for their roots, for a home, in the ruins of history.

Clambering over those ruins, one finds a dim, borderline area, an area characterised by the historian E. J. Hobsbawm as a 'twilight zone'. 'For all of us', he says in the Overture to the finale of *The Age of Empire*,

> there is a twilight zone between history and memory; between the past as a generalized record which is open to relatively dispassionate inspection and the past as a remembered part of, or background to, one's own life. For individual human beings this zone stretches from the point where living family traditions or memories begin—say, from the earliest family photo which the oldest living family member can identify or explicate—to the end of infancy, when public and private destinies are recognized as inseparable and as mutually defining one another.

'The length of this zone may vary,' Hobsbawm adds, 'and so will the obscurity and fuzziness that characterizes it. But there is always such a no-man's land of time. It is by far the hardest part of history for historians, or for anyone else to grasp'.[5] That is why people might turn to writers to represent that zone—or to artists, since, as that homely, domestic object the family photo suggests, it could be a visual representation or image that becomes the only remaining, half-remembered trace of the point at which the past of an individual connects with the wider, collective pasts of family, society, and history.

In the chapters which follow I aim to penetrate that twilight zone, the uncertain zone between memory and history, as a way of trying to understand what I am calling postcolonial nostalgia—or rather, I refer to postcolonial nostalgias in the plural since, as soon becomes apparent, there are many forms of the phenomenon I am trying to identify, and it would be wrong to assume that these forms can be captured by one defining statement. I should add that I am not going to try to deal with the phenomenon of nostalgia in all its complex and pervasive embodiments here; rather, this is an attempt to look at some of the ways the feelings we commonly associate with it have affected the work of a selection of late-twentieth-century writers (mainly novelists) for whom the impact of European colonialism in one form or another has been crucial. I am especially, but not exclusively, interested in contemporary figures whose links with earlier times and places have been severed by migration or displacement, and who have consequently felt a sharper need to represent or explore their own memories, with more or less nostalgia. My selection of writers and writings reflects my own background and interests, which the reader will easily discern in what follows. My hope is that this will make it all the easier to engage with my arguments, and to think of alternative or counter-examples from other backgrounds and histories.

It is clear that nostalgia is a widespread, if not universal, phenomenon, although the term itself is profoundly European in origin. I am going to explore some of the ways in which it has emerged as a complex form of representation for writers concerned to express their relationship with the recalled or remembered pasts they identify with; in particular, those whose pasts have been shaped by empire and/or colonisation. The basic idea informing this exploration is a simple one: I will be arguing that the rosy, sentimental glow most commonly associated with nostalgia is only a part of the story, and that pursuing its manifestations with a proper sense of the complex of feelings and attitudes it engages, and the contexts upon which it draws, reveals its potential as a source of understanding and creativity. The suspicion and mistrust with which it has been viewed by progressives, as a source of individual self-indulgence or collective myopia, reflects a lack of understanding of the breadth and significance of the phenomenon—or perhaps the fact that the radical left has its own forms of nostalgia, too. Not only is nostalgia deeply implicated in the political life of people, it is a part of their historical sense of themselves.[6]

Nostalgia begins in desire, and may well end in truth. It can, and often does, serve as a key to the multiple pasts that make us who and what we are, for better or worse. This is particularly the case in relation to the histories and experiences that fall under the rubric of the postcolonial, a term that has enjoyed a dazzling marketing success, despite, or perhaps because of, much theoretical and political ambiguity, and so should not be deployed without at least some clarification.[7] I should say I used the term (in its hyphenated version) myself, in a book on *Post-colonial Literatures in English*, where I argued for the need to attend to the astonishing rise of 'new writings' from countries formerly under the sway of the Western powers. And as I concluded there, the ambiguities of the term being many, the writings under its rubric might be best defined in terms of the conditions of their production, reception, and evaluation, that is, who wrote them, where did they originate, who read them, and how were they interpreted and valued.[8] The answers involve constructing narratives that reach back, and forward, as writers and critics try to chart the changing world we live in, while engaging with its challenges. This is a difficult task, not least because of the utopian tendency of much postcolonial cultural criticism to always seek the moral and political high ground in relation to past and present injustices.[9] Here I will try to avoid excessive claims to relevance and radicalism, using 'postcolonial' simply to identify a range of experiences and representations produced by intercultural and transnational conflict, migration, and enforced settlement since the long withdrawing roar of empire in the twentieth century.

Not that empires as such ever end: the urge to dominate and control, 'bearing the sword, and often the torch' as Conrad's Marlow put it,[10] continues; but the European empires to which he was alluding have become memories, dreams—and nightmares. How, when, and where we exhibit a yearning after those times, while acknowledging the problematic of that yearning, is what concerns me most in this book. By 'we' I mean people who have recently emerged from the grip of colonialism, whether they are called colonisers or colonised—overlapping categories too often set against each other in a frozen binary, despite the work of critics like Ashis Nandy or Homi Bhabha, who insist upon their intimacy.[11]

Nostalgia, Memory, and Writing

It is of course possible to recall and reflect upon the past as an individual or a group without being affected by nostalgia, although it is often difficult to disentangle nostalgic feelings from the operations of memory more generally. Memory has for some considerable time now been the focus of a large and growing area of literary and cultural study, to the extent that, some would say, memory fatigue has set in.[12] But nostalgia has been relatively neglected, perhaps because it is so familiar—'the good old days', have we not all been there at some time? Or perhaps because it so often seems to have negative implications—'sentimental kitsch' is only one of the vast penumbra of dubious associations around the word.

Since nostalgia is such a familiar, everyday experience, it has been no surprise to find representations of it everywhere. What has surprised me, however, is how little, relatively speaking, has been written about it from a critical or analytical point of view.[13] Nonetheless, I will be referring in what follows to some of the key works that have appeared in recent years, notably Svetlana Boym's ground-breaking study of *The Future of Nostalgia* (2001). Yet struggling to survive in the present—a time not only of the end of empires but of increased globalisation, ethnic tension, and national self-questioning—creates a widespread need to redefine the self, and many works reflect this need. Hence, too, the renewed interest in family history, memoir, and heritage, and the commemorative mania that seems increasingly a feature of contemporary cultural life in the postcolonial world. These phenomena do not necessarily involve nostalgia; but insofar as they feature moments of melancholy, yearning, and what in German is known as *Das Heimweh* (or home-longing) nostalgia is part of what they represent.

Nostalgia is usually thought of in terms of longing and desire—for a lost home, place, and/or time. But it is also more than that: it is a longing for an experience—subjective in the first place, and yet, far from limited to the individual. It is possible to speak of a group or even a whole society as nostalgic. *Time* magazine once asked: 'How much more nostalgia can America take?' The answer was, apparently, that since all Western culture for the last two thousand years seems to have involved nostalgia (the Romans looking back at the Greeks, the Renaissance looking back at the Romans, the Pre-Raphaelites . . .), and since looking back was a source of pleasure in tough times, 'play it again, Sam—and again and again and again'.[14] The British, according to a recent popular history, have for some time been a nostalgia-filled people, but alas this, it seems, is precisely what has held them back.[15] Nostalgia and national identity are inextricably entwined, as 'Britain's favourite Nostalgia and Heritage Magazine', *Best of British*, demonstrates, its pages replete with 'all our yesterdays', combining 'affectionate glimpses of yesteryear with all that is special about this country today'.[16] In France, the national obsession with heritage and an idealised rural past, summed up in the term *le patrimoine*, has produced an extraordinary, indeed unique work: Pierre Nora's *Les Lieux de Mémoire* (1984–92), a three-part, seven-volume, 5,600-page collective opus attempting to collate all those places, concepts, and people which had for centuries made up French identity, but might soon be lost forever. Notably absent from this collective recreation of identity were Jews (one brief chapter) and Muslims (no mention at all). Selective nostalgia has inevitably been more apparent in Germany, although not always for the obvious reasons: how, when, and where to refer to the Holocaust has been one issue; another has been dealing with the ambivalence of memories of the Communist era, memories defined appropriately enough as *Ostalgie*.[17]

Selective nostalgia is even more of an issue when we think about the wider world. Recent work on memory in relation to history (by, for example, Dominick LaCapra) has been dominated by a concern with Holocaust memories;[18] less has been written about memories of the dispossession, trauma, and genocide associated with colonisation. On one level, there is an obvious reason for this: in the former colonies the historical narrative has often had to be constructed out of stories and myths, the documents of imperialism having been written, by and large, by the conquerors not the conquered. 'The powerful and the literate leave artefacts and documents for posterity' writes Jay Naidoo; 'the weak and illiterate leave dust and silence'.[19] And yet, as Gayatri Chakravorty Spivak proposed some time ago now, the silent dispossessed leave traces which may be pursued, despite a proper suspicion of 'clear-cut nostalgia' towards them; while Homi Bhabha argued for a deconstructive reading of texts produced under colonisation that, through a mimicry of the coloniser's voice, exposed and denied its authority. Either way, though, the colonised seem to remain prisoners of history.[20]

Then there is the continued narrowness of the range of Eurocentric thinking that, as Peter Hulme has noted, postcolonial studies is still dedicated to surpassing, including those 'most resistant categories' of thought so 'deeply embedded that we have come to think of them simply as parts of a natural geohistorical landscape'. None of these categories, he adds, has a 'deader hand' than that of historical periodisation.[21]

Hulme has himself done much to extend the range of postcolonial studies back beyond the twentieth century, unearthing documents and images that tell of what has been ignored or neglected about the earliest encounters between Native Americans and European travellers, for example, thereby making scholars at least aware of what was lost as well as found in these encounters. Contemplating this kind of work operates as a challenge to the narrowness, the amnesia of much historical investigation, suggesting that what has been called the provincialising of Europe, and indeed of North America, with respect to the South (America, Africa, Asia) is long overdue.[22] In the absence of records, of an archive in the traditional sense, what this implies is a willingness to read, and listen, 'against the grain', acknowledging that memory resides outside as well as within the library or museum. This implies also a new understanding of the nature of history as a construct, as thinkers since Nietzsche have proposed—perhaps most strikingly in Jacques Derrida's *Archive Fever* (1995), although the limitations of his psychoanalytically oriented approach become apparent in a postcolonial context.[23]

Clearly, it is through the inscription or reinscription of the past that this kind of insight into the complexities of memory, and hence of nostalgia, is being produced. From Plato and Aristotle onwards memory has been thought of as a kind of impression made upon the mind, such as that made by a stylus upon a piece of wax. Although that simple model has long been overtaken by a variety of metaphors, including the image of memory as a storehouse or archive, the metaphor of memory as imprinting continues to resonate—in Freud, for example, for whom the earliest memories impressed upon the mind continue to survive in the unconscious. The focus here is upon those who inscribe, their inscriptions, and how we read them—that is, upon writers: and, primarily but not exclusively, upon narrative—despite the obvious use of remembering in other literary or quasi-literary forms, in poetry and song, drama and story-telling—not to mention photography and film, where the role of nostalgia has been immense. Arguably memory tends in any case towards narrative representation even in strictly non-narrative genres, especially in the oral form which is, as Richard Kearney says, the 'quintessentially *communicative* act'.[24]

Memory, or Mnemosyne as the Greeks called her, was the mother of all the Muses, and invention or imagination depends utterly upon remembering. Moreover, situating ourselves in time and space involves us in constructing a thread of meaning that enables us to know, or think we know, who and what we are in the present: in other words, by narrative. Our consciousness, as thinkers from St Augustine to Hume and Locke, from Rousseau to Freud and Damasio have suggested, is held together by a narrative of memory. Indeed, when the neurologist Antonio Damasio attempts to describe the creation of a relatively stable self in the face of the flux in all things, he resorts to the language of narrative fiction: 'You know it is *you* seeing because the story depicts a character—you—doing the seeing . . . Knowing springs to life in the story . . . '.[25]

Memory and fictional creation appear to be inextricably entwined; and somewhere in there lies nostalgia, with all the ambiguities and contradictions it brings in its wake. Hence my emphasis here upon writers of narrative— which does not mean only the novel, but a range of literary and related genres, more or less fictional.[26]

According to Adam Muller: 'It would be easy to remain vague about nostalgia, risking nothing and letting our presumably shared intuitions do the work of establishing the pretence that we are in agreement about its central terms of reference, its power, and its deep implication in the fabric of our modern psychic lives'.[27] Perhaps it is time to try to clarify a little more the meaning of the term itself as it has come down to us.

Defining Nostalgia: From the Medical to the Psychological

According to the *New Oxford English Dictionary*, the current core sense of the term 'nostalgia' is 'a sentimental longing, or wistful affection for the past, typically for a period or place with happy personal associations'. Additionally, it is 'the evocation of these feelings, especially in commercialised form', for example, 'an evening of TV nostalgia'. This is accurate, if narrow. As Michael Wood once remarked, nostalgia was always universal, in the sense that most cultures 'dream of golden ages and gardens of Eden, and even so-called primitives dream of an even more primitive past, the original, unspoiled season described in so many myths'; while for most of us non-so-called primitives, 'we remember odd patches of our lives with especial affection, sometimes patches that were not in themselves particularly pleasant—they provoke a sort of tenderness just because they are fragments of our past, pieces of ourselves'.[28]

But if there is an element of temptation, difficult to resist, about our personal pasts when we think of looking back, this tenderness towards ourselves may easily blind us to the pasts of others. 'Nostalgia', remarked Raymond Williams, 'is universal and persistent; only other men's nostalgias offend'.[29] If so, this offending is a matter of concern, particularly where the problem of access to the voice of 'the other' is of pressing interest, as is the case for those who inhabit a postcolonial world, or who share an interest in its configurations. But, as Svetlana Boym says at the end of *The Future of Nostalgia*, we are all in a sense survivors of the twentieth century, and thus nostalgic by definition, whether we see ourselves as modern or postmodern.[30] Boym's is the most substantial attempt to date to account for the global epidemic of longing for an earlier time or place or home that besets us, while defining that 'us' almost entirely in terms of the contemporary urban experience of North America and Eastern Europe, including Russia. Less substantial but with a similar focus, Andreea Deciu Ritivoi's *Yesterday's Self* builds on Boym's approach while stressing the paradoxical nature of dislocation as a 'cure' as well as a 'poison' for those who migrate and long for their original home.[31]

The word 'nostalgia' comes from two Greek roots, though it did not originate in Greece; as Boym says, it is only 'nostalgically Greek'.[32] From '*nostos*'—returning home, and '*algia*'—pain or longing, the term was created by Johannes Hofer, in a 1688 medical dissertation for the University of Basel, in which he attempted to describe and name a condition he had observed among young Swiss abroad. His choice of terms sprang from what he saw as 'the grief for the lost charm of the Native Land', a grief his fellow Swiss called '*das Heimweh*', while among the French it 'merited the name *la Maladie du Pays*'. But lacking 'a particular name in medicine', Hofer proceeded to supply one, thereby helping both to identify and no doubt further increase the disease. Its aetiology was a mystery: the disease appeared to spread from the brain through the body, the sufferer's afflicted imagination having been aroused by the idea of the recalled native land, resulting in nausea, sleeplessness, loss of appetite, fever, cardiac arrest, and even attempted suicide. According to Hofer, the sole cure was a prompt return to the homeland, although drugs could mitigate the condition.[33]

The Swiss, who were often employed abroad as servants and soldiers, were it seems particularly prone to nostalgia. Swiss scientists began to note the importance for nostalgics of taste and sound—mothers' soups and Alpine folk tunes having a notable impact. Soon others were observed displaying similar symptoms. Scots Highlanders away from home were liable to be incapacitated by the sound of bagpipes being played (there is a word in Scots Gaelic for nostalgia—*cianalas*); and when the Russian army entered Germany in 1733, it was only the threat of being buried alive that dispelled the appearance of nostalgia among the ranks.[34] Despite American doctors claiming their young country was free of this conspicuously European ailment, by the time of the Civil War in the 1860s it was observed there too, especially among young conscripts from rural homes. Hofer claimed homesickness was an expression of patriotic fervour; but for American military doctor Theodore Calhoun it revealed a lack of manliness that disgraced the nation. Either way, the medicalisation of nostalgia reinforced the sense that here was an ailment to be taken seriously.[35]

The connection with displacement from home persists into modern times, when however the clinical and military resonances disappear, and a psychological and psychiatric discourse takes over. Nostalgia becomes a state of mind rather than a physical condition, although the somatic continues as an undercurrent of implication.[36] Proust is a key figure in this development, leaning on Freud and Bergson to emphasise the inward, sensory nature of memory with his massive '*Recherche*' into lost time, in which he set up a distinction between voluntary recall, and the involuntary return of past scenes created by scents, tastes, and images. For Proust, the involuntary return to 'lost' times brought a kind of truth of the past into the present, reviving not merely the past moment, but the epiphanic experience of the past in its entirety. As this suggests, there is a profound association between the development of the modernist sensibility and the idea of nostalgia as a pathway to spirituality—even if, as in Baudelaire, nostalgia for the past was expressed in a very physical way. The importance of the senses as a source of potentially transformative early memories is clearly noticeable in modernist literary texts, from James Joyce's *A Portrait of the Artist as a Young Man* (1916) and *Ulysses* (1922) to Virginia Woolf's *Mrs Dalloway* (1925), originally named *The Hours*.

Although still widespread in contemporary culture, however, nostalgia eludes clear definition; it remains, as Davis concludes, 'susceptible to semantic vagueness, drift and ambiguity'.[37] Yet the yearning for a different and previous time/place/experience remains fundamental. Echoing Susan Stewart's *On Longing* (1996), Boym sees nostalgia as a generalised desire for origins, for unmediated experience, that tries to defeat time. Figured as the 'mourning of displacement and temporal irreversibility', it is, she argues, at 'the very core of the modern condition', a symptom of the age.[38] Nostalgia does seem to be a particularly seductive phenomenon for people who have literally been displaced, as all those earlier young soldiers were displaced. Avoiding the temptation is not necessarily sensible, even if it is possible; succumbing to it can and indeed should be a first step upon the path of knowledge. Exploring nostalgia can and should open up a negotiation between the present and the past, leading to a fuller understanding of the past and how it has shaped the present, for good and bad, and how it has shaped the self in connection with others, a task that may bring pain as well as pleasure.

Such negotiation involves a level of self-reflexivity about or within nostalgia. Only in this way may the sense of the difference between present and past at the heart of nostalgia counteract its undeniably negative tug towards self-indulgence and misperception. It is potentially the source of a double perspective: towards the past in its relation to the present, through the memories of the self as both actor and spectator. This doubleness is encouraged by the distancing effect of both aesthetic and historical consciousness. Milan Kundera defined nostalgia as 'the suffering caused by an unappeased yearning to return'.[39] This was in a novel about two former lovers who return from exile to their Czech homeland to find that their memories no longer match. Their nostalgia defeats them, because it is too absorbed in itself, it is ignorant of history. The more conscious we are of our own nostalgia, the more we reflect upon it, the more aware we may become of our history. If nostalgia is often enough characterised in negative terms, then it seems as if history is what might rescue it.

Nostalgia, History, and Politics

Despite the lack of clear borders to the concept, some historians have argued that the conditions in which nostalgia will develop can be identified. In particular, it has been suggested, modern societies share a view of time as 'linear, with an undetermined future'. According to this argument a cyclic view of time, or a view of time as reaching an apotheosis, would make nostalgia unattractive, whereas a view of time as linear and secular would promote it. A second requirement would be 'some sense that the present is deficient'. Shifting power structures within societies and between countries lead to an erosion in confidence in the present, and an elegiac turn to the past. The fall of empires, like the collapse of a class or regime, provides an obvious example. Thirdly, it is a requirement for nostalgia that 'objects, buildings, and images from the past should be available'. Modern technology (photography, film, DVDs, and the Internet) has ensured such availability. In short, a sense of time that includes linearity, secularity, and inadequacy supplies the necessary, if not sufficient, requisites for nostalgia.[40]

What this seems to indicate is that nostalgia is a feature of what is loosely called modernity. The difficulty of this is identifying it in terms of history, since the very concept of history itself comes under question in defining the modern, as Nietzsche forcefully demonstrated.[41] Earlier attempts to bring about a rational and humane order to human affairs have been radically undermined by the catastrophic developments of the recent past, with the result that, for someone like the émigré T. S. Eliot, the use of myth becomes 'a way of controlling, of ordering, of giving a shape and a significance to the immense panorama of futility and anarchy which is contemporary history'.[42] The readiness to move towards a nostalgic reverence for authority and tradition out of this sense of the immediate past reminds us, if reminder were needed, of the conservative, even reactionary potential of the phenomenon.

For others, such as Walter Benjamin, the catastrophes of the present lead to a critique of the progressive, linear sense of history, summed up in his famous description of a Paul Klee painting, 'Angelus Novus' or 'The Angel of History', whose 'face is turned toward the past':

> Where we perceive a chain of events, he sees one single catastrophe which keeps piling wreckage upon wreckage and hurls it in front of his feet. The angel would like to stay, and make whole what has been smashed. But a storm is blowing from Paradise; it has got caught in his wings with such violence that the angel can no longer close them. This storm irresistibly propels him into the future to which his back is turned, while the pile of debris before him grows skyward. This storm is what we call progress.[43]

For Benjamin, the defining representation of the present involves a superimposition of the past and the future—a future of which we might dream, but which cannot be realised. A German Jewish refugee from Nazism who lived the last years of his life in France before (apparently) committing suicide on the Franco-Spanish border in 1940, Benjamin's dark vision is echoed in the words repeated on his tombstone: 'There is no document of civilization which is not at the same time a document of barbarism'.[44] An inveterate collector of the matter of modern urban civilisation, the memorabilia of Parisian shopping arcades, Benjamin's nostalgia was radical, self-aware and ironic, fully conscious of the incongruity, even absurdity, of seeking out images from the past in a present that seemed doomed, yet which anticipated the future.

For Svetlana Boym, Benjamin's iconic Angel 'exemplifies a reflective and awe-inspiring modern longing that traverses twentieth-century art and goes beyond *isms*'. The key word here is 'reflective'. Boym offers a typology of modern nostalgia that distinguishes between two extremes, 'reflective' and 'restorative'. Reflective nostalgia 'dwells on the ambivalences of human longing and belonging and does not shy away from the contradictions of modernity'; restorative nostalgia, on the other hand, 'does not think of itself as nostalgia, but rather as truth and tradition'. Another way of putting this is to say that restorative nostalgia focuses on *nostos*, and tries in spite of history to reconstruct the lost home, or homeland; whereas reflective nostalgia thrives on *algia*, the longing itself, but 'wistfully, ironically, desperately'. The key difference between these two different perspectives lies in their attitude towards history in the present: *restorative* nostalgics try to restore the past, as in national and nationalist revivals everywhere, turning history into tradition and myth and monument; *reflective* nostalgics realise the partial, fragmentary nature of history or histories, and linger on ruins and loss.[45] Of course, as Boym acknowledges, these kinds of nostalgia are tendencies rather than absolute types; but they provide a useful template for thinking about the structure of feelings that hover beneath the sign of nostalgia, and I will return to them as I pursue the representations of postcolonial nostalgics.

At stake here is a politics of what one might call representability. Michael Hardt and Antonio Negri's *Empire* (2000) offers a new vision of the times as a regime of globalisation that has overtaken imperialism so as to 'do away with any nostalgia for the power structures that preceded it', hence to enable 'the multitude' to 'invent new democratic forms'. Critics of their vision (which is what it is) point out its implicit Eurocentrism, its flattening out of local and regional histories and memories: the 'small things' emphasised by the very title of Arundhati Roy's *The God of Small Things* (1997), which shows how the processes of globalisation capture and overwhelm individual lives and communities. Roy, herself a well-known activist in India and abroad, uses her fiction to demonstrate how globalisation shapes the post-independence state into a site that forgets its own history, with dire consequences. If, as David Punter suggests, the text of her novel is haunted by 'a prior history that cannot be verbalised', that is, the history of empire and colonisation, it therefore requires a re-reading that remembers that history in order to create the conditions for resisting what seems like the inevitable silence of forgetting.[46] The loss of the past in the globalising present is a common theme among

Anglophone authors abroad, including for example Nigerian Chimamanda Ngozi Adichie, as we shall see in Chapter 6.

The 'Tough Aesthetic' of Postcolonial Nostalgias

I want to suggest that nostalgia has not just a continuing interest but a special resonance for those of us entangled by the long histories of colonialism and decolonisation. According to its author, the origin of one of the canonical postcolonial texts, *Midnight's Children* (1981), lay in memories of a return visit to his childhood home in Bombay, when Salman Rushdie realised 'how much I wanted to restore the past to myself, not in the faded greys of old family-album snapshots, but whole, in CinemaScope and glorious Technicolour'. Having been away so long that he had become 'almost' a foreigner in his homeland, Rushdie was 'gripped by the conviction that I, too, had a city and a history to reclaim'. But there were dangers: 'writers in my position, exiles or emigrants or expatriates, are haunted by some sense of loss, some urge to reclaim, to look back, even at the risk of being mutated into pillars of salt'. And so, while it is impossible to reclaim precisely the thing lost, 'we will, in short, create fictions, not actual cities and villages, invisible ones, imaginary homelands . . . '. Writing from outside your country while trying to reflect that world one has come from, the writer 'is obliged to deal in broken mirrors, some of whose fragments have been irretrievably lost'.[47]

Dealing in broken mirrors (the visual metaphor is strikingly apt) does not mean—or should not be taken to imply—a descent into the 'ungeneralizable subjectivism' that one postcolonial critic has irritably identified in Rushdie.[48] Rushdie's remarks about his own writerly position usefully highlight the problems of representation faced by all those, writers, artists, and critics alike, who find themselves obliged to deal in broken mirrors, and there is no simple solution to these problems. As I have been suggesting, the imaginative reconstruction of the past may be a conservative and parochial activity, reflecting a 'restorative' desire for belonging that overrides distance; equally, it may be a radical and disturbing activity, reflecting a challenging sense of the inadequacy of recalled or (to use Rushdie's language) reclaimed images of earlier times and places; or it may in complex ways address both possibilities. In any case, nostalgia has a power that can be used in a multitude of ways, which is what makes it worth exploring; it is also what raises the issue of the ethics of remembering, and/or forgetting.

A good example of this was provided by the D-Day commemorations in June 2004, when the world's media was focused on the northern coastline of Normandy, and in particular the beaches where, sixty years before, body parts and blood littered the sand. D-Day veterans were depicted hobbling along those same beaches, living testimonies to one of the greatest battles for freedom in history, men soon to be replaced by archives. And as one commentator remarked, the ceremonies represented 'a passing of the torch—out of the aged hands of living memory and into the grasp of history'. At the same time, 'a nostalgic yearning' for what liberation had come to represent was everywhere apparent—a yearning for 'the age of great moral clarity', echoed by U.S. President George Bush, while quoting Anne Frank's words when she heard of D-Day: 'It still seems too wonderful, like a fairy-tale'.[49] But a closer look at Frank's diary reveals not only joy at the invasion, but also the uncertain mood of the Dutch, some of whom did not want to welcome the British when they arrived—instead, the diary records, the Dutch should instead like to see them 'restore the Dutch East Indies to its rightful owner and then return . . . to Britain'.[50] And as we now know, it was their Dutch neighbours who betrayed the Franks to the Nazis, an act people would understandably prefer to forget.

The point is, although it might seem easy in nostalgic retrospect to identify friend and foe, oppressor and oppressed, on closer inspection such moral clarity is difficult to sustain, especially when we take into account elided memories of empire and colonisation. The oldest photo that emerges from the twilight zone within my own family is of my German maternal grandparents sitting upright and elaborately well-dressed in a horse-drawn cart beside which, standing to attention, is a young black man in worker's clothing, while another black man in semi-military dress holds the horses' heads. This is, as I was told, 'Windhoek in Südwestafrika', a place to which my grandfather had trekked to avoid the war between the Boers and the British, his life having been saved en route by a Kalahari 'Bushman' who showed him how to find water. So he, and therefore my mother and I, owe our lives to a people at the time allocated the lowest rung on the evolutionary ladder, and who were already almost wiped out by starvation, disease, and the aggression of pastoralists from elsewhere in both Africa and Europe. As the photo implies, my grandfather went on to become a successful trader, eventually purchasing a German baronial fantasy house that is now a heritage location in postcolonial Namibia. His fortunes later collapsed, but not before he turned himself into a British citizen in 1939 so as to signal a different identity from other German-speakers in the colony on the eve of war. Thus, within one small family, the contrary roles of friend and foe, of coloniser and colonised, have been inextricably entwined and interdependent.

I mention this because I share Stuart Hall's view that 'We all write and speak from a particular place and time, from a history and a culture which is specific. What we say is always in context, *positioned*'.[51] Hence that position needs clarification. A Jamaican who has lived all his adult life in Britain, Hall has reason for being preoccupied with what he calls 'the diaspora experience and its narratives of displacement', and for articulating the Caribbean inflection of that experience. Steeped in the thought of the English New Left of the 1960s, he also has reason for exploring the abstract contours of identity and its representation among hitherto marginalised peoples like his own, and for challenging postcolonial critics for their apparent reluctance to analyse their own positions, sometimes because of a nostalgia for 'a clear-cut politics of binary oppositions'.[52] My position is evidently that of a displaced colonial too, but from the settler community, and a more recent one at that; and my nostalgia brings forth a receding set of images, of myself refracted through many pasts, including childhood memories in the old colonial setting of the Cape, but behind that, my parents' childhoods, within the European empires of Germany and Britain. South Africa is just one extreme example of the degree to which, in societies with long histories of exploiting difference to maintain inequalities of power, the sense of identity is a site of profound uncertainty and struggle. As events in the former Yugoslavia highlighted not long ago, what you call yourself, what others call you, and how that has come about, may be a matter of terrifying uncertainty elsewhere than the countries of the South.

Rushdie's image of a broken mirror is a potent one, suggestive of reflecting others as well as oneself—if in a fragmentary, partial way. In recalling my pasts I realise that I must not forget those pushed aside or made dependent by the arrival of my ancestors, the dark side of nostalgia. Derek Walcott has suggested (in a remarkable essay on 'The Muse of History') that merely serving 'historical truth' has led 'New World' writers to produce 'a literature of revenge written by the descendants of slaves or a literature of remorse written by the descendants of masters'.[53] In their 'rage' for identity, 'Third World' poets 'respect only incoherence or nostalgia'. The point is that it is not enough simply to recall the past, and turn it into a personal narrative of anger or guilt: recalling involves coming to terms with the past in an ethical as well as heuristic sense; it is to connect what you remember with the memories of others, colonisers and colonised and in-between. It is what Trinh Minh-ha has called writing 'from' the self, meaning with others in mind, rather than writing 'about' the self. The celebratory poetry of Guyanese writer-in-exile Grace Nichols's *I is a long memoried woman* provides a good example. Otherwise, the tendency towards narcissistic nostalgia may dominate—a tendency all the more likely in postcolonial discursive contexts, which have often sidelined the voices of women as well as others.[54]

It seems to me that this is where the term 'postcolonial' can still provide a useful conceptual paradigm, if handled with due caution and critical sensitivity. It needs to be used to identify processes that are narrated as neither simply local or national, here or there, then or now, yours or mine—but as fragmented, multi-perspectival, or in Hall's terms, in seeking to capture stages in the 'long-drawn out and differentiated affair, in which the recent post-war movements towards decolonisation figure as one, but only one, distinctive "moment"'.[55] This multiple, non-linear, and yet historically and politically informed perspective can and should reveal what the representation of memory tells us in today's divided world, in which new empires are taking over from the old, in technology as well as in territory, and nostalgia can be seen as neither intrinsically good or bad, but part of what we all experience and which may or may not lead to desirable effects. It is sometimes forgotten that postcolonial (or 'post-colonial') was contested from the start of its widespread deployment as an account of certain specific discursive formations, well before being interrogated almost to extinction. Despite claims of its demise, it stubbornly continues in use. However often it is said to have been transcended or sidelined by apparently more nuanced terms such as 'hybridity', or less nuanced terms such as 'globalisation', it refuses to be consigned to the dustbin of history, as Ania Loomba for one makes clear in an excellent summing-up of current debates.[56]

One of the lasting benefits of Edward Said's founding critique of what he identified in 1978 as the West's '*Orientalism*' was to have created a wariness about totalising discourses more generally, while focusing attention upon the experiences of the wretched of the earth, including, in his case, those of a Christian Palestinian brought up in Lebanon and Egypt, then settled in the United States. The sense is of how far personal and cultural identities are not simply given, but are contingent and must be constructed, as often as not through picking up the baggage of memory, rather than history. Despite subsequently writing a memoir with an awareness that he was living through his last days as he did so, Said was clear that, after a period during which it was too painful to even think about his past, nothing was more painful and at the same time 'paradoxically sought after' than memories of the 'many displacements from countries, cities, abodes, languages, environments that have kept me in motion all these years'.[57] The resulting account of his growing sense of himself as an outsider, despite his many achievements as a major public intellectual in the world, reveals how, in Walcott's phrase, the 'truly tough aesthetic' of postcolonial nostalgias can and does operate, eschewing both remorse and recrimination while dwelling on the past life in a way that offers a challenging perspective for the future of one of the most vexed postcolonial arenas of the world today—Israel/Palestine.[58]

Ironically, the majority of those who live in, or are forced out, of such areas are unlikely to be in a position to express their nostalgia for loss of home or homeland. Not having the access to the media of communication from print to the Internet of privileged, educated intellectuals and writers such as Said (or Walcott, Rushdie, or Hall), the vast majority of late-twentieth-century migrants are poor and illiterate. As Rey Chow has suggested, it is important to beware of talking indiscriminately about 'lack, subalternity, victimization and so forth' without some awareness of one's own position, and the potential for over-dramatising it.[59] As the exiled Breyten Breytenbach once put it, isn't it true that exile is not only about being marginal, weak and poor, but 'a chance, a break, an escape, a challenge? The courage and the perseverance, the futile quest for survival of these stowaways, wetbacks, throwbacks, and other illegal humans always astonish me'.[60] What this highlights is the continuing struggle for those who aim to deal with issues of representation to avoid over-identifying with the objectification of people by the discourses under analysis.

Like all forms of nostalgia, postcolonial nostalgias have both positive and negative aspects: usually the latter is fore grounded, as the source of an insecure idealism or sentimentality, casting a beneficent glow over past suffering and anxiety; but there is also a positive side, which admits the past into the present in a fragmentary, nuanced, and elusive way, allowing a potential for self-reflexivity or irony appropriate for former colonial or diasporic subjects trying to understand the networks of power relations within which they are caught in the modern world, and beyond which it often seems impossible to move. Such a move depends upon the politics of the present, including in the old imperial nations negative or in Boym's terminology 'restorative' nostalgia of the heritage or, more subtly, apologetic variety; and in the 'new' nations, a sometimes dangerous tendency to forget colonial pasts, and their distorting effects. As Kimberly Smith suggests, the 'theory of nostalgia not only tells us whether memory is reliable, but *whose* memories are reliable—whose past is politically relevant'. Since nostalgia is universal, she argues, and has its roots in the modern crisis of industrialisation—and imperialism, I would add—its use is central to political debate as well.[61]

But a tough aesthetic that uses what the past has delivered, including the colonial language, as part of a complex negotiation between remembering and forgetting is essential if we are to remain clear-eyed. There is a long history of colonial and postcolonial writing that invokes nostalgia as a means of resuscitating the forgotten or obscured histories of both colonised and coloniser, for a variety of reasons. When it becomes especially noticeable is during the rise of nationalist feeling in the colonised and decolonising territories, as writers seek to transform their sense of cultural disinheritance and loss into new identities for themselves and their communities. Elleke Boehmer has pointed out that from W. B. Yeats' evocations of an ancestral 'romantic Ireland' to Claude McKay's 'jungle jazzing', the 'artifice of nostalgia' has been valued by writers taking the initiative in aiming to shape the future by recalling the past in terms of nativist pastoral or romance. But, as she also points out, the results could be highly ambivalent, nostalgia and/ as reconstruction legitimating or camouflaging 'the more "advanced" of an élite's progressive or modernist attitudes'.[62]

According to Hobsbawm, the 'age of empires' is dead, since most colonies or former dependencies have become independent states, amongst which the memory of the past remains ambiguous. And as he points out, the memory of struggle and liberation requires a good deal of historical scepticism.

> Such narratives tend to exaggerate the independent role of the forces of liberation, to underestimate the local forces not involved in the liberation movements, and to oversimplify the relationship between an empire and its subject population . . . The relationship between empires and their subjects is complex, because the foundation of the power of lasting empires is also complex.[63]

Where, when, and how to identify nostalgia in postcolonial contexts is therefore a tricky task, fraught with the potential for misunderstanding and misrepresentation. This is particularly difficult when considering the articulation of past trauma, when forgiveness and forgetting are often at odds with remembrance and a wider politics.

Some of the sharpest examples arise out of South Africa's recent past, as the editors of a recent collection of essays on the 'making of memory' in that country have demonstrated. The revelations of witnesses before the Truth and Reconciliation Commission have made it more important than ever to disentangle the memories of victims and oppressors; and yet, the process is fraught with difficulties that, far from disappearing as the past recedes, become ever more challenging. This means that, for South Africans today, 'contradictory voices should be heard', and the 'task' of memory understood as not so much about making whole as reconstituting 'turbulence and fragmentation'.[64]

This is easier said than done. Among the contradictory voices the editors do not take into account are those of the many South Africans who went abroad, as refugees, exiles, or various kinds of migrant, many of whom like myself continue to live outside their former homeland. But understanding that the recollections, nostalgic or otherwise, of South Africans are likely to be at least ambivalent, if not contradictory and 'turbulent', is clear. The recent past does not submit to obvious interpretations. Former exile Lewis Nkosi has expressed astonishment at what he perceives as the 'absence of nostalgia' in modern South African literature, which generally 'shows a certain incapacity for generating nostalgia'. Instead the past is remembered, even by white writers, as 'a bad nightmare'.[65] This was not true of earlier writers like Alan Paton or Ezekiel Mphahalele; and it simplifies the situation today, as the recent 'memory plays' of Athol Fugard demonstrate.[66] And a controversial book by South African journalist Jacob Dlamini, *Native Nostalgia* (2009), suggests what it means for Black South Africans to remember their lives under apartheid with fondness. A mixture of personal anecdote and reflective meditation, Dlamini's book challenges the master narrative of 'the struggle', according to which the black masses all 'experienced apartheid the same way, suffered the same way, and fought the same way against apartheid', whereas there were class, ethnic, age, gender, and regional differences as there are everywhere. Dlamini remembers a happy childhood, despite the lack of basic services, in the township of Katlehong, and uses what he perceives as his own and others' nostalgia to show that the world of apartheid was not as polarised as is often assumed, but 'a world of moral ambivalence and ambiguity in which people could be both resisters and collaborators at the same time'.[67] An approach to postcolonial nostalgia that captures this kind of complexity will have to be tough, and it will have to be nuanced.

The Ethics of Memory

Nostalgia is not innocent—least of all, perhaps, when indulged by those who have benefited from past structures of oppression; yet it can be shown to reside equally strongly in the minds of those who have been oppressed. Pursuing the often wayward, ambiguous paths of nostalgia as they have been represented beyond, but also within, Europe, so as to identify some of those processes of communal and individual experience that constitute the present and, by implication the future (nostalgia often involves a projected future), reveals a process that reconnects the individual to his or her past, and to a community. It resists postmodern attempts to deny the temporal, or to transform it into a fixation upon a consumable present, thereby avoiding the demand of the Other, to engage in or bear witness to the histories that envelop and continue to challenge us. Recovering the memories of those subject to imperial and colonial processes means inevitably facing trauma as well as celebration, with all that implies. When South African filmmaker Deborah Hoffman was asked why she had made her documentary about the Truth and Reconciliation Commission—*A Long Night's Journey Into Day* (2001)—she said it was because although her family were Holocaust survivors, they had kept that history secret from her as a child, and here was an opportunity at last to 'bear witness'.[68] Bear witness to what, exactly? And to whom? To the complex, remembered and forgotten, partial or denied lines of affiliation between Germany, Israel, and South Africa, all connected with each other through history, migration, and politics.

To pursue such complex lines of affiliation—which I will be doing in what follows—is to confirm a suggestion made by the philosopher Avishai Margalit in *The Ethics of Memory*, to the effect that although we think of memory as primarily to do with individuals, there may be such a thing as a *community* of memory, which goes beyond 'natural' communities of memory such as families, clans, tribes, religious communities, and nations, but which also responds to the moral claims of the past. It is important to stress that this idea is something different from that form of postmodernism that turns everyone into others, a carnival of otherness that, as Margalit puts it, simply changes masks at will. For Margalit, there is an obligation on all of us to admit some 'minimal shared moral memories', memories of 'striking examples of radical evil and crimes against humanity', such as 'enslavement, deportations of civilian populations, and mass exterminations'. This obligation implies a very difficult project: institutions to store and diffuse such memories tend to be bureaucratic and soulless; networks of people carrying out the division of mnemonic labour are not always coherently connected; and there is the problem of 'biased salience', which may make it easier for some people to remember Kosovo rather than Rwanda (or vice versa), depending upon the current media interests of their own environment, as well as their personal pasts, for example. Nonetheless, we are all under an obligation *to remember*, precisely because of the efforts of 'radical evil' (a Kantian notion introduced by Margalit) 'to undermine morality itself by, among other means, rewriting the past and controlling collective memory'.[69]

As John Su has pointed out, in an important study of *Ethics and Nostalgia in the Contemporary Novel*, a range of contemporary philosophers, from Martha Nussbaum to Richard Rorty have 'looked to narrative to provide a means of sharing, debating, and negotiating communal ethical values'. Narratives can provide 'an opportunity to identify with potentially unfamiliar descriptions of the world', thereby encouraging readers to 'empathize with the values and needs of others'; they 'challenge the truth claims of existing histories and beliefs by redescribing reality from alternative perspectives'; and they may 'expose the ambiguities and aporias of any ethical project'.[70] This is laying a very large set of claims upon narrative, however broadly defined: and upon individuals—who, after all, has the power to absolve or exonerate the evils of the past? Nonetheless, this does seem part of the postcolonial project, as it has been articulated by a host of writers and critics, from Ngugi wa Thiong'o to Chinua Achebe, from Edward Said to Diana Brydon: that is, to provide narratives that meet at least the claim to challenge 'existing histories and beliefs' by recalling and retelling the past in terms of what they argue are in some sense 'alternative' values.

What does this imply? I would like to think that those of us committed to the postcolonial project, through the 'thick' relationships of family or friends, or the 'thin' relationships of institutional or other connection—that we share a sense of the importance of remembering the radical evil of apartheid, just as we recall instances of slavery and genocide marking the long histories of empire and colonisation, as part of our contingent sense of who we are in the present. One way of creating or sustaining such a community of memory is through responding to the force of certain quite specific representations of the past—representations that acknowledge an ethical dimension to the struggle to understand the meanings of identity, identification, and reflective recall prompted by nostalgia. Such representations may not be aesthetic or literary; although the mix of experiential intensity and reflective detachment characteristic of artistic forms carries the potential to affect debates about who we are and how nostalgia may or may not contribute to that fragile, contingent sense of ourselves in a way that is more than merely conceptual, or issue-driven.

Chapter Summary

The selection of recent and contemporary writers, texts, and arguments under consideration in the chapters that follow are viewed as test cases for my general argument that the varieties of nostalgia are worth pursuing in postcolonial contexts. In each case—and they are intentionally varied in origin and reach—the twilight zone between memory and history is shown to be occupied in ways that encourage a fruitful dialogue between present and past, personal and public. A critical, that is to say, properly reflective approach to nostalgia as both an individual and communal phenomenon, should encourage a sense of responsibility for the way we engage with it, and this is what I finally aim to establish.

The first issue that requires addressing is that of 'identity', a notion by its nature elusive and ambivalent, yet a key concept for understanding personal experience and social life in a world of global change. As I show in Chapter 2, drawing on V. S. Naipaul's *The Enigma of Arrival* (1987) as well as his other work, reinscribing oneself as a writer becomes fundamental to overcoming the melancholy of loss for the self-exiled novelist. *Enigma* is Naipaul's most compelling yet finally ambiguous attempt to define who he is, and where he comes from. Mingling nostalgia and ironic critique, *Enigma* seeks to engage with both present and past, exploring the author-narrator's newly established home on an English estate and the multiple journeys that have brought him there, while challenging easy assumptions about the formation of identity for the postcolonial subject, including all those who have taken Naipaul to be on the side of the colonisers. Identifying with the nostalgically imagined, idealised 'other' of England brings simultaneously the warmth of recognition, and the chill of understanding that this other home is a construct: not so much an identity found, as an *identification* made, based on nostalgia. A perceived lack of fit, and the emptiness or excess between narrating and narrated selves, or in Derridean terms, between presence and absence, is what engages Naipaul in his search for identity. What he is unable to do is seek ways of narrating the self that bear witness to events that have disrupted our frames of reference entirely—events such as the Atlantic slave trade.

For diasporic subjects, remembering not just 'home' but 'the homeland' has opened up the scope for multiple forms of identity within and beyond the nation-state. Yet this also implies an increasing lack of certainty or finality about home as a place of origin, undermining nostalgia as a phenomenon of positive identifications and affiliations, even while it is more widely and profoundly felt. In Chapter 3 I explore further some of the ways in which home, and the homeland (which invokes both the private and the larger, public or national space) offer a troubling source of re-membered, or recreated identities. In particular, I consider how the figure of the primal inhabitant of southern Africa, the nomadic hunter-gatherer figure of the 'Bushman', has been constructed and deconstructed by certain writers, including poet-journalist Antje Krog, nostalgically redefining postcolonial nationhood from within, rather than from diasporic spaces like the one I inhabit and from which I write this book.

There certainly seems to be a hunger, a yearning for the past, which becomes a yearning for something more, something harder to define, in what we might call, after J. M. Coetzee, 'white writing'. Coetzee himself has written a fictionalised autobiographical trilogy, characteristically detached, intertextual, and increasingly postmodern so as to distance himself from nostalgia, although, like Lessing and many others from the settler communities of Africa, he has finally left his home country for abroad. Earlier colonial writing, according to him, was characterised by its dream-like, 'retrospective' gaze, typically mythologising the indigenous peoples as idle primitives, thereby all the more readily displaced by or made subject to the needs and desires of incomers.[71] But as we can see from Chapter 4, in her best 'African' work, such as *The Grass is Singing* (1950) or the story of 'The Old Chief Mshlanga' (1951), Lessing's retrospective gaze generally resists this paradigm, despite her dreams for something lost in the past, something out of reach of the present which, paradoxically, becomes a vision of the future in *Mara and Dann* (1999). She recognises the other, although at times with anguish and a sense of threat. And there are times when her remembering takes her towards the more dubious aspects of white settler nostalgia, sharing the mythologising tendency of colonial predecessors like Karen Blixen and Laurens van der Post. Nonetheless, as the 'African' sections of *The Golden Notebook* (1962) demonstrate, she was aware of the dangers.

Chapter 5 concerns the work of German expatriate writer W. G. Sebald. Sebald is not much studied by postcolonial theorists or critics, but the issues his work raises concerning the literary mediation of what I call the 'hidden endings' of empire, are highly pertinent. Sebald's work expresses a preoccupation with memory, nostalgia, and exile grounded in a deep knowledge of the multiple histories, including colonial histories, that haunt us in the present. In works like *The Emigrants* (1993), *The Rings of Saturn* (1995), and *Austerlitz* (2001) he shows how the histories of the present are inextricably interwoven with memories from within and beyond Europe to an extent that makes most writing today appear provincial. It is too easy to forget, as many postcolonial theorists and critics forget, that the British Empire was only one among many, even if at its apogee it was the largest empire the world had seen. Sebald's writing reminds us of the deep, if sometimes barely visible connections and affiliations across as well as within empires. The common perception of nostalgia as a facile glossing of the past seems particularly limited as we pursue it here, its promptings bringing these hidden ends into clearer focus so as to enable a better understanding of the past, and of our responsibilities to the present.

Like Naipaul, Sebald creates an authorial persona whose many journeys tend towards an inner, even spiritual dimension, glimpsed through the various masks or characters he creates, and who are often grounded in real people and places encountered or read about, and experiences which, through hidden echoes and connections, blur the boundary between the found and the made, fact and fiction, history and memory. The end of his work is to create an awareness of complicity with the histories of earlier generations, and a deeper understanding of connectedness through empire. Haunted by the multiple pasts of individuals and societies, he provides a unique template for remembering histories mislaid or forgotten, by means of the nostalgic yearnings and hidden, involuntary memories of travellers, migrants, and exiles like himself.

Chapter 6 returns to Africa, and to the work of two writers for whom nostalgia functions as the generative source of a profound critique of the bitterly remembered postcolonial homeland: Nigerians Chinua Achebe and Chimamanda Ngozi Adichie. For them, nostalgia involves connecting their authorial selves with their recalled childhoods, so as to reflect critically upon their memories and the histories they bring. National revival in the postcolonial nation-state has led to the reconstruction of collective identities through commemoration and memorialisation, a context in which the realist novel has been found well suited to rewriting the recent past, including the violence of civil conflict and mass killing, by writers in the Achebe mould. But drawing on earlier, 'traditional' cultural forms has been transformed by the work of a younger generation, notably Achebe's acknowledged 'heir' Adichie, who provides a feminist slant upon the structures of the past. Adichie's writing, particularly her civil war novel *Half of a Yellow Sun* (2006), represents a step beyond the familiar paradigm of African female empowerment; it reflects the violent dislocations in space and time characteristic of the diasporic realities of the globalised world she knows as a Nigerian abroad, while not forgetting the longing for home and wholeness. The result is a complex aesthetic, in which predominantly realist representations of the past in all its remembered everydayness are shot through with intimations of deeper, spiritual realities.

In Chapter 7 I consider the work of J. G. Ballard, for whom nostalgia was anathema, and yet whose finest work, *Empire of the Sun* (1984), was the product of nostalgia—reflected and refracted through a remarkable fusion of autobiography, fantasy, and history. For Ballard, interested above all in the present ('the next five minutes'), exploring the present seemed at first to mean imagining the future, and for many years he wrote futuristic fantasies developing the imagery and narrative conventions of science fiction; with the publication of *Empire of the Sun*, it became clear that writing about the present also meant revisiting his past, and in particular his shaping experiences as a prisoner of the Japanese in Shanghai during World War II. Despite his lifelong rage against nostalgia for pre-war, imperial England, he found that through an ironic mixture of science fiction, war story, popular adventure, and the traditional *Bildungsroman*, he could undermine not just the desire for the simple moral map of the last war, but the whole Western version of twentieth-century history, while exploring the psychopathology of everyday life in a postcolonial, post-nuclear world.

If nostalgia is still thought of as the sentimental return to an imaginary, idyllic past, this is also how Ballard himself tended to see it. Scathing about the nostalgia of those who look back towards some mythical domain of village greens, cathedral closes, and imperial vistas, he came by the time of his last book, *Miracles of Life* (2008), if not before, to realise that memory had been essential for him, providing an archive drawn on throughout his career as a writer, whatever the surface form taken by a particular work. The traumas and catastrophes he had witnessed as a youth ensured that even his most far-fetched fantasies were glued to the past. Avoiding direct representations of that past in terms of social realist or more traditional 'literary' fiction, he found his inspiration in the classic modernism of Kafka and the surrealists, creating a shifting collage of perspectives in which memory and history operate at different levels. In *Empire of the Sun*, acknowledging the larger movements of history meant creating a perspective cleansed of imperial and colonial delusions. The more sentimental nostalgia towards history was to be found in Spielberg's popular film version of the novel.

The continuous interweaving of future as well as past perspectives counteracts the simplistic implications of popular war narratives: for such fictions, history is a matter of stereotyped, providential conflict, in which good overcomes evil, and established class, race, and gender positions are predictable and privileged; the book *Empire of the Sun* challenges such stereotyping, while relying on popular realist elements to make itself accessible. Its engagement with history is a reminder of the value of nostalgia in the present, whether it is consciously acknowledged or not. The problematic relationship between coloniser and colonised at the heart of the imperial mission, whether conducted by Western or Eastern powers, is shown to be the issue we have to deal with now when—as Ballard emphasises—the American *imperium* has taken over, although another, the Chinese, waits in the wings.

2 'How is it going, Mr Naipaul?'
Remembering Postcolonial Identities

'... the old colonial anxiety of having one's individuality destroyed'.
V. S. Naipaul, Interview, 1981[1]

'I wished to explore who I was ...'.
V. S. Naipaul, *A Writer's People*, 2007[2]

'When the strength for fiction fails the writer, what remains is autobiography'.
Salman Rushdie, review, 1987[3]

Identity 'under erasure'

The global movements of people over the last century have highlighted as never before the questions we all ask ourselves at some point: 'Who am I?' 'Where do I come from?' With the result that, as Stuart Hall remarks at the beginning of a wide-ranging collection of essays exploring *Questions of Cultural Identity*, 'There has been a veritable discursive explosion in recent years around the concept of "identity", at the same moment as it has been subjected to a searching critique'. As he points out, various disciplinary areas have been engaged in an 'anti-essentialist critique of ethnic, racial and national conceptions of cultural identity and the "politics of location" to the extent that the question arises, 'What, then, is the need for further debate about "identity"? Who needs it?'[4]

My immediate answer is, *we* do—and if, for now, I take 'we' to denote those of us interested in postcolonial writings, this chapter is an attempt to frame an affirmative answer, drawing in particular on V. S. Naipaul's *The Enigma of Arrival* (1987), while referring to some of his other work. Inhabiting the uncertain territory between fiction and autobiography, *Enigma* is Naipaul's most compelling yet finally ambiguous attempt to define who he is, and where he comes from. Mingling nostalgia and critique, *Enigma* seeks to engage with both his present and his past, exploring his new home on an English estate and the multiple journeys that have brought him there. It offers a continuing challenge to easy assumptions about the formation of identity for the postcolonial subject, including all those (and they are many) who have taken Naipaul to be on the side of the colonisers.[5] It also suggests how and why memory, including nostalgia, is central to such formation.

Naipaul has always been one to challenge easy assumptions, especially as far as his own position as an expatriate former colonial subject is concerned. Born in 1932 in impoverished, rural Trinidad to a family of East Indian descent, he left his country (a Crown Colony until 1967) in 1950 on a scholarship to Oxford, thereafter making his home in England, despite extensive travel abroad. By 1964 an established 'Commonwealth' writer with six books behind him, his response to the first Commonwealth Literature Conference at Leeds University was to note how soon everything was becoming 'codified' in this new field, including 'the West Indian with his search for identity'. Students already 'write or even telephone to say that they get the impression from my works that I am engaged in a search for identity. How is it going? At times like this I am glad to be only a name'.[6] It was not long before he was much more than only a name; and now that a major biography has been published, anyone who wishes to may check up on how Naipaul's identity has developed, as a writer and as a man.[7]

As the grandson of indentured labourers brought from India to replace freed African slaves on the sugar plantations of Trinidad, Naipaul's identity always seemed to him something improbable, created by others.[8] What he was really objecting to about the instant institutionalising by Literature Departments of the West Indian 'search for identity' is a tendency that long predates the Leeds Conference and the subsequent development of Commonwealth and then postcolonial criticism: the tendency for Anglophone writers located outside the English 'centre' to have a troubling sense not just of being boxed and labelled, but of having been immersed in a long struggle for representation within a colonising culture that both nurtured and rejected them.

There is, for example, the revealing account in R. K. Narayan's comic and poignant novel *The English Teacher*—which appeared in 1946, just before Indian independence—of the teacher Krishnan's decision to resign from his post at Albert Mission College, Malgudi:

> I would send in a letter which would be a classic in its own way, and which would singe the fingers of whoever touched it. In it I was going to attack a whole century of false education. I was going to explain why I could no longer stuff Shakespeare and Elizabethan metre and Romantic poetry for the hundredth time into young minds and feed them on the dead mutton of literary analysis and theories and histories, while what they needed was lessons in the fullest use of the mind. This education had reduced us to a nation of morons; we were strangers to our own

culture and camp followers of another culture, feeding on leavings and garbage.[9]

Nevertheless, as Krishnan argues with himself, 'What fool could be insensible to Shakespeare's sonnets or the *Ode to the West Wind*?' And 'what about examinations and critical notes? Didn't these largely take the place of literature?' All the ideas had been uttered 'a hundred times before', and merely attacking the system would look like 'a rehash of an article entitled "Problems of High Education"', which appeared again and again in a weekend educational supplement—the 'yarn' some 'educationist' was spinning out for ten rupees a column. 'This is not what I want to say', Krishnan mutters to himself. 'There is something far deeper that I wish to say.' But instead, he writes 'Dear Sir, I beg to tender my resignation for personal reasons. I request you to relieve me immediately . . . '[10]

Narayan does not even attempt to tell the reader what that something 'far deeper' is that his narrator wishes to say, but, ironically, his English teacher goes on to use that same functional register the imperial masters have taught the cultural 'morons' of India as a way of resolving his dilemma, while avoiding the oppositional clichés of the local 'educationists'. Anticipating what Gauri Viswanathan was to go on and show at much greater length in *Masks of Conquest* some forty years later, about the imposition of English studies as an instrument of colonial control and cultural assimilation,[11] Narayan's narrator nonetheless desires to maintain a grip on the classics of the English canon that have shaped his sense of who he is (as they also shaped Narayan, whose father was an English teacher). In other words, at the same time as he raises questions of personal, cultural, and national identity, Narayan avoids direct engagement with them, leaving them, so to speak, 'under erasure'.

This Derridean notion, originating in *Of Grammatology*,[12] helps us towards one kind of answer to the question of why it is worth continuing to discuss identity as a form of self-representation, despite the apparent tiredness of the issue. Stuart Hall suggests that unlike those forms of critique 'which aim to supplant inadequate concepts with "truer" ones, or which aspire to the production of positive knowledge, the deconstructive approach puts key concepts "under erasure"'(1). What this means is that although they have not been entirely superseded, and we have to continue to think with them, we do so in terms which take us beyond the paradigm in which they were originally generated: operating 'under erasure' means trying to think through the interval between reversal to an earlier model and the emergence of a newer way of thinking. But where might we find a set of discourses that promote this sense of identity, hovering between reversal towards an older model as a matter of geographical and religious and historical fixity on the one hand, and a newer model as a process of struggle towards something decentred and deferred?

To develop such thinking beyond the over-familiar discourses of the decentred self, it is helpful to look first at the work of writers rather than that of critics or theorists. It seems to me that the critical and theoretical exhaustion to which Hall's essay alludes (and of which it is also symptomatic) requires a good dose of writerly oxygen. And one important source is the work of the aforementioned V. S. Naipaul, whose resistance to being labelled is itself part of what intrigues readers and critics. So is the fact that, for him, identity is as central as it is complex and unresolved, or indeed crucially deferred, and generates a continuous rewriting of the same memories from different perspectives and within different genres—most consciously and substantially in *The Enigma of Arrival*, although typically that work has been, not superseded, but qualified and redefined, as it is bound to be, by subsequent autobiographical or semi-autobiographical books, including *A Way in the World* (1994), *Reading and Writing* (2000), *Half A Life* (2001), and *A Writer's People* (2007).

As Naipaul remarks in *Reading and Writing*, Narayan's 'world is not as rooted and complete as it appears'.[13] Indeed not. Yet Narayan's method, though lighter in touch than Naipaul's, anticipates the later author's urge to record the reactions of people caught within situations of profound and continuing cultural and historical disjuncture, by using narrators who are themselves entangled participants in the larger, global lines of force they dimly perceive through their memories. Naipaul's vision of the struggles of his protagonists and alter egos to find themselves in relation to both past and present involves a level of alienation, violence, and despair that contrasts sharply with Narayan's quietly affirmative view of the continuing validity of Hindu mythology in the present, whatever complexities Narayan may reveal in relation to his Anglophone inheritance.

It is difficult to imagine Naipaul's writing supporting a narrator who, like Narayan's English teacher, ends up communicating with his dead wife, a wife who appears to him in person at the end of his narrative so that, in the epiphanic words of the concluding paragraph of *The English Teacher*,

> We stood at the window, gazing on a slender, red streak over the eastern rim of the earth. A cool breeze lapped our faces. The boundaries of our personalities suddenly dissolved. It was a moment of rare, immutable joy—a moment for which one feels grateful to Life and Death.

The boundaries of Naipaul's characters never 'dissolve'—except perhaps as a sign of mental breakdown, for instance in the central (Green Vale) section of his third novel, *A House for Mr Biswas* (1961), when the disintegration of the eponymous Biswas' character takes the reader into another, non-realist realm. But apart from such moments, Naipaul's characters are distinct in their often precarious apartness; nor does his kind of realism allow for an acceptance of the kind of collective, remembered (rather than merely recalled) fantasy or myth apparent in Narayan (or Caribbean contemporaries such as Wilson Harris). However, Naipaul's *narrators* do share a driving need to define themselves, often in terms that involve taking up a position in relation to the remembered 'classical' or canonical traditions of English literature—or indeed, in relation to the newer traditions of Commonwealth or postcolonial literatures, despite the author's explicit objections to the premature codification of issues generated by their institutional arrival.

Thus Derrida's notion of a concept lying 'under erasure', with its implications of thinking in or across margins, or indeed more materially of writing as re- or over-writing, seems an apt concept to breathe life into our sense of the nature and achievement of Naipaul's ongoing project. This project was clearly changing, as Stuart Murray has observed, from *Finding the Centre* (1984) onwards, and became most fully transformed in *The Enigma of Arrival* (1987), a work Murray rightly calls a new departure, making it 'increasingly difficult to accommodate him within the paradigm of postcolonial writing'.[14] What this means is that the current 'paradigm' needs revision, not necessarily discarding: remembering, not forgetting. But the question then becomes: how does Naipaul's 'new departure' affect the parameters of what might still count as postcolonial? The answer has to do with how we define departures and arrivals, and the shifting relationship between them, for the migrant writer, which means that 'postcolonial', too, is a concept that might best thought of as shifting, under erasure.

That 'new departure' is defined by Naipaul's disarmingly frank passages in *The Enigma of Arrival* about his own writing. After the success of his first 'inspiration'—writing fast and very simply about the remembered street in Port of Spain where he had spent part of his childhood—he realised that his subject was not his 'inward development', but 'the worlds I contained within myself'.[15] This is a significant remark, suggesting both his ambition and his sense of an identity not something simply given, dependent upon his personal history and memory, but rather a construction of the many histories, memories, or 'worlds' within him. Those worlds, the author-narrator continues, made it necessary to 'acknowledge more of myself', before going on to explore 'India' (surrounded with scare-quotes to highlight its recalled, constructed nature), the India of his forefathers and an India that he had, as he says,

> partly grown up in, the India that was like a loose end in my mind, where our past suddenly stopped. There was no model for me here, in this exploration; neither Forster nor Ackerley nor Kipling could help. To get anywhere in the writing, I had first of all to define myself very clearly to myself. (140–41)

But that clarity eludes him, as he goes on to pursue the earlier self that travelled from Queen's Royal College in Port of Spain, Trinidad, to 1950s

London, upon a journey he identifies with the journeys of all those whose 'restlessness and the need for a new idea of the self' had driven them from the New to the Old World (145).

What this sense of unending restlessness in the search for 'a new idea of the self' represents is one of the more compelling yet unexamined aspects of nostalgia, the positive and ongoing relationship between migrants' homelands and their final places of settlement and work, not merely their fruitless longing to return to an idealised version of their past. It is a relationship defined in part by the multiple (unconsciously) remembered *and* (consciously) recalled associations that the everyday lives of diasporic subjects frequently if not continuously throw into relief, as they proceed through the familiar (yet for them fractured) cycles of family, occupation, and leisure in the new homeland. The stories of asylum-seekers and refugees are dramatic and sometimes terrible; they are the extremes of experiences deeply embedded within the lives of many millions throughout the world today, whose allegiances are at once temporary, and yet permanently strung out along long lines back to their points of origin, creating an ongoing disjunction or fracture between social and national identities. The result is that there is an increasing multiplicity of identities available to the subject, often on different levels of consciousness, to be dreamed or yearned after, if not fully remembered or recalled or understood.

Part of the difficulty reflects the uncertain, complicated, and paradoxical hold of nostalgia, variously defined, upon the present. According to Andreea Ritivoi in her wide-ranging investigation of 'nostalgia and the immigrant identity', nostalgia is 'a genuine *pharmakos*, both medicine and poison: It can express alienation, or it can replenish and rebuttress our sense of identity by consolidating the ties with our history'. Ritivoi considers how far it is possible to assimilate into an unfamiliar world without self-alienation or despair, suggesting that this ultimately depends upon the nature of the engagement with otherness and difference. She proposes a 'narrative' view of personal identity, involving a 'dynamic incorporation of change and sameness', a story 'in constant making and remaking', a 'locus for change and stability' which tempts enquiry. Yet 'the case for nostalgia' suggests that maybe 'we should not look too hard' since, like precious, ancient frescoes under a strong light, the detailed images of what we find may disappear.[16]

Ritivoi's use of visual imagery is telling: nostalgia often relies on the visual, especially in the sense of being multilayered, yet fragmentary. This reminds us that the quest for continuity apparent in Naipaul's work, although often prompted by a sense of crisis, may lead to a greater sense of rupture and alienation, after all. Hence the need for Naipaul to continue his travels into the past through the present, calling up the histories that his attempts to settle bring with them, fully aware of their fragility. Hence, too, the longing for return as an unachieved ideal, articulated throughout his work.

Arrival, Restlessness, and Longing

In *The Enigma of Arrival* Naipaul invites the reader to follow his narrator's attempt to root himself within the Old World, in an ancient, rural English landscape, the landscape of centuries of cultural and historical association, going back to the times of the prehistoric monoliths still standing stolidly upon the land. This was Wiltshire—where the author found a house in which to write (Teasel Cottage, in the grounds of Wilsford Manor), after first returning from a failed attempt to re-root himself in his place of origin, Trinidad, to work on a commissioned 'history', *The Loss of El Dorado* (1969).[17] The 'arrival' of the title is the story of arriving in a new homeland, of a migrant and former colonial who puts down roots in the land of his former oppressor—or so it appears at first.

The first section tells of how, in his early middle age, the narrator has settled in rural Wiltshire; the second section recalls his first journey from Trinidad to England; in the third he returns to Wiltshire, rewriting the earlier material but with a different emphasis; and the fourth shows him observing his neighbours afresh as time passes and an increasing sense of change and decay overtakes him. The narrator's new attempt to earth himself in England seems at first to succeed, but it is then defined as a 'mere' writer's fantasy, so that in the final, fifth section of the novel, which begins as a metanarrative about trying to write a book called *The Enigma of Arrival*, it is admitted that 'the story had become more personal, the writer defined by his writing discoveries, his ways of seeing, rather than by his personal adventures, writer and man separating at the beginning of the journey and coming together again in a second life just before the end' (309).

That complex 'end' is both the end of this narrative, and the end of Naipaul's narrator's life up till then. But it also refers to the end or completed life of his younger sister Sati, whose funeral rites he has returned to Trinidad to take part in, a return that forces him to face the extinction of self he has been fearing night after night in his new English home in terms of the repeated dream of an exploding head. Coming together with his grieving family enables him to experience 'a real grief where melancholy had created a vacancy . . . And that was when . . . I laid aside my drafts and hesitations and began to write very fast about Jack and his garden' (318). 'Jack's Garden' is the title of the first section of the narrative. Accepting his familial mourning as part of his present identity has apparently enabled him to write about someone else: Jack, the farm labourer neighbour who had come to stand as an image of that rooted, communal yet hierarchical Englishness he desired, and wished, vainly, to identify with.

Vainly, because although there is a sense in which the narrator—who both is, and is not, the author Naipaul—*does* nostalgically identify with this vanished or dying Englishness, most notably in that part of the novel when he remarks that he 'felt at one with my landlord' (174), he is at the same time crucially *unable to forget* the history that lies between them, the history of empire: empire which has provided the wealth on which the landlord's ancestors relied, as well as the exploitation of the tenant's migrant Indian ancestors whose labour generated that wealth in the first place. So that while he feels 'in tune with what I saw, or thought I saw' on the Wiltshire estate, the narrator is also 'nervous' of undoing the 'magic of the place' (175), because it means the end of the sense of permanence, of settled origins or destinations, that it seemed at first to promise.

And so it turns out. Despite having 'trained' himself 'to the idea of change, to avoid grief', the 'second life' he has found for himself in the heart of rural England seems only to confirm change, as Jack falls ill, dies, and his garden is destroyed, concreted over, and surrounded by barbed wire, just as the earlier forms of agriculture have been destroyed, and replaced by large-scale mechanisation and industrialisation.

> I had lived with the idea of change, had seen it as a constant, had seen a world in flux, had seen human life as a series of cycles that sometimes ran together. But philosophy failed me now. Land is not land alone, something that simply is itself. Land partakes of what we breathe into it, is touched by our moods and memories. And this end of a cycle, in my life, and in the life of the manor, mixed up with the feeling of age which my illness was forcing on me, caused me grief. (300–1)

For the narrator, then, no place is immune to decay and corruption, not even the imagined, idealised, orderly, and seemingly powerful centre to which, like other colonial migrants, he long yearned to go, and to which he returns, but where he has apparently found little more than indifference to his presence. The further implication of his discovery is that the *idea* of Englishness to which he has been attached is just that: an idea, or concept, constructed historically, thus open to deconstruction at any time and, given the changes that are part of modern life, especially fragile now.

For the author Naipaul, *The Enigma of Arrival* was to prove a turning point in his career, bringing a degree of literary recognition that had previously eluded him. Yet it was never enough, and *Enigma* reveals why. His life, his past, seems to him finally characterised by those key elements of nostalgia, 'homelessness and drift and longing' (152). Hence the repeated attempts to rewrite his life, involving multiple returns and new starts, but also arrivals, like this one—here, in England, on the quintessentially English estate, in the grounds of a great house. The irony is that the older structures of rural life in England had been changing for centuries, as literature since the eighteenth century attests.[18]

Identifying with the English 'other'

Yet, recording his arrival in what for Naipaul betokens the almost mythically familiar landscape of literary and artistic tradition—he refers to Constable,

Wordsworth, and Hardy as he remembers that first arrival—brings with it a jolting self-awareness: he is, he realises

> A man from another hemisphere, another background, coming to rest in middle life in the cottage of a half neglected estate, an estate full of reminders of its Edwardian past, with few connections with the present. An oddity among the estates and big houses of the valley, and I a further oddity in its grounds. I felt unanchored and strange.

But his colonial sense of dislocation enables a deeper sense of history. The passage continues:

> Everything I saw in those early days, as I took my surroundings in, everything I saw on my daily walk, beside the windbreak or along the wide grassy way, made that feeling more acute. I felt that my presence in that old valley was part of something like an upheaval, a change in the course of the history of the country. (19)

Naipaul does not spell out which 'upheaval' this refers to: but it is plain from what he writes elsewhere that it is the post-war migration from the Caribbean he has in mind, of which his own family partook, and which is also part of the broader, long drawn-out drift of peoples subject to first colonisation and then decolonisation. As Robert Winder points out, if America was the nearest employer for West Indian migrants, Britain, thanks to Empire, was the more familiar.

> The colonial administration had given West Indians a grounding in Queen and Country, in Shakespeare and Tennyson, in W.G. Grace, *Kennedy's Latin Primer* and the Lord's Prayer. They had grown up singing 'There'll Always Be an England' and 'Land of Hope and Glory' at assembly. Many of their Christian names—Nelson, Milton, Winston—derived from British heroes. A reverence for Britain had been carefully planted. Now, modern steamships brought the land itself within reach.[19]

Not for Naipaul a Christian name derived from a British hero. His forenames, Vidiadhar Surajprasad, indicate his origins in a community that saw itself as differing from the larger group in terms of history, culture, religion, and class. In histories such as Winder's, the necessary distinctions are skirted: Sam (Selvon), Derek (Walcott), and Edward (Brathwaite) are referred to as if they belong to the same community as V. S. Naipaul, boxing him in with those with whom of course he has much in common, but beside whom he also wishes to identify himself as different—hence the many clashes between Naipaul and his fellow-migrant writers, although to begin with he was satisfied to be linked with all those other 'Caribbean Voices' struggling for recognition.[20]

Nonetheless, Naipaul also writes as an inheritor of what he perceives as the English tradition, specifically its literary tradition, with which his reading as a colonial British subject has made him thoroughly familiar—just as Selvon, Walcott, and Brathwaite were familiar with it, although in ways that differed, too. Significantly, the *Enigma* narrator finds analogies between what he sees and that much older landscape of early English literature, going back to *Gawain and the Green Knight*, which he re-reads on the bus back from Salisbury one autumn day, recalling the winter journey of the old poem—'So in tune with the landscape had I become, in that solitude, for the first time in England' (24–25). The precision and cadence of the writing hint at the nostalgic charge created at such moments of isolation—created, since as we know Naipaul was in actuality accompanied by his wife Pat, who is never mentioned in his saga of arrival (nor is Margaret, the mistress who was also part of his life at the time and later).[21] He is more interested in watching his neighbours and their affairs, consciously apart and solitary, yet increasingly, he feels, 'in tune' with the physical environment familiar to him from his reading.

Identifying with the nostalgically imagined, idealised 'other' of England brings to the narrator simultaneously the warmth of recognition and the chill of understanding that this other is a construct: not so much an identity found, as an *identification* made, based on desire, the characteristic mood of nostalgia. Thus there is the telling realisation that, when the narrator later describes himself in the first days of his original, first departure from Trinidad, he does so as someone tensely aware of other migrants: 'In each [of whom] there were aspects of myself', as he admits. The displaced Naipaul-narrator *can*—if only momentarily, yet it is a moment he feels compelled to record—identify with the black man, whose awareness he shares of the excluding, racist classification invoked by the ship's purser who wants to put them together in a cabin en route from New York to Southampton. Here Naipaul for once records an experience of identifying with those he is so often accused of expressing prejudice towards, although it is an experience of identification that he simultaneously wants to resist, because he believes it will diminish him: 'Racial diminution formed no part of the material of the kind of writer I was setting out to be', he says. But he is obliged to admit that at that unsympathetic point: 'Thinking of myself as a writer, I was hiding my experience from myself; hiding myself from my experience' (115–17).

Naipaul's honesty is revealing. Clearly hiding from his experience of racial classification, while he records both the experience and his inadequate self-reflection upon it, suggests the wider issues at stake here, while also delivering Naipaul at least momentarily from the usual identification of him as among the racists.[22] The writer's uncertain relation with his own experience of himself and his self-definition points towards a second kind of answer to the question of how and why we might continue to think about identity and memory in a revised version of the postcolonial dispensation. This is that we have to think about what sort of problems arise in relation to identity when faced by the apparent irreducibility of the concept. Erasure is, as the metaphor implies, never complete—traces of the original always remain, in memory at least. This raises problems: problems of agency and politics, here highlighted by Naipaul's account of the process of his own temporary subjectification to the politics of exclusion. There may well be a need to reconceptualise identity as a question of 'identification'. For Hall, this reconceptualising of identity in terms of identification draws meanings from both the psychoanalytic and the discursive or Foucauldian repertoires, without being limited to either, and it certainly seems relevant here, if not preferable to discussions of identity exclusively.

Why, then, might 'identification' be more useful a problematic than 'identity'? If the familiar, common-sense definition of identification involves the recognition of some common origin or shared characteristics with another person or group, with the closure of solidarity and allegiance this implies, then adopting the more discursive, historically specific approach suggested by 'identification' might enable us to see identity as, once again, a construction involving memory, hence a process never completed. It is Naipaul's anguished awareness of the nostalgic incompletion of his identity at moments such as that in which he recalls being momentarily made to belong to an excluded group that brings to the fore the constructedness, temporality, and hence fragility of his sense of self—*and* the pressing need to keep recalling through rewriting it. As Hall says, identification is a process involving certain conditions of existence, including 'the material and symbolic resources required to sustain it'; yet it is 'in the end conditional, lodged in contingency. Once secured, it does not obliterate difference'. There is, in other words, 'never a proper fit', instead either an 'over-determination or a lack' (2–3).

I doubt that it is possible to manage all of this, and certainly not simultaneously. Nor am I interested in pursuing further Hall's theorising polemic, since, as he goes on to admit, not only are the Lacanian and post-Althusserian tides receding, but attempts such as Judith Butler's to propose a postmodern, performative space for identity (as in *Bodies That Matter*, 1993), leaves us with a 'tangled and unconcluded argument', the end of which is simply to acknowledge both the necessity and the 'impossibility' of identities (16). Again, an awareness of the pressures that produce migration for those oppressed by the identities they have been given, as 'other' to a dominant or more powerful group, suggests just how sterile and pointless such theorising can become. And the greater the amount of compulsion involved—whether as a result of internecine conflict, human rights violations, or sheer poverty—the less relevant such debates appear.

More fruitful, it seems to me, as my interpolation of references to Naipaul's fictionalising of identities and memories within this account of Hall's argument might suggest, is to look at where the narrativisation of the self has been taking place in some historically specific if discursively ambiguous instances of narrative. Moreover, these instances highlight a significant common theme in relation to both identity and identification—neither of which is either stable or timeless—and which implicitly pulls both the personal and the political into a revised postcolonialism. That theme, as I have been suggesting, is memory and in particular that mode of memory variously defined as nostalgia, or the yearning for home, origin, place. In the case of *The Enigma of Arrival*, it is precisely nostalgia as a means for creating, at least provisionally, a sense of identity, that the postcolonial critique of the present retains some purchase.

Writing, Seeing, and Remembering

One reason for the relevance of memory in the context of debates about identity is pretty obvious. Narrativisation takes place through and by means of time; and it relates closely to the long-standing and familiar western or specifically Lockean sense of identity as a construct based on memory. Critics and scholars with an investment in the construction 'postcolonial' generally remain wedded to the desire to assert or imagine alternative, non-western kinds of narrativisation, and these are certainly available, although given our mixed and muddled or plural inheritances, not in any pure or unmediated form. But, as Nayantara Sahgal remarked in an address at another key moment in the narrative of postcolonial studies, the Silver Jubilee Conference of the Association for Commonwealth Literature and Language Studies at the University of Kent in 1989, if it has long been time 'for interpretation to flow many ways instead of only west to east', 'the question of direction is itself no longer relevant when the migration of cultures is leaving cultures open-ended, and when migration can take place without ever leaving one's soil'. After all, 'Where does one culture begin and another end when they are housed in the same person?'[23] But even for Sahgal, with a sense of her self as identified simultaneously with ancient Hindu culture and a western-inflected modernity, a crucial aspect of the construction and negotiation of identity today lies in the complex relations between present and past, on a personal as well as on a social and historical basis.

The past figures importantly in people's self-representations in general, because it is through memories of the past that we represent ourselves to ourselves, and often through narrative; although those narratives are not necessarily literally written, as is commonly assumed, but may be oral, tactile, visual, dramatic, or may even rely on the sense of smell and taste, as Proust's immense researches in *À la Recherche du Temps Perdu* demonstrate at length. For Naipaul, who commonly refers to his writing in terms of observation or seeing, 'ways of looking',[24] the imagery of memory seems to be predominantly visual—most strikingly so in *The Enigma of Arrival*, the title of which is derived from a disquieting De Chirico painting of 1912, reprinted on the cover of first and subsequent editions of the book.[25]

The Enigma of Arrival revolves around this painterly image, found in memory, and itself about memory. Just days after the narrator arrives in the Wiltshire valley where he aims to settle, he comes across a small paperback booklet in 'The Little Library of Art' about De Chirico's early paintings. Initially, the reproductions strike him as flat, facile: 'arbitrary assemblages, in semi-classical, semi-modern settings, of unrelated motifs—aqueducts, trains, arcades, gloves, fruit, statues—with an occasional applied touch of easy mystery: in one painting, for instance, an over-large shadow of a hidden figure approaching from round a corner' (91). But among the reproductions one, 'perhaps because of the title', catches his attention: 'The Enigma of Arrival'. Despite his initial rejection of De Chirico's 'easy mystery', he feels that 'in an indirect, poetical way' this refers to something—as yet inexplicit—in his own experience. He learns that the title was not the painter's own, but given by Apollinaire 'who died young in 1918, from influenza following a war wound, to the great grief of Picasso and others' (91).

Illness, death, and grief permeate the texture of the writing of *Enigma*: a 'sad pastoral' Salman Rushdie called it on its appearance, 'one of the saddest books I have read in a long while, its tone one of unbroken melancholy'. Naipaul, he said, 'unlike most of his fellow migrants . . . has chosen to inhabit a pastoral England' for his 'rebirth'.[26] But if a new world appears to have been gained, much has been lost: the narrator speaks of his spirit having been broken, of his exhaustion and illness. Yet, as if out of nowhere, the apparently inconsequential details of the remembered De Chirico image, reinforced by what he learns about it, provide a focus for this seemingly enervated narrative. Significantly, the picture 'was always a surprise', because it 'changed in my memory'. However superficial the writer's conscious, critical mind might find it, the image tugs at something deeper within that requires or demands definition—repeatedly. To begin with, it prompts him to imagine

> A classical scene, Mediterranean, ancient-Roman—or so I saw it. A wharf; in the background, beyond walls and gateways (like cut-outs), there is the top of the mast of an antique vessel; on an otherwise deserted street in the foreground there are two figures, both muffled, one perhaps the person who has arrived, the other perhaps a native of the port. The scene is of desolation and mystery: it speaks of the mystery of arrival. It spoke to me of that, as it had spoken to Apollinaire. (91–92)

Like other members of the avant-garde of the first two decades of the twentieth century, both De Chirico and Apollinaire were restless wanderers driven by the desire to arrive, to find a home, to establish an identity. We can think of them as the two figures in the painting, transformed by Naipaul into a visitor and a 'native', allegorising the archetypal colonial experience. For Guglielmo de Kostrowitzky or, as he came to be known when he had 'nativised' himself as the Parisian Apollinaire, the premature death alluded to by Naipaul interrupted all journeying. While for De Chirico, born 1888 in the seaside town of Volos on the Greece-Ottoman border of Italian parents, meeting and being taken up by Apollinaire in Paris provided the most important stage in his travels, since it was there that he first gained recognition for his 'metaphysical landscapes'— as Apollinaire called them when reviewing the Salon d'Autumne of 1913.[27] Yet thereafter, sojourns in various Italian cities, the United States, and, finally, Rome, where De Chirico settled at last, reflected a lifelong search for a reality imagined in terms of reverie, nostalgia, dream, and foreboding—themes he was to revisit endlessly, to the extent even of making copies of his own earlier paintings, much to the annoyance of collectors.[28]

Not that I am suggesting Naipaul knew all this about De Chirico; yet with a sensibility open to the childhood memories and early experiences of the contrast between transitoriness (trains, broken columns, ships) and permanence (classical statuary, figures from myth) that intrigued De Chirico, Naipaul is also fascinated by the classics, ancient Rome, and the concept of Empire.[29] So he is led in *The Enigma of Arrival* to consider the possibility of writing (it is told in the subjunctive) a brief story based on the De Chirico picture. The result is a narrative inserted within the main story which becomes something, as Rushdie noticed, 'utterly unlike anything Naipaul has ever written'.[30] The story would be set in classical times, says the narrator, in the Mediterranean, and he would arrive at the 'classical port' of De Chirico's picture, and 'would walk past that muffled figure on the quayside' to 'a gateway, or a door', where he would enter 'and be swallowed by the life and noise of a crowded city'. He would have 'encounters and adventures', entering houses and temples; and

> Gradually there would come to him a feeling that he was getting nowhere; he would lose his sense of mission; he would begin to know only that he was lost. His feeling of adventure would give way to panic. He would want to escape, to get back to the quayside and his ship. But he wouldn't know how. I imagined some religious ritual in which, led on by kindly people, he would unwittingly take part and find himself the intended victim. At the moment of crisis he would come upon a door, open it, and find himself back on the quayside of arrival. He has been saved; the world is as he remembered it. Only one thing is missing now. Above the cut-out walls and buildings there is no mast, no sail. The antique ship has gone. The traveller has lived out his life. (92)

This projected Borgesian tale generates the kind of frightening clarity of De Chirico at his best; and the obscure 'religious ritual' at its centre (to which, by an ironic touch, the narrator is led 'by kindly people') can be understood as a ritual of commemoration, a way of saying that what he cannot recall is the whole of his past life of travel, while he remains forever in thrall to the memories that life has generated, memories which have inescapably made him who he is. Naipaul's 'mission' is that of the writer, writing himself; the tension and frustration involved is powerfully evoked by this little allegory that otherwise sits brilliantly yet enigmatically within the narrative.

Since remembering, like writing, is a process without an end—or at least the end is death—Naipaul cannot leave it at that; he must rewrite the remembered image from De Chirico yet again. The second time, the images of the ship and the town recur, but now that he is writing the 'African story' (which the reader of Naipaul knows to be the long title narrative of *In A Free State*, 1971) that had been waiting in his memory for expression, causing pain and a fear of death, the De Chirico painting has become 'a point of rest', a 'refreshment, a promise of release', with which he can 'play' (Derrida's term comes to mind). This is how he does so:

For two days they had sailed, staying close to the shore. On the third day, the captain wakened his deck passenger and pointed to the city on the shore. 'There. You are there. Your journey's over.' But the passenger, looking at the city in the morning haze, seeing the unremarkable city debris floating out on the sea, unremarkable though the city was so famous—rotten fruit, fresh branches, bits of timber, driftwood—the passenger had a spasm of fear. He sipped the bitter honey drink the captain had given him; he pretended to get his things together; but he didn't want to leave the ship. (156–57)

But the traveller has to land, have adventures in the city that seemed so 'classical' from the ship, but 'so alien within'. He becomes a 'man on the run' who, once again, goes through a doorway to find his life's journey is done. The italicisation and use of simple narrative past tense suggest a story told: because the writer's subject has meanwhile been found—memories of himself, in Africa, recreated through writing in Wiltshire, where he now has 'a second life' (157).

If, as the author writes later, the past for him, 'as colonial and writer', was 'full of shame and mortifications', as a writer he could 'train' himself to face them. 'Indeed, they became my subjects' (221). In this sense, he *has* arrived in the foreign city, and does not need to leave it. Recreating himself through memory is the writer's, this writer's task, which, as the narrative proceeds, he finds he can address himself to with less pain and anxiety: until finally, in the concluding section of the book, he records having

> thought for years about a book like *The Enigma of Arrival*. The Mediterranean fantasy that had come to me a day or so after I had arrived in the valley—the story of the traveller, the strange city, the spent life—had been modified over the years. The fantasy and the ancient-world setting had been dropped. The story had become more personal: my journey, the

writer's journey, the writer defined by his writing discoveries, his ways of seeing, rather than by his personal adventures, writer and man separating at the beginning of the journey and coming together in a second life just before the end. (309)

The affiliations and parallels between Naipaul and De Chirico could be pursued further,[31] and among the more interesting might be the extent to which both reacted to the loss of the father in their art. De Chirico's father was a railway engineer, Naipaul's a journalist, and both figure indirectly and obsessively in their work. In many of De Chirico's early paintings (*Gare Montparnasse* or *The Melancholy of Departure*, 1914, for example) the shadow of a train represents the memory of his father, darkly present. In *A House for Mr Biswas*, Naipaul's own yearning for home and a secure identity was superimposed upon a commemoration of his father Seepersad as his predecessor, whose 'teaching' and example he repeatedly acknowledges as having given him a 'high idea of writing'.[32]

As he explained in *Finding the Centre* (his first attempt at an autobiography), the 'disorder' of his early life derived a focus from the memories of his father writing stories, stories which narrativised the family history.

> He didn't write a great deal. He wrote one long story and four or five shorter stories. In the shorter pieces my father, moving far from my mother's family and the family of his uncle by marriage, recreated his own background. The people he wrote about were poor, but that wasn't the point. These stories celebrated Indian village life, and the Hindu rituals that gave grace and completeness to that life. They also celebrated elemental things, the order of the working day, the labour of the rice-fields, the lighting of the cooking fire in the half-walled gallery of a thatched hut, the preparation and eating of food. There was very little 'story' in these stories. But to me they gave a beauty (which in a corner of my mind still endures, like a fantasy of home) to the Indian village life I had never known.[33]

Thus a memory-fantasy of rural India, handed down through his father's writing to the son, created a nostalgic fantasy of 'grace and completeness', of the celebration of ordinary things, absent from Naipaul's own upbringing in rural Trinidad. And it turns out that the fantasy of rural England, created by his reading of English literature, adds another, yearned-for layer which suddenly seems on his 'arrival' in Wiltshire to have become complete.[34] But of course it has not; nor can it be more than a temporary refuge for his sense of self.

Naipaul's anxiety about identity has driven him into a continuous rewriting of his own journey from the former colonial home in Trinidad through a multitude of narrative genres and perspectives, touching on the migrations of people worldwide, while always returning to the figure of the writer, and

40   *Postcolonial Nostalgias*

the question of who he is and where he belongs. Often attacked or dismissed for his lack of sympathy towards progressive movements among former colonial societies, he does however at times find a complex connection between himself and what he calls his family's 'remembered India', a 'wounded civilization' that bewildered him even as he tried to discover his own Hindu past there, in an idealised, pre-imperial, pre-Muslim homeland.[35] At the same time, returning to his childhood, as he has done numerous times in his writing, Naipaul's journey has included the discovery that the country town where he was in fact born in Trinidad, Chaguanas, had 'an aboriginal name', the name of 'a troublesome small tribe of just over a thousand' who had acted as river guides for some seventeenth-century English raiders, before being wiped out by the Spanish for some unspecified crime, and whose 'name had disappeared from the records'.[36]

Remembering India

It is a common experience for the reader of Naipaul to have this sense of a writer whose insights, whose identifications, go beyond his opinions, themselves expressions of an everyday, invented and cynical self created in order to challenge and resist any questioning of his background, race, or class. This has been most in evidence in his treatment of India. If Indian and African in the Caribbean have been, as his earlier books suggest—but many contemporaries would disagree—left in a void by the processes of history, then at least the Indian can grasp the root of an earlier, identifiable culture, having been spared the transatlantic slave trade—or so the reasoning might run. But what did Naipaul find when he went to India? The titles of the three books he has written about the country suggest what he thought he found: *An Area of Darkness* (1964); *India: A Wounded Civilization* (1977); and *India: A Million Mutinies Now* (1990). As he confessed early in the first account

> Even now, though time has widened, though space has contracted and I have travelled lucidly over that area which was to me the area of darkness, something of darkness remains, in those attitudes, those ways of thinking and seeing, which are no longer mine.[37]

It is a darkness he must continue to explore: 'But increasingly I understand that my Indian memories, the memories of that India which lived on into my childhood in Trinidad, are like trapdoors into a bottomless past'.[38] His Indian identity is unreachable, threatening. Even when, in the third and last Indian book, he introduces people who have 'ideas now about who they are and what they owe themselves', he cannot relate to them.[39] Early on in that book he reiterates the childhood emotions which first took him towards India, an idea rather than a place, but an idea offering both refuge and imprisonment, like a neurosis, the neurosis of the colonial subject:

> I grew up with two ideas of India. The first idea—not one I wanted to go into too closely—was about the kind of country from which my ancestors had come . . . Migration to the New World, shaking us out of the immemorial accepting ways of peasant India, had made us ambitious; but in colonial and agricultural Trinidad, during the Depression, there were few opportunities to rise. With this poverty around us, and with this sense of the world as a kind of prison . . . India . . . became in my imagination a most fearful place . . . This India, or this anxiety about where we had come from, was like a neurosis.
>
> There was a second India. It balanced the first. This second India was the India of the independence movement, the India of the great names. It was also the India of the great civilization and the great classical past. It was the India by which, in all the difficulties of our circumstances, we felt supported. It was an aspect of our identity, the community identity we had developed, which, in multi-racial Trinidad, had become more like a racial identity.[40]

His failure to settle in India brought with it the realisation that what he found, instead of a land of achievement based on a whole, living and long-standing culture, was another fractured culture, a mixture of mimicry of the West and 'oriental' resignation. No wonder, then, that the dream recorded on the last page of *An Area of Darkness* compares his search for identity to a piece of patterned cloth unwoven to trace the figures, which unravels until the unravelling spreads 'from the cloth to the table to the house to all matter, *until the whole trick was undone* '.[41]

The image is doubly suggestive: of profound, existential frustration at the outcome of his search for a common, historically grounded identity; and of the complex tangle of narrative forms or ways of writing, which represent his continuing search for a secure sense of self. The sense he displays of a threatened identity failing to recover itself emerges in such works as the multi-genre, fictional, and non-fictional *In a Free State*, the writing of which features within *The Enigma of Arrival* as yet another failure to recover himself through a proper relationship with the past. The difficulty remains that which perhaps faces all postcolonials: of which history to claim, which of the many histories, before, during, and after the dominant imperial histories are truly theirs. The different stages of Naipaul's journey through India become ideas, constituents of his psyche that he yearns to make whole, but cannot.

As the writer becomes aware of this nostalgia for wholeness, *The Enigma of Arrival* signals a turning point, a moment of commitment to an identity which, paradoxically, will be represented not as the stable and autonomous subject of conventional autobiography and memoir, but as shifting and dependent upon the subject itself in the present. This subject embodies the act of remembering so as to give meaning to the remembered self (or selves) of the past. That meaning, or rather, set of meanings, reflects the uncertainty of the provincial, the colonial, that he repeatedly calls himself—most strikingly when he remarks that, growing up in Trinidad, 'I was used to living in a world where the signs were without meaning or without the meaning intended by their makers' and 'of a piece with the abstract, arbitrary nature of my education' (120).

Insofar as his writing remains focused upon this personal past as a matter of return, it remains nostalgic, but in a more complex, self-aware sense: he realises both the negative and idealising dangers of nostalgic reminiscence on the one hand, and on the other hand the limitations of all such harking back. Hence the mood of acceptance that overtakes the last section of the book, when he realises that, as his sister's Hindu burial ceremony reminds him, after all the family's travelling, 'There was no ship of antique shape now to take us back' (317).

Remembering the Modern Self and History

As the neuroscientist Eric Kandel has suggested

> Recall of memory is a creative process. What the brain stores is thought to be only a core memory. Upon recall, this core memory is then elaborated upon and reconstructed, with subtractions, additions, elaborations and distortions.[42]

In *The Enigma of Arrival*, Naipaul recounts his first arrival in Wiltshire through recalling the figure of Jack, his neighbour, and others in the landscape. As he retells that arrival, with varying emphases and interspersed with other memories, it turns out that, as if mirroring his own condition, none of the people around him are as rooted as they seem: they, too, are subject to change and decay.

And so he proceeds, creatively revising, elaborating, subtracting, and identifying himself with different images of himself arising in memory. His remembered, repeated yet revised story of the figures in the De Chirico painting is of something Mediterranean, and classical. 'The idea of living in my imagination in that classical Roman world was attractive to me. A beautiful, clear, dangerous world, far removed from the setting in which I had found myself' (92). The 'antique-quayside story' can, it seems, provide a release from the feelings of menace and threat that memories of his African experience engender in him as he writes the story of that experience (96). But, as the repetitions and revisions continue, the sense of self is of an idea in suspension, sustaining only the continuing search.

The instability and contingency of a narrative such as *The Enigma of Arrival* are what we would expect from anything so thoroughly dependent upon memory—which, as St Augustine pointed out in the first truly modern attempt to understand it, only exists in the present. I referred earlier to the western, Lockean tradition of identity as a construct created through memory; but it is revealing to turn further back, back indeed to Augustine, whose life was spent in the Mediterranean and classical world Naipaul imagines he sees depicted in the De Chirico painting. As soon as Augustine turned to himself to ask 'Who are you?' the answer, beyond those creaturely functions we share with animals, was to be found in memory—a vast storehouse of images, a cloister of secrets, an immeasurable sanctuary (as he variously characterises it)—memory, to which we address ourselves and yet which remains a puzzle, although without it, as Augustine says and neurologists such as Oliver Sacks have proved, we could not even speak of ourselves.[43]

Augustine does not in any simple sense anticipate our understandings, however. His account of memory in Books X and XI of the *Confessions* may indeed be where we can discern the first signs of modernity, if we think of Augustine's conception of time linking events not merely in the classical, linear, chronological way, or simply by cause and effect, but in terms of a singular horizon of interpretation, the omniscient God. These terms, says Thomas Docherty, anticipate the modernity of thinkers from Descartes onwards who call, not on God, but on a conception of the unified human self as a subject existing through and beyond time.[44] Docherty is persuasive for example in construing T. S. Eliot's ruminations in *Four Quartets* (1943) upon memory, time, and timelessness as another migrant writer's escape into a constructed present, but these cannot be taken as representative of even western modernity, insofar as anybody's can; nor does Augustine present so unambiguously modern a conception of memory, even assuming we can simply replace his call on the wholeness of God with a call on the wholeness of the unified human self.

More striking is the fact that memory is questioned, indeed radically defamiliarised by Augustine, for whom it is more than just an ability to remember or an act of remembering (or forgetting). He still conceives of memory as the *source* of his sense of self; nor is there any gap between what he remembers himself to have been, and what he finds himself to be in the present; moreover, what he remembers himself to have been is demonstrably narratable, as in those earlier books of the *Confessions* about his childhood and early life that precede his reflections upon memory. For Augustine, there is an unbroken link between the narratable past and the present in which it may be narrated, unlike the sense of memory as a more arbitrary phenomenon, which arrives with the European Romantics, who sever this link between past and present, while yearning for its recovery.

For Romantics like Wordsworth, the individual in his or her solitude can be imagined by the poet to live in relation to nature and the past. In *The Enigma of Arrival*, Naipaul readily infuses his neighbours with Wordsworthian associations—Jack's father-in-law seen from afar with 'a load of wood on his bent back' could be the subject of a poem that 'Wordsworth might have called "The Fuel-Gatherer"' (26). Does this prove that the narrator has finally managed to overcome his colonial alienation, his knowing in apartness—reflected in Naipaul's well-known early essay 'Jasmine', in which he remarked on 'Wordsworth's notorious poem about the daffodil. A pretty little flower no doubt; but we had never seen it'?[45] Or rather, does it suggest how far the migrant who arrives in a new land has to adjust his or her perceptions in order to feel secure, a process which it turns out is—not futile, but never-ending? Sent some poems about Krishna and Shiva by his landlord, he notes that they are written out of a 'romance' of India, giving the author, for all the feebleness of his literary efforts, a sense of being 'rooted in England, wealth, empire, the idea of glory, material satiety, a very great security' (192–93). Whereas the narrator, who admits to himself some element of the man's 'accidia' and withdrawal, the truth is that unlike his landlord, 'I had set myself up as a writer—as deliberately as that', and had 'engaged myself with the world' (197–98). In short, he has willed an identity for himself and, as he sees it, created it out of nothing; although it is a nothingness into which he may fall, lacking a strong enough sense of home or place. He is the traveller whose ship has left, and who therefore does not, can not finally know where or who he is. He must simply keep on writing, writing himself into the only identity in which he feels—paradoxically, since it is always a fragile construct—secure: that of the writer.

The instability and uncertainty of this conception of identity in its profound questioning of the multiple selves of the past, and their various points of view or 'truths', has a source in Romanticism, most evidently in Jean-Jacques Rousseau. Here was another writer in exile who, in his *Confessions* (1781–88), was, as Frank Kermode has well put it, in 'hot pursuit of a closure to be achieved by leaving nothing out, by inserting, and then later supplementing, innumerable bits of truth and leaving the reader to make them whole'.[46] The opening words of Rousseau's *Confessions* characteristically express a double untruth, while claiming the truth: 'I am resolved on an undertaking that has no model and will have no imitator' he begins. 'I want to show my fellow-men a man in all the truth of nature; and this man is to be myself'.[47] The gap between the narrating, fictionalising 'I' and the self which is its subject in Rousseau may be discerned variously inscribed in all those nineteenth-century *Bildungsromane* from *Werther* and *Jane Eyre* to *Great Expectations* and *The Story of an African Farm*, all of which display the progress (or, latterly, the decline or degeneration) of the self by means of a double perspective, internal and external, if not literally first-person and third-person. But as another wanderer upon the face of the earth, Rimbaud, famously wrote in his *Lettre du Voyant* (1871), 'Je est un autre',[48] summing up the increasing sense of disconnection or splitting that troubles the modernist inheritors of Romanticism's nostalgic yearning for past selves: a splitting already there in Rousseau, in the multiplicity of remembered selves his writing generates, and the incompatibilities between them. But for the postcolonial, self-questioning goes further.

Yet it is this lack of fit, and the emptiness or excess between narrating and narrated selves in Rousseau's writing, or, in Derridean terms, between presence and absence, that engages Naipaul in his search for identity. What he is unable to do is seek ways of narrating the self that bear witness to events that have disrupted our frames of reference entirely—events such as the Atlantic slave trade.

To say 'such as' here is already to imply that the Atlantic slave trade is not unique in human history, or at least that there *is* a frame of reference within which it becomes narratable. The paradox is that we are unable to write or indeed talk without referring to or inhabiting in some sense what we inherit or recall, which leads to some difficulty—if we accept Primo Levi's insistence in *The Drowned and the Saved* (1988) that only the 'drowned' or murdered could truly bear witness to the extreme experiences that he survived to remember, despite the fact that 'all, or almost all the factors that can obliterate or deform the mnemonic record are at work' in such remembering.[49] The result is bound to be fragmentary, incomplete, and in need of decipherment. The dispersed nature of the process of interpretation is a function of the multiple possibilities of modern or contemporary texts in their changing contexts, which include the inability to come to terms with, or properly remember, the most extreme events we can think of—mass enslavement, murder and torture on a scale previously unimaginable.

This has obvious implications for postcolonial writers. Naipaul once notoriously claimed that the Caribbean had no history. What he should have claimed, and indeed was testifying to whether or not admitting it, was the loss or erasure of history, of many histories, through the extreme events of mass slavery and indentured labour, and his own inability to represent these losses. 'The history of the islands can never be satisfactorily told' was what he actually wrote. 'Brutality is not the only difficulty. History is built around achievement and creation; and nothing was created in the West Indies'.[50] As he later remarked in a flash of self-awareness in *A Way in the World*, 'that feeling of the void had to do with my temperament, the temperament of a child of a recent Asian-Indian immigrant community in a mixed population: the child looked back and found no family past, found a blank'.[51] It was as if there was no memory, not even the fantasy of a ritual nostalgia, available to him, produced by the lack in the community in which he had arrived, like the mysterious figure on the dockside in De Chirico's picture.

Yet it is this lack of fit, and the emptiness or excess between narrating and narrated selves in Rousseau's writing, or, in Derridean terms, between presence and absence, that engages Naipaul in his search for identity. What he is unable to do is seek ways of narrating the self that bear witness to events that have disrupted our frames of reference entirely—events such as the Atlantic slave trade. One has to turn to much younger writers, such as Fred D'Aguiar (born 1960), who sees himself as black British rather than West Indian or Caribbean, for an acknowledgement of that past—in *The Longest Memory*

(1994) for example, or *Feeding the Ghosts* (1997), which is based on a true account of a slave who survived being thrown overboard with 132 others.

The question that remains is: what are the terms in which it might become possible to mourn the extreme events of the past, insofar as they are recollectable? To begin with, we have to bear in mind that memory does not, cannot belong to the individual alone, any more than it can belong to the community or collective alone: it is an arena or, in De Chirico's iconography, a place of arrival and departure, where the shadows of the past are long and mysterious, but they affect all of us irresistibly, profoundly. Personal memory may appear to go unrecognised in the public realm of history, or at least to be undermined for its lack of rigour or precision; but it provides the momentum as well as the detail without which that kind of approved memory could not exist. This is what takes the everyday sense of witnessing, upon which historians rely, to the level of an act of recognition or acknowledgement that has an ethical and no doubt a political dimension as well.

In the next chapter, I will look at how identity and memory intersect from a more personal perspective, considering the question of what is meant by the nostalgically invoked 'homeland' in Southern Africa: specifically, how the search for an originary 'primitive' figure in the landscape reflects a new drive to create a 'home' for the decolonising, if not yet fully postcolonial nation.

3 'The Broken String'
Remembering the Homeland

> My Father
> Sang (that)
> The string has broken. . . .
>
> [Diä!kwain, 28 July [1875]][1]

> Oh! Fond farewell to savages and explorations!
>
> Claude Lévi-Strauss, *Tristes Tropiques* (1955)[2]

Home is Where One Starts From

Some one hundred and twenty years ago a group of German-speaking immigrants in the new city of Johannesburg decided to trek west across the Kalahari desert. Their motives were twofold: to get away from the impending war between the Boers and the British over control of the gold fields; and to seek their fortunes in a territory recently annexed by Bismarck as part of the scramble for Africa. The central Kalahari remains one of the more inhospitable areas of the world, and it was not long before the Europeans found themselves in difficulties. They had African ox-wagon drivers, and their leader was an experienced explorer; but they ran out of water, and some were already dying, when they met one of the Kalahari's nomadic tribes-people, possibly a G/wi.

The G/wi Bushman showed the dying trekkers how to dig down deep into the hard desert earth for the tubers of a scrubby-looking plant which, when squeezed, produced water. And so the trekkers eventually reached their goal, the small settlement of Windhoek, where by 1898 the leader of the expedition had become a successful trader, with his own 'house' on the Kaiserstrasse. His name was Albert Liebenstein; and he was my grandfather. As he told me, he owed his life to the Bushman. And therefore so do I. Which means I have good reason for wanting to remember the Bushman people, when I think about my own origins, ancestry, or homeland; although whether or not, or how far, that remembering should include or refer to the Bushman peoples is an interesting and important question, for reasons I will discuss in what follows.

It should be clear from the outset that there is no 'typical' or 'essential' Bushman. The stereotypical descriptors (diminutive, high-cheek-boned, yellow-skinned, nomadic people speaking languages remarkable for their 'click' sounds) in fact apply to an extinct people of the Cape Province. Anthropologists and ethnographers have until recently used the term 'San' in preference to 'Bushman' (from Dutch 'Bosjemans') on the grounds that the latter is both racist and sexist. But 'San' is the Khoikhoi (formerly 'Hottentot') word for forager, once aimed at those who had lost their cattle, and so also used to mean 'vagabond', 'tramp', or 'rascal': hence a more recent preference for 'Bushman', despite its negative associations. And while other terms have relevance, from the Tswana 'Masarwa' (plural Basarwa), originally signifying small people, to G/wi, an ethnic self-designation for specific southeastern Kalahari groups, 'Bushman' remains as an internationally recognised English-language term, embraced as well by many (although not all) activist groups.[3] So I shall use 'Bushman' in what follows, and other terms where appropriate, clarifying my usage through context as best I can.

I should also point out that I am not going to engage with the vast and ever-increasing academic and popular discourses around the figure of the Bushman, except insofar as they touch on my chosen theme. I will be referring to certain key texts and moments as I proceed, but in any case the reader who wishes to pursue the debates further could well start with the first issue of the online journal *Critical African Studies* which, significantly, opened with an essay by anthropologist-ethnographer Edwin Wilmsen on the representation of the Bushmen, summing up the argument of his many articles and books on the subject. This was followed by responses and comments from other scholars in the field. Wilmsen's argument is that a Bushman image has become 'part of our society's—professional and public—network of signs', a 'mythologized' construct providing a form of security for an age in crisis. Many challenge his assumptions and argument, although it seems reasonable enough to suggest as he does that the modernist search for a form of secure identity in a time of crumbling certainties may fix on the symbolic primitivism represented by the Bushman figure—a primitivism that has attracted many artists and writers not necessarily familiar with that figure in any explicit way.[4]

Amongst a wide range of works, Wilmsen cites T. S. Eliot's *Four Quartets* as an instance of the yearning for 'a reintegration for the human spirit' in modern times. It is not necessary to subscribe to Wilmsen's overall thesis of how this yearning—a form of nostalgia—has come to be expressed in developments within ethnography or anthropology to agree that Eliot's work represents the urge of the modern exile to find a 'home' or 'homeland'. 'Home is where one starts from', as Eliot pointed out in the 'East Coker' section of *The Four Quartets*. The small Somersetshire village which provided the focus for this quartet was not where Eliot started from; but it was where he chose to end, having his ashes laid to rest there. Only by an act of what I would call *re-membering*, recreating his sense of who he was through an act of literary-historic recuperation, could Eliot claim East Coker as his 'home', its churchyard both his end and his beginning. Eliot's familial ancestors left East Coker for the New World in the seventeenth century, and did not return. Even after he became a British citizen, Eliot used to sign himself 'metoikos', Greek for 'resident alien'.[5] He was behaving in a way now made much more familiar by the forces of recent globalisation, which include, although they go beyond, the earlier impact of empire. As Robin Cohen suggests, for diasporic subjects, remembering the homeland has opened up the scope for multiple forms of identity within and beyond the nation-state.[6] Yet this also implies an increasing lack of certainty or finality about home as a place of origin, undermining nostalgia as a phenomenon of positive identifications and affiliations, even while it is more widely and profoundly felt.

In this chapter I will be exploring further some of the ways in which home, and the homeland (which invokes both the private and the larger, public or national space) may provide a troubling source of re-membered, or recreated identities, and in particular how the figure of the primal inhabitant of southern Africa, the nomadic hunter-gatherer Bushman, has been constructed and deconstructed by certain South African writers nostalgically redefining postcolonial nationhood from within, rather than from diasporic spaces such as the one I inhabit, and from which I write this as part of my own continuing engagement with my beginnings.

Re-Membering the 'Lost' Native Land

People may and do often feel alienated from the place where they are, even when they have been born there; although a sense of alienation is more likely if you have been obliged to depart from your place of birth and upbringing, and make a new home for yourself elsewhere—when, as the old Cape Bushman trope has it, the string is broken. Such feelings of alienation are often sharpened, if they have not already been created, by historical and political circumstances, notably the many migrations—voluntary or enforced—of empire and its aftermath. Such migrations have had many causes, from exploration to enslavement; but they have led to a common anxiety about the past, and in particular those pasts that have been misinterpreted, forgotten, or erased by the processes of colonisation, just as the various peoples of colonised countries have been misinterpreted, forgotten, or erased. To overcome this anxiety many colonial and postcolonial writers have tried to re-imagine or recreate their homelands, using memory, but also memory's stepchild, nostalgia.

As I have pointed out earlier, everyone is sometimes affected by nostalgia, especially at moments of personal anxiety; but it is also a phenomenon arising at moments of public crisis or redefinition, since it goes beyond individual psychology, permeating both popular and elite cultures on a global scale, and affecting the way people identify themselves as members of a group, community, nation, or state. The idea of a homeland is always also bound up with the individuals who remember it. In my case that means tied up with the country of my birth and upbringing, and its struggles to achieve an identity as a modern, democratic nation-state within the southern African region as a whole, which includes the adjacent state of Namibia, formerly South West Africa, formerly Deutsch-Südwest-Afrika. Namibia thus becomes another part of my personal 'homeland' narrative. To acknowledge that narrative as a construction is to place it under erasure, framing it provisionally so as to view it critically within certain defined contexts.

We think we know our identities as a result of a kind of internal narrative we construct for ourselves out of our memories: a process of knowing that can be and often has been seen as analogous to what happens in nations, the product not only of a sense of shared language, culture, and territory, but crucially also of a real or, as Benedict Anderson's *Imagined Communities* insists, imagined ancestry. 'All profound changes in consciousness,' Anderson notes, 'by their very nature, bring with them characteristic amnesias. Out of such oblivions, in specific historical circumstances, spring narratives.' Narratives give us the help we need to associate 'this naked baby in the yellowed photograph' with our adult selves. And the photograph, 'fine child of the age of mechanical reproduction, is only the most peremptory of a huge modern accumulation of documentary evidence which simultaneously records a certain apparent continuity and emphasizes its loss from memory'. Out of this 'estrangement' emerges an identity which, because it cannot be simply remembered, must be narrated. 'As with modern persons, so it is with nations'. Yet such extrapolation from person to nation is not quite as straightforward as it seems. Persons have natural beginnings and ends: not so with nations, which must invent their originary moments, a 'fashioning' through time that proceeds from the present into the past, thus inverting conventional genealogy.[7]

There seems to be no question that nations and indeed empires yearn for ancestry, or 'tradition', usually embodied in a narrative of origin that connects their peoples through a shared sense of longing and belonging, linking them to what in German is called *Die Heimat*, the homeland.[8] The word 'Heimat' has immense and continuing resonance in the German context, as Edgar Reisz' controversial epic film series of that title (1984, 1992, 2004) well demonstrated. The feelings such material evoked went deep, not least because of the long and troubled history of nation-building in Germany, which lacked the centralised statehood which contiguous nations such as France or Holland or Britain had achieved by the eighteenth century, when what we now think of as Germany was still governed by hundreds of princes, many of whom rattled around in stuffy little provincial courts.

When German unification finally became an accomplished fact in the closing decades of the nineteenth century, the concepts and ideology of empire were serving as a means of incorporating colonisers and colonised within a larger vision of imperial command and control. This involved the imposition of retrospectively created or 'remembered' traditions—however vague or plural—upon the subject colony, and in order to define themselves as the 'natural and undisputed masters' of the colonised, white settlers also drew upon European invented traditions 'both to define and justify their roles, and also to provide models of subservience into which it was sometimes possible to draw Africans'.[9] Colonial ceremonies of state and local control often incorporated what was believed to be—whether it actually was or not—indigenous custom, such as, in Africa, kingly or chieftainship investiture proceedings. In short, an exchange of meanings took place. The stereotypical postcolonial concept of the direct imposition of ideology and control, while bearing witness to the realities of power in the colonial situation broadly defined, is too simple by far, and fails to capture this element of interchange, which marked in different and complex ways the circumstances of different times, places, and encounters.

Within such exchanges, the idea of a homeland has a peculiar potency. To begin with, the image of a homeland has served generally as a symbol of continuity through time and the vicissitudes of history. It is more than a matter of 'home'; although as Rosemary George has pointed out, if the idea of 'home' may seem at first sight to refer exclusively to the private domain, the word's 'wider signification' is to the place or space where people feel they belong: it is an 'imagined location'.[10] 'Homeland' incorporates 'home' as a focus for thinking on a multiplicity of levels, including the individual, family, community, society, and nation; it also functions as an indicator of the spatial aspect or geographic location of imagined belonging. The complex nature of 'home' and hence too of 'homeland' as a so-called 'spatial imaginary' has been well demonstrated by Alison Blunt and Robyn Dowling, who show how far these concepts can invoke both a sense of belonging and of alienation, and in particular how the interplay of ideas of home, nation, and empire helped determine the configuration of past imperial power on one level, and domesticity on another.[11]

One of the dangers (for others if not also themselves) of homeland imagining on the part of Europeans has been their tendency to include within it a space identified with both past and present colonising ambitions. For example, in a 1926 novel with the prophetic title *Volk Ohne Raum* ('People without space'), by Hans Grimm (who thereby gave the Nazis one of their most potent slogans), the space identified as homeland for the German people took in all those areas of the world Germany had lost through the Treaty of Versailles, including South West Africa.[12] In an uncanny parallel, in Laurens van der Post's *Lost World of the Kalahari* (1958) the quest to find what the author called the 'unique and almost vanished First People of my native land'[13] took in not just South Africa, but also the adjacent territories where his Dutch ancestors trekked in their search for farmland, thereby helping to destroy those First People as surely as the German and then South African colonisers almost finished them off—almost, because the remnants may still be found; and indeed of those remaining there are some who are still struggling to reclaim what they have lost, by legal and other (i.e. cultural) means, aided, ironically, by the present German government, as well as by the new South African democracy, both of which have apologised for past crimes towards indigenous peoples.[14]

It is these crimes, during the long, drawn-out process of colonial invasion and settlement, that have created what van der Post remembered as 'the profound quality of melancholy which lies at the heart of the physical scene in Southern Africa', a melancholy generated by the air of death he perceived hanging over his homeland.[15] What has gone is the 'pure' Bushman he kept searching for, but could not ultimately find, because it is the product of a nostalgically essentialising imagination, sorrowfully reconstructing a complete people out of the fragments of the past—the myths, stories, and rock art of the desert, where Bushmen lived for tens of thousands of years, in an area covering all the southern African nation-states of today.

Van der Post's imagining was far from unique. Three years after the publication of *Lost World*, Athol Fugard noted his friend 'J van R' remembering being 'fascinated by the Bushmen paintings in a cave in the hills' on the Free State farm he roamed as a boy, saying 'I can understand how people are fascinated by them, especially children. They are fantastic and beautiful—and so old. For me they hadn't been painted by people. It was a holy place. Spiritual, you know'.[16] Clearly for J van R 'spiritual' signified something outside the beliefs and practices of organised religion, something personal, intuitive, and experiential, connecting him with his remembered place. William James once defined religious experience as the feelings of individuals in solitude towards whatever they apprehended in relation to themselves as divine: feelings prior to the theologies and institutions that may grow out of them.[17] For J van R, the remembered feelings evoked by the Bushmen paintings represented a spirituality both ancient and impersonal. It is to his credit that he found spirituality outside his church, since at the time all the Afrikaans churches supported apartheid, and indeed famously threw out the few heretics who disagreed. Nevertheless it is dismaying now to note the emphasis upon the Bushman paintings' appeal to children, and the lack of interest in who was responsible for producing them.

Initially prompted by the same kind of childhood memory, van der Post went further, seeking the Bushman painters themselves; although underlying his journeying lies a seductive complex of feelings:

> I love my own time too much and would not have chosen to live in any other even if that had been possible. Yet, if forced to an alternative I would choose to be the first European in Africa free to see, before we laid our blind, violent hands upon it the vast land glowing from end to

end in the blue of its Madonna days like some fabulous art gallery with newly restored and freshly painted Bushman canvases of smooth stone and honey-coloured rock. For so, apparently, it existed for many centuries. As fast as a painting faded it was either restored or a new theme painted over it. At the same time entirely new pictures were added to the great store. It is astonishing how in this late hour, they burn within the aubergine shadows of cave and overhang of cliff and krans, and what power they still possess to provoke an almost unbearable nostalgia for the vanished painter and for the spirit that possessed him. True, their fire is dying and the ruby coals are blown silver with the ashes of time. But underneath there is enough authentic flame to show the Bushman and his chosen companions on the enigmatic spoor.[18]

Madonna days, aubergine shadows, ruby coals, and enigmatic spoor—this is the kind of thing that gives meaning to the phrase 'purple passage'. And yet, van der Post presents an image of the land that acknowledges the deep past of some of its people, revealed in the fabulous art that remains.

The Lost World of the Kalahari was the first of two popular and widely influential memoirs that came out of an expedition van der Post mounted to the Tsodilo Hills (Botswana) in the mid 1950s in search of the Bushmen for what became a world-famous BBC documentary. Despite starting off by denying that he would wish to live in an earlier time, he admits 'unbearable nostalgia' for the vanished Bushman painter and 'the spirit that possessed him', a spirit inhabiting the pre-colonial landscape while, alas, the individual human bearers of it have become little more than a dying fire in his overheated imagination, stoked by the ideas of J. G. Frazer's *Golden Bough* (1890) and C. G. Jung's *Modern Man in Search of a Soul* (1933)—the latter in particular. Within four years of its publication in London in 1958, Commonwealth sales of *Lost World of the Kalahari* amounted to 225,000, despite criticism from figures such as Doris Lessing, who wrote in the *New Statesman* that white African writers like van der Post were using the continent as a peg to hang their egos on, or the reviewer who said van der Post was 'ridden with mystical fancies' and overladen with 'symbolism and Meaning'.[19]

It is too easy to knock van der Post for his nostalgic-essentialist fictionalising of experience. He once remarked that when he was a prisoner of war of the Japanese, he was forced to realise what it was like to be on the other end of race prejudice, finding himself 'in the position which is the nearest equivalent to what I imagine is the position of the black man in Africa today'. He concluded that it was the fear of the 'dark' side within that we projected on to others, scapegoating them as the Nazis scapegoated Jews and Gypsies, and a 'clue' to 'a way out of prejudice' could be found in the Bushman painting in the Brandberg, 'The White Lady'—a vision of the 'feminine', the 'loving, caring side of life'.[20] We can perhaps appreciate this vision for what it is, while being aware that the famous figure from which van der Post articulates his vision is a male shaman: that is to say, 'The White Lady' is neither white nor a lady. As his recent biographer J.D.F. Jones points out, even the Bushman woman van der Post said he remembered nursing him, and to whom he dedicated *Lost World*, is best understood as a mythical figure, changing shape from book to book; and her stories, like those of other Bushman people he claimed to have met, may well derive from other sources. But if van der Post created an image of the Bushmen as primitive, unspoilt Stone Age people, with whom he felt some special, spiritual affinity, whether they were (in his words) 'tame' and domesticated, or 'wild' and still living in desert isolation, the twinkle-eyed old explorer also asserted that their way of life, their folklore, customs, and above all their belief systems were of great value and should be preserved.[21] And this at a time when the Bushmen were still regularly portrayed within southern Africa and abroad as inferior people, at the lowest end of the evolutionary scale, and, like aboriginal peoples everywhere, subject to Darwinian notions of the difference between themselves and the so-called 'developed' peoples of the world—a view which in more attenuated form, survives. The experience of Fugard's friend is not uncommon, and continues. When writer Michael Cope was a boy the family lived on a farm in the Lowveld, an area 'uninhabited before white people came, I was often told'. One weekend the family set off to climb a local landmark to visit the Bushman paintings found there.

> The endurance of the paintings seemed to imply permanent habitation. But there were no Bushmen, or people looking like what we imagined Bushmen to look like, in the area, and the orphaned paintings seemed to emerge from a primeval and magical prehistory shared or perhaps created by Rider Haggard and other colonial romanticists. How, I wondered, had these people survived the tsetse-flies?
>
> I now surmise that they left their mark during seasonal visits, their nomadic habits enabling them to survive the flies long enough to make the paintings.[22]

The writer's awareness that his earlier perception of the Bushmen living in some magical realm outside time might be the product of the nostalgia of 'colonial romanticists' suggests a more critical, historically informed view of that kind of nostalgia is developing. Yet the idealising continues, as do the memories.

Idealising Disappearing Cultures

It is a striking irony that Darwin himself—whose theories of evolution and natural selection were so readily taken up by racists to justify slavery and colonial oppression—also argued that the different races had a common ancestry, and were therefore not so different after all. Coming across aboriginal people in New South Wales in 1836, he sensed what their fate would be:

wherever the European has trod, death seems to pursue the aboriginal. We may look to the wide extent of the Americas, Polynesia, the Cape of Good Hope and Australia, and find the same result . . . It was melancholy at New Zealand to hear the fine energetic natives saying that they knew the land was doomed to pass from their children.[23]

Ambivalence towards the aboriginal inhabitants of colonised territories may be found in many quarters. From late Victorian Cape Town, where he was busy recording the language and culture of the /Xam (Cape) Bushmen, German philologist Wilhelm Bleek sent a request to his aunt in Germany to contact zoologists for information about 'the sounds made by apes . . . specifically whether apes also make click-sounds with their tongues and lips'.[24]

Bleek was typical of the time in his assumption that languages, like the people who spoke them, gradually evolved into more advanced, that is to say, Northern and European forms. On the other hand, Bleek, like George Stow, another late Victorian observer and mediator of the culture of the Bushman peoples, tended to depict their beliefs as having a richness absent from those of the indigenous Zulu, Xhosa, Sotho, and Tswana peoples whom it therefore became easier for the coloniser-settlers to denigrate later on—when the prevailing ideology accorded Bantu-speakers less right to the land than the overseas settlers whose arrival was supposed to have occurred simultaneously.

The fact that most of the indigenous Ur-peoples of the subcontinent were dispersed or wiped out by incomers from north and south, not only motivated Bleek and a few others to record as much as possible of their cultures before it was too late, it also removed them from threat, thereby making them fit subjects for nostalgic idealisation at home and abroad, then and later. Early on in Olive Schreiner's influential *The Story of an African Farm*, begun during the 1870s, three farm children sit on a shelving rock 'on the surface of which were still visible some old Bushman-paintings', prompting the boy Waldo (the author's mouthpiece) to reflect that the Bushman painter 'did not know why he painted but he wanted to make something' which, if strange and laughable to them, 'to him they were very beautiful'. 'Now the Boers have shot them all, so that we never see a yellow face peeping out among the stones' he continues, a 'dreamy look' on his face; 'And the wild bucks have gone, and those days, and we are here . . . '.[25] Eugène Marais, the Afrikaans writer and naturalist who argued that humans and apes shared an inherited memory of suffering and yearning, believed that the Bushman, 'this ape-like being', was 'the only true native South African artist . . . a poet and story-teller whose genius would compare favourably with that of any human race of a far higher degree of culture'.[26] Marais' *Dwaalstories* (1937: 'Wandering/Wanderers' Tales') were versions of tales told him by an elderly Bushman, whose world, as Annie Gagiano says, was thereby vividly portrayed as 'an intact, different, but recognisable culture'.[27] But it was—as Marais acknowledged without recognising the contribution of his own people to this—a fast-disappearing culture. More common was the assumption, especially but not exclusively among Afrikaners (as an ethnic-linguistic-ideological community), that earlier cultures were invisible, as they created their pastoral idyll on the vast and supposedly empty spaces they found. As J. M. Coetzee points out, in the writing of 'meetings with the silence and emptiness of Africa' there is a certain 'historical will' to see 'as silent and empty a land that has been, if not full of human figures, not empty of them either'.[28]

Coetzee himself has allegorised the nostalgia of the settler-farmers so as to acknowledge the absent presence of the original inhabitants. For example, in his *In the Heart of the Country* (1976), published at a time when the growing resistance to apartheid had been temporarily checked at the cost of many lives, the central consciousness of the isolated spinster Magda expresses the psychopathology of the settler in terms of a retreat into pastoral delusion, and (in the concluding paragraph of the novel) a 'nostalgia for country ways'. In a lengthy passage addressed to her dead father, repeating 'Do you remember', she nostalgically recalls a childhood family expedition to the seaside, the years of the great drought, and details of the servants and animals on the farm. But there is nobody to listen to these stereotypical recollections. Her solipsistic yearning is an expression of a failure to connect with those around her, the 'ghostly brown figures' that have accompanied her whole tale, and which radically undermine her sense of Afrikaner identity, leaving her with nothing but a sense of failure.[29] As many critics have suggested, the struggle at the heart of Coetzee's fictional (and indeed metafictional) project is the struggle to find a way to represent the persecuted Other, as a means for discovering a proper, that is, ethically viable sense of self.[30] Magda's backward-looking fantasy reveals the corruption at the heart of those forms of nostalgia that look for a homeland that never existed, except in the imagination.

The story of the persecution of the Bushman peoples has often been told—one recent narrative receiving a royal imprimatur from the Prince of Wales, according to whom it was van der Post's *Lost World* 'that first alerted many of us to an extraordinary civilisation that had survived in its pristine state at the heart of Africa for thousands of years', a civilisation whose 'secret . . . was and still remains their complete immersion in the natural and spiritual rhythms of existence'; the Bushmen were, for those in 'the developed world . . . the essence of Africa', he said.[31] So deeply embedded has been this nostalgic-essentialising tendency that even the more historically informed and politically aware can falter. Freda Troup's 'Historical Introduction' to *South Africa* in Ronald Segal's oppositional Penguin African Library (1975), could still refer in her account of pre-settlement southern Africa to 'small and scattered groups of San, dwarfed and direct descendants of the proud first men who once roamed the African homelands almost unchallenged':[32] as if the Bushmen were even in pre-colonial times alas, a lowly, meek version of those fabulous Africans of the more distant past, familiar from many a nostalgic colonial narrative.

But it should be remembered that writers, whether or not inflamed with semi-mystical, prophetic apprehensions of their homeland, have always contributed to the process of creating national narratives of belonging: from the familiar, ancient classical and biblical stories used to identify and justify the founding of Greece, Rome, or Israel to the more modern narratives of the European nation-states. For some, like Scottish Marxist Tom Nairn, the motive is inevitably regressive and inward-looking, as societies 'propel themselves forward . . . by drawing more deeply upon their indigenous resources, resurrecting past folk-heroes and myths about themselves. These idealistic and romantic well-springs adhere to every form of nationalism'.[33] This is how it must appear to progressives. But progressive or not, at least we should be able to agree that national identity is not monolithic, rather it is both relational and contingent;[34] and it is best understood as a negotiable interaction between different histories or narratives, including the histories of empire: histories characterised by the ambivalences of nostalgia, as much as they are characterised by the ambivalences of homeland—a place of nurture but also, too often, oppression.

How we identify ourselves depends upon the situation in which we are called upon to do so, since in practice everyone, migrant or not, has more than one identity and even, often, more than one place to call home. For most but by no means all people in long-settled and unified countries like the United Kingdom, the question of who we are, what we call ourselves, or where our homeland lies is less of an issue than for people in, or from, the former colonised territories of the world, where national identity has been a more troubled and troubling phenomenon, and far from settled or agreed. Europe's colonial divisions in Africa created states out of hundreds of diverse groups, enclosing people without common languages, cultures, or histories. But this is not to say it is *only* in states once part of a colonial empire that nationalism is profoundly at issue, although that does take in a surprisingly large portion of the globe: the problematic status of the post-communist nations of Eastern Europe shows that often disturbing new formations are still coming into being.

Nationalism and the Homeland

The focus upon southern Africa here is, as I have said, partly because of my personal history and connections, but it is also because South Africa and to a lesser extent Namibia have within the last two decades taken on new national identities as part of a remarkable and dramatic decolonisation process—from new systems of government to new sets of official languages; from new anthems to new coats of arms and flags; and sets of new names, although in the case of South Africa not the name of the country itself, which might have been Azania, if one of the smaller and most violent black liberation groups had had its way.[35] Many commentators have pointed out that the growth of national identity in South Africa is both a recent and a violently divided and divisive phenomenon. Two South African historians have put it like this:

> For much of the twentieth century, an exclusive form of white Afrikaner nationalism, with its explicit objective the capture of the state by the white Afrikaner 'nation', has confronted its counterpart, a pan-South African black nationalism, which has sought the incorporation of Africans into the body politic. The exclusivism of Afrikaner Christian nationalism with its roots in late nineteenth-century European nationalism has been confronted by a black nationalism which, despite strong Africanist underpinnings, has in general espoused the nineteenth-century liberal values of multiracialism.[36]

One of the nearer roots of Afrikaner nationalism was National Socialism, with its evocation of German historical and symbolic myths. The white Afrikaner movement soon adopted the familiar idea of emphasising the sacred history of a nation within the state, attempting to dominate the latter through the mechanisms of party rallies, folk songs, and staged demonstrations, as well as—during World War II—paramilitary, neo-Nazi organisation. A key figure in the development of post-war nationalist ideology, Geoff Cronjé, who had studied in the Third Reich before becoming head of sociology at Pretoria University, produced a blueprint for apartheid entitled *'n Tuiste vir die Nageslag* (1945: 'A Home for Posterity'), the main aim of which was to show that the only way to preserve the culture and traditions of the Afrikaner was through racial partition, creating separate 'homes' for the different peoples or race-nations of the country, to prevent racial mixing as well as to ensure the protection and preservation of the 'pure' whites.[37]

The Africanist tradition, on the other hand, urged the opposite: as may be found in the early writings of the general-correspondence secretary of the African Native National Congress (forerunner of the ANC), Solomon Plaatje, whose historical novel *Mhudi* (1930) employed a nostalgic-romance mode to suggest that an inclusive, supra-tribal form of nationalism should prevail in southern Africa (the territory covered by his novel ranges well beyond today's national boundaries). For Plaatje and those who came later, nationalism involved a retrieval of past identities as a way of opposing settler-colonial imposition. This position has had an extraordinarily long life, as may be gathered from the recent transformation of South Africa and to a lesser extent the former South West Africa into new nations, through the retrieval and redefinition of what is meant by 'homeland': a redefinition that has been aided by literary and cultural production, and in particular by the nostalgic representation of the displaced and ignored if not utterly destroyed early peoples of the land, whose occupation extended historically beyond colonial as well as more recent national boundaries.

It is important to recall that the word 'homeland' has a specific, historically inflected resonance for South Africans and South West Africans/Namibians alike. It was one of the fundamental principles of apartheid, where indeed it differed from earlier forms of segregation, to stress the need to give the various black peoples of the subcontinent the opportunity of preserving and developing separate 'national' identities. It was a key part of the ideology of apartheid—proposed by thinkers like Cronjé—as it was gradually introduced after the 1948 elections, that these peoples were to be encouraged to live in areas considered for many years their places of origin, broadly speaking those areas of African residence laid down by the Land Act (1913), and moreover that those areas should become self-sufficient, self-governing 'ethno-national' states. Implementation of the homeland theory became the responsibility of two key figures: Werner Eiselen, brilliant son of a German missionary, and at the time secretary to the Minister of 'Native Affairs', Hendrik Verwoerd, a Dutch-born academic who, like Eiselen, held a PhD in one of the social sciences and was a former colleague at the breeding ground of apartheid ideology, Stellenbosch University.

Both argued that there was a need to protect 'native' tribal culture from the bad effects of 'Westernisation', by which they meant modernisation. Great stress was to be laid on the development of Bantu languages and culture in the Bantu 'homelands': an emphasis that appealed to others swayed by ideas about the desirability of blacks developing according to their own traditions and cultures. Like the Afrikaners themselves, battling for recognition of their language and culture, Africans were to be granted the opportunity to develop their forgotten or erased tribal structures, returning to the past for which they yearned, and as citizens of the various homelands they were to be allowed to exercise limited political rights. Unfortunately, this also meant removing all their *other* rights, including the right to vote, work, or reside, in those parts of the country *not* their official homeland; and none of this applied to those, like the millions of Coloured and Asian (and far fewer Bushman) peoples, who had no traditional territories, although they were to be given certain limited rights and institutions of their own.[38]

This distorted homeland vision was widely accepted, and not only by the ruling white minority: indeed, it was encapsulated in school textbooks, in terms which subtly undermined any originary claims by black people over the land, by suggesting that, contrary to all the evidence, the early Voortrekkers found beyond the Orange River 'lands practically void of inhabitants, since the natives had been massacred by the Zulus and the Matabele while all the survivors had hidden themselves'; hence the white settlers' occupation of those lands offered a kind of deliverance to the 'natives', rather than their dispossession. Again, the Bushmen hardly counted in this narrative, except as reminders of the Stone Age, 'simple people' who had not reached the cattle-rearing 'stage of development' and yet at one stage were 'becoming so destructive' towards those who did rear cattle, hunting their beasts as they would wild animals, 'that they had to be chased out like vermin'—that is, shot on sight.[39]

What was extraordinary about the apartheid Balkanisation of the country into ten pseudo-nations set aside for the majority of the population, yet covering a mere 13 per cent of the land and that among the poorest and least industrialised, is how far it got, before the 'homelands' were finally reincorporated into the new South Africa in 1994. Moreover, it had been recognised as an unworkable ideal by some of its own supporters even before it began to be implemented, since with rapidly increasing urbanisation and the dependence of the economy upon black labour, many black people had already developed a strong sense of common nationhood across the old ethnic and tribal divisions, as the African National Congress was quick to recognise. Perhaps only KwaZulu, the most populous of the 'homelands', yet scattered across some sixty different bits of land (wealth-producing, white-owned land being generally protected by omission from the 'new' territories)—was the one homeland that had a sense of identity amounting to nationhood, nurtured for his own ends by Chief Mangosuthu Buthelezi, and which continues to this day. But the 'homeland' authorities, who had their own flags, anthems, police, judiciary, army, and civil servants, behaved like tyrants, exploiting the genuine need among many of their people for a sense of identity involving some continuity with their pasts, leaving a legacy of bitterness and confusion that still prevails.

Ironically, just as the Bantu 'homelands' were being dissolved, some white Afrikaners were launching a new 'homeland' of their own at Orania, in the semi-desert northern Cape, under the direction of Dr Verwoerd's son-in-law, Carel Boshoff, who assisted a group of families in buying land and clearing it of all those who might be thought to sully the purity of 'traditional' Afrikaner culture. Orania survives, an anomalous, Ruritanian community of about 650 white Afrikaners, in which all work is carried out by the Afrikaners, whose ideal of self-reliance is represented on their flag, which depicts a small boy pulling up his sleeves, upon a blue and orange background, recalling the old Dutch colours. The self-proclaimed 'Volkstaat' reflects the undying nostalgic fantasy of a group seeking a space for themselves in a country that has left them behind.[40]

The situation in Namibia, in effect a South African colony despite attempts by international institutions to redefine the Mandate relationship established after the defeat of its German rulers by South African troops in World War I, mirrored that of its powerful neighbour. South Africa's apartheid government was determined to extend its scheme of 'separate development' into its neighbour, despite the protests of the international community. The Development of Self-Government for Native Nations of South West Africa Act of 1968 duplicated the Promotion of Bantu Self-Government Act of 1959, and ten 'national homelands' were set up within a few years, including a 'Bushmanland' on the South West Africa/Botswana border which substantially restricted the territory of those herded into it, such as the !Kung. These homelands were all dissolved in May 1989, as a prelude to Namibian independence negotiations.

This recent history of fraudulent, ethnic nationalism, devised to divide and rule the majority of the population, helps explain the real urgency with which the new, democratically elected governments of southern Africa have wanted to find ways of redefining their people through redefining a common homeland. It also helps explain why that redefinition has involved going back to pre-colonial times, creating an ancestry for everyone that is, in a profound sense, imaginary. A whole network of cultural markers from the more distant past have been brought back into play—with some questionable or at least ambivalent results. These markers include a redefinition of southern Africa's First People, or the Bushmen—a name back in use as the various Bushman peoples are being imagined or, to be more accurate, re-imagined, since that imagining is a new version of a cultural process of incorporation that goes back a long way—at least to the earliest literary productions in English emerging from southern Africa.

'The Broken String'—Consolation or Reflection?

The earliest literary productions in the broadest sense, that is to say including oral forms such as chants and prayers, myths and tales, were of course produced by the Bushman inhabitants of the region themselves. However, everything we know of that material has been mediated through written means and by people who came later. In what way did they attempt to represent the Bushman? If we look at the earliest written materials of literary ambition in English, we immediately come across the well-known poem written by Scots immigrant Thomas Pringle in 1824, shortly after the arrival of the first major influx of British settlers. The opening stanza of this influential and much anthologised poem is worth quoting at length:

> Afar in the Desert I love to ride
> With the silent Bush-boy alone by my side:
> And, sick of the Present, I cling to the Past;
> When the eye is suffused with regretful tears,
> From the fond recollections of former years;
> And shadows of things that have long since fled
> Flit over the brain, like the ghosts of the dead:
> Bright visions of glory—that vanished too soon;
> Day-dreams—that departed ere manhood's noon;
> Attachments—by fate or by falsehood reft;
> Companions of early days—lost or left;
> And my Native Land—whose magical name
> Thrills to the heart like electric flame;

> The home of my childhood; the haunts of my prime;
> All the passions and scenes of that rapturous time
> When the feelings were young and the world was new,
> Like the fresh bowers of Eden unfolding to view;
> All—all now forsaken—forgotten—foregone!
> And I—a lone exile remembered of none—
> My high aims abandoned,—my good acts undone,—
> Aweary of all that is under the sun,—
> With that sadness of heart which no stranger may scan,
> I fly to the Desert afar from man![41]

Coleridge madly referred to this as one of the two or three 'most perfect lyric poems in the language'.[42] But it is easy to see why: the poem reignites the whole complex of standard Romantic attitudes towards the construction of the self through nostalgia: regretful tears, fond recollections of childhood and home, the past imagined as a timeless Eden from which the poet feels exiled and alone, and 'remembered of none'. The standard trope of longing for a rural home within the national British landscape has been transposed to a colonial setting, where longing for the so-called 'Native Land' from across the seas was to become all the more deeply felt, and part of a lasting literary tradition within the new environment. Lasting, yet apparently blind to the condition—not to mention the identity—of all those displaced people the white incomers relied upon, through a nostalgic self-absorption rooted in a desire, conscious or unconscious, to return to their distant European homeland.

And yet, in the illiberal context of Pringle's time, 'Afar in the Desert' *can* be read as expressive of a more ambivalent sensibility than its consolatory nostalgia implies.[43] Pringle, who fought successfully for press freedom and the abolition of slavery in the colony, and who translated Ntsikana, the first Xhosa poet to have his works written down, was of course caught within the contradictions of a colonial system. That he was also aware of this becomes apparent from his later poems, such as 'The Song of the Wild Bushman', where the figure of the mute 'Bushboy' becomes defiant, exclaiming 'I am Lord of the Desert Land', and *refuses* to become—as he puts it—the white man's hound, to watch flocks for the white man's gain.[44] This is some distance from not only that mute Bushboy, but the contemptible creature of an earlier (perhaps the earliest) South African English reference (1812): 'Scarce human form the squalid figures boast, / Filth is their ornament, their cov'ring grease!'[45]

Perhaps the quality of Pringle's own sense of loss and yearning after all gave him a glimpse of the sense of loss, and even anger, on the part of those whose land the settlers had come to occupy? If so, this would certainly qualify his writing, taken as a whole rather than simply on the basis of one poem, as a more critical or constructively reflective kind of nostalgia. And generally, the experience of exile and loss, suffering and struggle, embodied in South African writing in English has tended to swing between the poles of this kind of nostalgia and the more sentimental, indulgent, and unreflective kind, before the transformation of the country into—in Archbishop Desmond Tutu's famous, if retrospectively ironic phrase—the 'rainbow nation' of the 1990s.

What has been emerging during the post-apartheid decades, amidst an outpouring of writing from a variety of cultures and traditions, is a significant new focus upon creating a re-imagined national past involving new representations of the Bushmen. There were, as I have suggested, earlier attempts to write the Bushman into the national narrative, most obviously by van der Post, but also in many other areas of twentieth-century discourse, scientific as well as humanistic, popular as well as academic, in which they were commonly stereotyped as pre-modern, noble savages who, sadly but inevitably, were almost entirely eradicated.[46] It should therefore be no surprise that the image of the Bushman should have been wrapped in nostalgia; although what that means is far from straightforward. The very absence of written records creates a space for nostalgic mythmaking, although to their eternal credit, one relatively objective record was provided by the aforementioned philologist Dr Wilhelm Bleek, and his sister-in-law Lucy Lloyd, during the 1870s and 1880s—coincidentally when my grandfather's life was saved in an archetypal moment of interaction with the Bushman peoples of the Kalahari.

Bleek, who was born in Germany in 1827, and earned his doctorate in linguistics at the University of Bonn, was fascinated by African languages, which he believed expressed in their structures the spirit of the peoples who spoke them. After an earlier visit to East Africa, he came to South Africa initially to aid Bishop Colenso in his dealings with the Zulus of Natal. But it was in Cape Town as curator of Governor Sir George Grey's library that he first came across the /Xam prisoners whose language prompted a lifelong enthusiasm. Despite the influence of contemporary philological assumptions about the existence of an inherent hierarchy of languages, with the 'primitive' languages of non-Bantu-speaking indigenous peoples at the bottom, he evinced an imaginative responsiveness that led to the creation of the sole surviving source of one of their unwritten languages—/Xam or Cape San. It had come to Bleek's attention that some twenty-eight /Xam were working as convicts on the Cape Town harbour breakwater, serving time for crimes ranging from stock theft to murder; and, realising that their language was doomed, he arranged with the governor to have six of them transferred to his home, where he and his sister-in-law spent the next five years interviewing them, learning their language, and then devising a script for it.

This became one of the most remarkable transcriptions of oral literature extant, 138 notebooks comprising more than 12,000 pages, now kept in the University of Cape Town archives. Here may be found set down the words of the Bushmen convicts in Cape Town, alongside a word-for-word translation into English. They reveal, as one might expect of an oral culture, circling, repetitive, digressive, and overlapping stories. How far they represent precisely what the narrators were attempting to convey, who can say? No-one today can speak the /Xam language, there is no comprehensive grammar available, and even the dictionary published by Bleek's daughter Dorothea in 1956 remains incomplete; so anybody wishing to translate their original words has to rely on clues provided by anthropologists, archaeologists, and students of rock art to guess their meanings and cultural references.[47]

But at least this meant that, for example, in the influential *Penguin Book of South African Verse* of 1968, what was called there 'our earliest poetry, the literally stone age songs and recitals of the Bushmen and Hottentots', with their 'archaic click languages' could be—through the Bleek/Lloyd material—included.[48] The two editors, Jack Cope and Uys Krige, combining English- and Afrikaans-language skills between them, divided up their chosen poems by language which, although perhaps intended to suggest the multitude of languages in which poetry had been created in the subcontinent, privileged 'English', and then 'Afrikaans', followed by an 'African' section, itself subdivided, as if into so many Bantustan homelands. This kind of racialised stratification of thinking was of course pervasive: witness the immense popularity of Jamie Uys's box-office hit film *The Gods Must Be Crazy* (1980), in which whites, Africans, and Bushmen are clearly stereotyped, the latter depicted as comically likeable innocents whose closeness to nature enables them to outwit or assist the blundering incomers.[49]

However, Cope and Krige did begin their 'African' section with a 'Bushman' subsection, subtitled 'Traditional', in which they included eight poems acknowledging their source in Bleek, yet discreetly modified by Cope, himself a writer and poet of distinction. Reading the abrupt, repetitive, and truncated lines of one of these 'songs' gives the illusion of contact with an archaic, long-dead culture—as one can see from this version of the short narrative, related to the Bleeks by one of his Bushman narrators, Diä!Kwain, whose father sang it as a lament in memory of his friend, a shaman or rainmaker.

THE BROKEN STRING

They were the people, those who
broke the string for me
    and so
this place was a grief to me
    for what they did.

Since it was that bow-string which broke for me
and its sound no more in the sky, ringing,
hereabouts it feels to me no longer
like it once felt to me

> just for that thing.
>   For
> Everything feels as if it stood open before me
> empty, and I hear no sound
> for they have broken the bow's string for me
> and the old places are not sweet any more
>   for what they did.⁵⁰

The elegiac tone is inevitable, since this clearly represents a lament for the death of a whole culture—a culture in which the rain-dance was a central survival activity. It is difficult to know what word to use to capture the profound sense of loss expressed here; yet nostalgia in all its complexity is surely what it is.

And then, just as the apartheid system finally collapsed, two decades after the publication of 'The Broken String' in the *Penguin Book*, the Cape poet Stephen Watson produced new versions of the 'songs' in the Bleek and Lloyd collection, on which he had evidently been working for some time, including, again, 'The Broken String' which he called in his version the 'Song of the Broken String'. The opening stanza begins

> Because
> of a people,
> because of others,
> other people
> who came
> breaking
> the string for me . . .

Words and phrases are repeated and echoed, to mimic the circularity of oral performance; yet there is also more of a narrative drive towards the change which has broken the string. Continuing in this vein, Watson's poem concludes by repeating with variation the opening short lines—'Because / of this string, / because of a people / breaking the string', his earth, his place, is the place of 'something' that does not stop 'sounding' and 'breaking' within.⁵¹

Cope's Penguin version was arranged in two or three irregular sections, involving a circling, repetitive progression typical of oral narrative, with the refrain 'for what they did' emphasising the historical event of colonial settlement which destroyed the people. This was in fact little advance on the version published by George Theal in W.H.I Bleek and L. C. Lloyd's *Specimens of Bushman Folklore* of 1911, in which the refrain is rendered as 'On account of it', that is, of the string having been broken.⁵² Whereas Watson's version has a consciously modernist shape, strung out in a thin column *like* a string, and its emphasis is turned inwards, towards the breaking string within, something he imagines continues in the present. Watson is not trying to get close to

Bleek and Lloyd, but to the modern South African reader. This leads him to use the song to announce a once dispossessed nation, although the Bushmen peoples did not recognise such a concept. He is reflecting his own and current anxieties, while ventriloquising the /Xam Bushman oral poet's father. For Watson, the characteristic note of South African poetry, indeed its 'most powerful governing myth', is 'homecoming'—a homecoming which however remains frustrated, because of the extent to which 'South Africans of all complexions have either lost or been fated never to know a harmonious, integrated connection with their world', producing the 'version of melancholy' which appears in so much of their work[53]—including, I would add, his own.

Duncan Brown suggests that, since it is apparently constructed around a central metaphor, 'The Broken String' functions in a way similar to the Western lyric. This has made it a popular item for anthologising, while other songs and narratives with a more religious or medicinal and less personal role have been relatively neglected. The breaking of the string may obviously refer to a musical instrument, the subject himself a singer, composer, and rainmaker (a musical bow was used in rainmaking), who would now fall silent, in the silence of death. This also suggests the breaking of a hunting bow, one of the most prized possessions, hence the 'larger breakage' in Bushman society which the death of a shaman portended. Further, the 'people' identified in the song as responsible for the breaking are the farmers whose arrival in the area would change their world and their history: the power of the song lies 'in the fact that, even as it is a moving personal lament on the death of a great figure, it is also a haunting anticipation of the destruction of /Xam society'.[54]

But how metaphoric *was* the discourse of the Bushman peoples? How can we know? In any case, the overall effect of 'The Broken String' as it has been reproduced and disseminated, alongside other nostalgic reworkings of the Bleek transcriptions, has been to encourage the inclusion of an image of these first peoples' culture within a new, reconciliatory national narrative, while confirming the image of the Bushmen as non-violent and unresisting victims. Dia!kwain had much else to convey about the customs and myths of his people, whereas for an older man, //Kabbo, an increased longing for home—Bitterpits in the northwestern Cape—became the dominant theme of his narrations until, after two years living with the Bleek family, in the winter of 1873, he provided the best-known of his stories, '//Kabbo's Intended Return Home', as it was called by Bleek and Lloyd in their *Specimens of Bushman Folklore* (1911). This text was rendered by Watson as a poem entitled 'Return of the Moon', in which the speaker refers to his overwhelming yearning, his desire for the moon to enable him to return to his place so that he may hear again his people's stories: whereas the people with whom he now lives do not know his stories; their servants are gardeners, not hunters.[55]

Significantly, a 1992 South African anthology entitled *Broken Strings*, coming at a time 'regarded as a watershed in South Africa's history' according to the editors, led with the last stanza of Watson's 'Song of the Broken String' poem as its epigraph, and then opened with Pringle's 'Afar in the Desert', thereafter pursuing the same image of the passive Bushman through the collection, with a poem by Jack Cope of a 'Motionless' 'Khoi San' and another Watson version of the title 'song', reworked as 'Xaa-ttin's Lament' ('a sign of the end of the /Xam way of life, and therefore of the /Xam as a whole').[56] Yet Bleek's Bushman informants were convicts precisely because they *had* resisted the settlement of the Kalahari by white farmers, a fact conveniently elided by these representations of their utterances. As the Namaqualand magistrate Louis Anthing had already noted in 1863, were not their acts of stock theft 'perhaps acts of retaliation, part of a system of retaliation, for wrongs inflicted? For kinsmen murdered?'[57]

No Bushmen appear in André Brink's Namibian novel, *The Other Side of Silence* (2002), about a German woman's epic journey through the Kalahari desert with a ragtag army of female and indigenous victims of the Second Reich. This journey allows the narrator to resuscitate the lost names and memories of the dispossessed Nama people, who are depicted not just resisting but taking vengeance upon their tormentors; but at the same time they and their land become incorporated within a hegemonic South African national narrative, despite the fact that Namibia, the former 'protected' illegal dependent of South Africa, became independent before South Africa held its first democratic elections. Recalling that Brink is an Afrikaner, and writes first in Afrikaans, it is striking that his representation—or lack of it—of the Namibian Bushman peoples belongs on one level to what little Afrikaans fiction about South West Africa was previously current: mainly adventure-romance-settler fantasy, in which, if they appear at all, the Bushmen figure as alien, isolated, pre-civilised if skilful hunter-gatherers.[58]

Brink's novel contributes to the growing sense that this 'watershed' in history is time for a nostalgic incorporation, or re-membering, of the scattered and massacred desert peoples of the whole region, who were more vigorously opposed to colonisation than is usually assumed, even by the revisionist histories of German South West Africa which naturally emphasise the appalling actions of the colonial authorities. The worst of these was the German action towards the Ovaherero, whose rebellion prompted General von Trotha's notorious extermination order of 1904.[59]

If there was to be—as newly elected president Thabo Mbeki announced in 1994—an African Renaissance led by South Africa, then the histories and peoples of the surrounding territories were it seems to be gratefully included within this new transnational vision. But not everybody was happy. In 1996, a moment of national trauma as the first Truth Commission hearings were being broadcast, an exhibition called 'Miscast' appeared in Cape Town. Curated by artist-historian Pippa Skotnes, it was aimed at foregrounding the past misrepresentation of the Bushman peoples.[60] But the displays prompted protests from self-identified Khoisan activists claiming a 'pure' biological identity with the victims; and since then there has been a veritable outpouring of books attempting to recover these same victim identities—from Trudie Bloem's *Krotoa-Eva* (1999) to Elana Bruigen and Belinda Kruiper's *Kalahari Rain Song* (2004); and, joining the bandwagon, outsiders with exiled or migrant South African backgrounds, such as Rupert Isaacson in *The Healing Land: A Kalahari Journey* (2001); and Neil Bennun's *The Broken String: The Last Words of an Extinct People* (2004), a dreamily incoherent, nostalgic account of the Bleeks' writings, with another version of 'The Broken String' serving as his epigraph.[61] The only discordant note in this chorus was sounded by Zoë Wicomb's satiric allusion to the new 'rainbow-nation poetry' of the past which shopkeeper Mahmoud in *Playing in the Light* expresses as a 'rap' on 'the San people and their dispossession'.[62]

But such exile or migrant South African contributions to the representation of the Bushman peoples as a lost or broken race have been overshadowed by the work of the poet-journalist Antjie Krog, who gained national and international renown for her self-questioning account of the Truth and Reconciliation hearings in *Country of My Skull* (1998). Like other Afrikaner writers trying to recapture their identity from its white-oppressor inheritance, Krog has turned increasingly to autobiography. Yet her more recent ventures, from her contribution to photographer Paul Weinberg's *Once We Were Hunters* (2000), a glossy, illustrated account of journeys among the indigenous communities of South Africa, Namibia, Maputa, and Kenya, to an equally glossy collection of poems, *the stars say 'tsau'* (2004), reflect a different impulse.

Once We Were Hunters offers a nostalgic rendering through a range of narratives of the losses of indigenous peoples among whom the various contributors have journeyed, including Krog's modernist versioning of voices heard in the Richtersveld, formerly a 'Coloured' area in the arid North West Cape, become a National Park for the protection of the indigenous peoples, with mixed results.[63] *The stars say 'tsau'*, its title taken from one of the songs in Bleek/Lloyd, offers transcriptions devised to give readers access to what Krog calls 'the world of the First People', a venture that filled at least one local critic with 'a nostalgia close to grief';[64] and here we find—once again— 'the broken string', running in now familiar form, as 'the broken string / people were those / who broke for me the string', the 'ringing sound' in the sky no longer heard, the 'place' no longer feeling as it once did, but now made 'strange' because the string is broken, 'on account of it'.[65]

Krog finds a nostalgia in her material more poignant than Watson's in her attempt—as she puts it—to allow the 'original' to speak for itself. This ignores the question of what the 'original' means, when 'texts' were not fixed, but were mobile and being adapted with the people who created and repeated them.[66] Krog says she discerns traces of Afrikaans in the syntax of the archival material, declaring that she is 'tempted to imagine' that this could be 'the starting-point for a South African epic poem such as the Greek *Odyssey* or the ancient English *Beowulf*.[67] This seems implausible: the Bleek/Lloyd source was the creation of philologists struggling to identify and record the /Xam language, self-evidently a world away from Afrikaans—or indeed any other Indo-European language—although the Bushman interviewees may have spoken Cape Dutch, an early form of Afrikaans. But Bleek was able to translate directly from /Xam into English from quite early on, and Lucy Lloyd later became completely fluent in /Xam.[68] In short, Krog has her own new-nation agenda. In the opening words of her Foreword to Duncan Brown's *To Speak of this Land* (2006) she says: 'One of our country's earliest stories was told by //Kabbo through William Bleek and Lucy Lloyd', thus positioning the Bushman as the original and authentic South African voice.[69] Identifying with the Bushman lament apparently brings with it an imagined, new national narrative designed to include guilt-stricken white Afrikaners as well as liberal-English poets such as Watson.

Re-Imagining the South African Nation

As a result of the dramatic changes that overtook the country during the 1980s and 1990s, there has emerged a strong desire to use memory to reconnect with aspects of South Africa from which writers have felt cut off, disconnected, or alienated by their colonial pasts. This includes a sense of environmental or ecological loss, as well as spiritual yearnings.[70] There is for many of them, and not only for anguished white writers such as Krog and Watson, an inner exile of lived experience, as well as the more obvious exile of the migrant. The nostalgic reflections of dramatists and poets like Athol Fugard (*Valley Song*, 1996) and Mongane Wally Serote (*History is the Home Address*, 2004), however, avoid the fetishisation of the primal indigene apparent in Watson and Krog's work, and are concerned to express a more critical or counter-discourse of everyday and communal as well as individual memory.[71]

The urge to create a new sense of identity by invoking a real or imagined, remembered collective past or homeland, among people who continue to be deeply affected by the aftermath of colonialism, is shown, finally and most powerfully, by the attempted reconstruction of national unity through the country's new motto and Coat of Arms. These, as anthropologist Alan Barnard has pointed out, explicitly evoke the idea of the Bushman as ancestral man and original South African, despite the manipulation of the past this involves—or, indeed, its nostalgic re-imagining.[72]

This motto and Coat of Arms were officially adopted on 27 April 2000, to replace the earlier one dating from 1910, when the Union of South Africa was created out of two Boer republics and two English colonies. And what we have, in the same way as with the poetic re-versionings of 'The Broken String', is an apparent Bushman original which has been recalled, recreated and re-membered for a new purpose, overtly part of the national narrative of reconciliation. The source in this case is one of the most famous examples of southern African rock art, the Linton Stone, removed from a farm in the Eastern Cape in 1917, and deposited in the Iziko/South African Museum in Cape Town, where it sits in a room including artefacts collected by the Bleeks. On it are depicted a number of individual human figures, some dancing, some hunting, and one who holds a bow and arrow while standing on a so-called line of power. Today this figure reappears in the new South African Coat of Arms, *but* with its weapons and prominent genitalia removed, and doubled, so as to create two figures, apparently clasping hands—as in no rock art anyone has seen—to symbolise unity, according to the official description.

Now the motto, in the extinct /Xam language of the original 'Broken String' song, and which therefore nobody now speaks, or knows how to pronounce—this motto means, according to past-President Mbeki, 'diverse people unite'; and it represents, the president went on, 'a commitment to value life, to respect all languages and cultures and to oppose racism, sexism, chauvinism and genocide'.[73] The /Xam inscription runs 'ke e: /xarra // ke', the various punctuation marks derived from the Bleeks' invented phonetic system to indicate different kinds of clicks, the phrase itself traceable to one of the Bleeks' /Xam interviewees; but its meaning is far from settled, and the official translation expressed by Mbeki is only one of various possibilities. According to Skotnes, it was David Lewis-Williams, former Professor of Cognitive Archaeology at Witwatersrand University and a seeker after the spiritual meanings in rock art, who 'was able to assist the president in finding the phrase he was looking for', which she translates as 'people who are different come together'.[74]

But if it seems necessary for a nation to forget its violently divided past, this symbolic attempt at expressing a unity through re-membering a lost, pre-colonial, pre-genocidal homeland surely requires something more than such fetishising of the surviving remnants of the past? It requires the kind of critical and self-reflective harking back that promotes awareness and even restitution: which, as far as the remaining Bushmen peoples are concerned—not to mention *other* First Peoples worldwide—has at last begun, if in a stuttering and at times fraudulent way.

Thus Botswana's Tribal Land Act, which favoured non-Bushmen 'tribes' in the allocation of land, was amended in 1993 so as to define those eligible to receive land as 'citizens', yet Tswana claims continue to be favoured over Basarwa. And the Botswana High Court ruled in 2006 that the Bushmen had been wrongly evicted from the Central Kalahari Game Reserve because the Botswana government in alliance with international mining companies wanted to mine new diamond finds there.[75] The court's ruling was seen as a victory for indigenous peoples everywhere in Africa, but like all such victories its implications have yet to be fully understood or played out: does it signify the potential for a new Bushman 'homeland' within the state?—perhaps on the model of the Aborigine 'reserves' set up in Australia, territories defined in terms far from unproblematic as a means for protecting the rights of their 'original' inhabitants?[76] Self-determination and legal recognition of the right to own and control their land seem incontestable; but does that also mean the right to remain in poverty and ignorance? At the centre of the debates lies the question of how to re-member the past in the present—at a personal as well as communal and national level.

Meanwhile, in the central Kalahari area through which my grandfather passed, the minority peoples including the G/wi (of whom perhaps one thousand are identifiable as such), have resisted attempts to move, nor has much subsequently been done to help those who were moved to return; many survive in squalid resettlement camps on the fringes of the Central Kalahari Game Reserve. Ironically, despite early success, my grandfather ended up a sad figure living in a garage beside the baronial-style mansion he had once possessed, and which is now a declared 'heritage' site in the new Namibia: not for him the farms and businesses of most South West African whites of his time, but the small space of failed settlement, where he could but dream of the German homeland he had left.

In South Africa, where the Bushmen's need for their own place, for a homeland, has since the 1990s become even more pressing, so traditional or ancestral land—hard to identify for peoples whose mode of life was often nomadic—has finally been allotted to some of the few remaining groups, such as the people of Schmidstdrif and the Kalahari Gemsbok National Park in the northern Cape, bordering on Namibia and Botswana. The land restitution process, encouraged at the highest levels of government, has involved at least the #Khomani San being allotted a portion of what they claimed, an important step in giving scattered communities a sense of identity within the new polity, although they remain divided about how to manage their land. In Namibia, Bushman claims have been more successful, in part because the Ju/'hoansi were active for several years beforehand in preparing their case for securing rights in the Nyae Nyae region bordering on Botswana in the north—now officially recognised as their communal land.[77]

All these developments are merely beginnings and alas, for many surviving Bushmen people, beginnings of the end. Insofar as they are identifiable as such, or self-identifiable, they continue to be viewed as an underclass, their claims problematic. Re-membering—which is also recreating—the various pasts and histories that may appear to constitute a nation in the postcolonial context requires a new perception of the politics of the present, if those pasts are to be remembered for the good of all the nations of Southern Africa, including those whose string was indeed broken.

The next chapter explores how nostalgia for a mythical Africa constructed out of colonial childhood memories helped writer-in-exile Doris Lessing find a source for a vision that both acknowledges and attempts to transcend the pain and sufferings of the past. Veering towards the 'primitive' and mythic qualities perceived in her former home in colonial Southern Africa, the writer struggles to find a way of adequately representing personal and historic pasts, resulting in a complex 'nostalgia for the future'.

4 'Alone in a Landscape'
Remembering Doris Lessing's Africa

> 'You remember with what you are at the time of your remembering.'
> Doris Lessing, *Under My Skin: Volume One of My Autobiography* 1995

> 'That was the last year when I was part of the bush, its creature, more at home there than I've been since in any street or town.'
> Doris Lessing, *Under My Skin: Volume One of My Autobiography* 1995[1]

The Myth Country

In 1964 during an interview with Roy Newquist, Doris Lessing reflected upon her upbringing in colonial Rhodesia in the following words: 'I spent most of my childhood alone in a landscape with very few human things to dot it. It was sometimes hellishly lonely, but now I realize how extraordinary it was, and how very lucky I was'.[2] Like other lonely geniuses of the veld before her, such as Olive Schreiner and Eugène Marais—both of whom she admired[3]—Lessing's early years were spent in solitary communing with nature rather than with people, an isolation which left its mark in an intense, lifelong preoccupation with personal fulfilment, and an almost overwhelming sense of being an outsider. Lessing's trajectory from colonial backwater to metropolitan London and an international reputation as both chronicler and prophet of our times is well enough known. What is perhaps not so well appreciated is the extent to which what she refers to as her 'myth country' has remained colonial Southern Africa, and in particular that part of it once called Rhodesia, where the profound inadequacies of white settler culture led her to develop a more general sense of the inadequacies of the dominant civilisations of the world, and a consequent search for alternatives influenced by memories of her past, and indeed a nostalgia for idealised versions of it.

'The emotional impulse behind nearly all white writing . . . is a nostalgia, a hunger, a reaching out for something lost; hard to define but instantly recognizable', Lessing once remarked.[4] J. M. Coetzee came to a similar conclusion: earlier colonial or 'white writing', according to him, was characterised by its 'retrospective gaze', its 'dream-fare' consisting typically of a mythology of the indigenous peoples imagined as idle primitives, thereby all the more readily displaced by or made subject to the needs and desires of incomers.[5] Lessing's retrospective gaze generally resists Coetzee's paradigm, despite her hungry dreams for something lost, out of reach of the present; but there are times when her remembering appears to take her towards the more dubious aspects of white settler nostalgia. Certainly she shares a mythologising tendency with her colonial predecessors, including writers such as Karen Blixen and Laurens van der Post. In 1989, during a return visit to her homeland Zimbabwe, as it had become, she decided to make a 'quick trip' to her 'myth country, perhaps to make sure it was still there'. She had lived in London since 1950, when, famously, she had arrived with £20 and the manuscript of her first published novel, *The Grass is Singing*. But she still wanted to revisit the remembered 'dark stuffy bungalow on the hill' of her childhood north of Harare. The way being barred by a 'Trespassers Will Be Prosecuted' sign, she found instead, just before she left, what she clearly felt was, after all, an appropriate image: 'I glimpsed the past—all our pasts—in a light-stepping youth returning from a range of low hills, his eyes alert for the ghosts of vanished game. On his back was a spear, in his hand was a catapult, and he was accompanied by three lean hunting dogs'.[6]

This is one of those resonant images that, as Gaston Bachelard once remarked, seems to take the individual beyond history, 'or even, while remaining in history', detach us from our own past and 'the always too contingent history of the persons who have encumbered it'.[7] Barred from re-entering the parental house of her childhood, Lessing takes a glimpsed scene from the landscape and turns it into more than merely a signifier for her own remembered past, although it obviously is that, but rather a symbol for 'all our pasts' and indeed '*the* past', apparently detaching it entirely from history and the contingent. But there is more to Lessing's creative imagination than this: viewed as a whole, her work displays a dialectic between different forms of nostalgia that avoids the bad faith and essentialism assumed by those (such as Fredric Jameson) who denounce all nostalgia as de-historicising.[8]

What I aim to do in this chapter is reflect further upon the kind of imagination that is operating in moments like this, an imagination produced by the isolated, remembering self of one contemporary, postcolonial writer: and in particular, that writer's nostalgia, understood ultimately as a yearning not just for a lost or impossible home, but for something beyond individual memory and collective history—in short for the infinite. If at times this yearning seems to generate some of Lessing's best, most creatively challenging work, it is also at times deeply problematic in effect.

Remembering 'Africa'

To remember Africa is not to remember it; it is to remember 'Africa', that is, a construct of the remembering self. This is all the more apparent if we remind ourselves that Africa is a continent, not a country: too large and various to capture in any single, simplified phrase, although many have tried. Ironically, perhaps, one of the most famous examples of such generalising contains its own truth: Pliny the Elder's *Ex Africa semper aliquid novi*, itself a reworking in Latin of a remark made by Aristotle—as Thabo Mbeki pointed out in a speech to the European Assembly in November 2004 aimed at challenging prevailing assumptions about 'Africa', such as the view that, contrary to Pliny, *nothing* new was coming out of the continent today, just depressingly familiar stories of poverty, disease, war, and oppression. But as the unexpected, unpredicted transformation of South Africa from an apartheid tyranny into a multiracial democracy within a few years demonstrated, the continent may still surprise the outsider. As Africans, said Mbeki, we are proud of this miracle.[9] Mbeki was trying to promote the familiar Pan-Africanist idea of an African Renaissance, an idea which in its way also subsumes the individuality of its distinct, varied, and contradictory groups and countries within a simplified generality derived from past cultural formations.

The shiftiness of the signifier 'Africa' has to do with long histories as well as present politics: what this means is not that the word should be ignored, rather, that its use as anything more than a geographical expression needs to be located within an awareness of those histories and that politics. This applies as much to those whose territories were colonised, as to the colonisers. When, for example, Wole Soyinka's 1973 Cambridge lectures referred to the 'African world-view', it was as yet another attempt to promote a counteracting perspective to 'Eurocentric' conceptions of society and the human: conscious that this might appear to involve a return to the earlier, backward-looking perspective of the Francophone Negritude movement, Soyinka insisted that despite the lyrical, celebratory quality of some of its poetic practitioners, Negritude was trapped in a derivative relationship with the European intellectual traditions it wished to deny. However, his own struggle to define an essentially African self-awareness based on Yoruba myth and ritual suffered from the same problematic: of generalising from one specific group of cultural phenomena to a continent-wide and hence abstract, fictional, Africa.[10] Yet it is arguable that the first generation of modern African writers to gain worldwide recognition, writers such as Soyinka, and his Nigerian colleague Chinua Achebe, felt it necessary to argue that there was something distinctive about their work and the issues they dealt with, while not wishing to lose their individual, local rootedness. Achebe perhaps put it best when he remarked 'Africa is not only a geographical expression; it is also a metaphysical landscape—it is in fact a view of the world and of the whole cosmos perceived from a particular position'. What that position is, Achebe went on to clarify in terms of specific writers, obsessed with the 'monumental historical fact' of Europe as they may have been 'from Equiano to Ekwensi', but using the form of the novel, 'the African novel', according to their 'differing abilities, sensibilities and visions'. For Achebe, the African novel excluded Conrad (whom he repeatedly attacks for his Eurocentrism), but includes Lessing.[11]

The relevance and centrality of a nostalgically recalled Africa (as she repeatedly calls her part of the continent) for Lessing's imagination was clearly signalled by a passage that appeared in the 1964 Preface to her first collection of *African Stories*, fourteen years after she had left her country. To begin with, she remarked on the advantages for writers of having been brought up in Africa—'being at the centre of a modern battlefield; part of a society in rapid, dramatic change' which, however, can also be a handicap, since you wake up every morning with your eyes on 'fresh evidence of inhumanity'. After all, 'There are other things in living besides injustice, even for the victims of it'. Yet, 'I believe', she went on,

> that the chief gift from Africa to writers, white and black, is the continent itself, its presence which for some people is like an old fever, latent always in their blood; or like an old wound throbbing in the bones as the air changes. That is not a place to visit unless one chooses to be an exile ever afterwards from an inexplicable majestic silence lying just over the border of memory or of thought. Africa gives you the knowledge that man is a small creature, among other creatures, in a large landscape.[12]

It is this belief in an Africa as at once a place of remembered pain and suffering, of inner as well as outer exile, and yet at the same time the source of something 'just over the border of memory or thought', something that transcends, as it helps put into perspective, the human condition—it is this complex of thoughts, arising out of her own sense of isolation, that seems to have led the author paradoxically to abandon her specifically Southern African material after the mid 1960s, when she made these observations; and yet, how far did she abandon, how far has she really abandoned 'Africa'?

Before I answer this question, I have to confess that for many years I stopped reading Doris Lessing, because it seemed to me that *The Grass is Singing* (1950), the *'African'* stories (1951 onwards) and the *'Children of Violence'* series (1952–69), all of which had once spoken directly to me as a former colonial familiar with the part of the world from which they sprang—these early works had apparently been left behind by an author engaged with more speculative, impersonal and fantastic fictions, intent on depicting realms distant not only from Southern Africa, not only from the continent of Africa, but also from the mundane earth itself—until even the mirror-world of metafictions such as *Briefing for a Descent into Hell* or *Memoirs of a Survivor* was left behind, and Lessing became (as Lorna Sage put it), 'a fully paid-up alien', in the outer space of the *Canopus in Argos* series.[13] And yet, I also received reports that among these outer realms, there was a continuing obsession with empire, colonisation, and power, projected from some inner awareness of alienation and displacement. And then, an apparently random event prompted a re-assessment: in 1999 I attended a talk Lessing gave at the Commonwealth Institute in London to celebrate her latest novel, *Mara and*

Dann, subtitled 'an adventure'. Prompted by the author's powerful articulacy to buy a copy of the novel, I found on the very first page there was a map, immediately recognisable as the continent of Africa, down to the little segment at the bottom labelled 'Green Cape', which suggested to me the lush area I remembered as a place to which in the 1940s and 1950s white Rhodesians used to flock for rest and recuperation from the stress of managing the natives, often indeed to sojourn in the very hotel where I was brought up, and where I used to watch the coarse and red-faced farmers and businessmen carousing with their heavily-made-up wives and mistresses, while their offspring were taken to the sea they had never seen before by black servants forbidden to join them in the waves.

Reflecting on that memory I should in fairness also mention later memories (aware of what memories are like), of those several white Rhodesians whom I met at university in the Cape, and who, like Lessing, for all their rootedness in their place in Southern Africa, resisted the seductions of white privilege. This meant in several cases joining the liberation movements, as a consequence ending up in prison or fleeing abroad. Lessing herself was—apparently to her surprise—made a Prohibited Immigrant by the Rhodesian authorities, who feared (in the minister's words) she would be going around 'upsetting our natives' if permitted to return to the country where she had lived from the age of five until she left at thirty.[14] One of the best accounts of the particular moment of left-wing and liberal white resistance in 1960s Southern Africa, and the contradictory impulses of those involved, may be found in a fictionalised memoir called *Elegy for a Revolutionary* (1969) by the poet and student leader of the time C. J. Driver, who, as it happens, was briefly a schoolteacher in Marandellas, near Harare, where Lessing once lived, and where some of her stories are set.[15]

Nostalgia for the Future: *Mara and Dann* and *The Golden Notebook*

As if to justify the flood of memories that overtook me as I paged through *Mara and Dann,* the author's preface confirmed that this 'very old tale' was indeed set in Africa, although 'Ifrik', as she somewhat perversely renamed it, was represented in a mode far different from the closely rendered, moral-realist depiction of the familiar 'Africa', that is, Southern Africa, of her earlier fiction. The remorseless, socio-historical texture of, say, *Martha Quest* (1952), had been thinned-out into a lengthy, picaresque narrative in which the two foundlings of the title wander northwards after an ice age many centuries hence has redrawn the globe. Yet everywhere Mara and Dann go, they find evidences—the coins, stones, and towers—of previous empires, suggestive of the Zimbabwe ruins near Mutare, where stand the haunting stone walls and courtyards of a vanished civilisation that the white regime stubbornly refused to believe could have been built by the indigenous Shona, preferring the fantasy that a white Queen of Sheba, perhaps, was responsible. Or, as Lessing recalled, describing a visit with her young husband and new baby, 'the Arabs'. Sitting alone on a rock above the ruins in the mid-afternoon, she heard a sound that

> has haunted me ever since. Somewhere down there, in a hut I could not see, or from under a tree where someone sat came two notes on a drum, a high note, then a lower, then an interval, then the two notes again. These notes are not to be found on a piano, and the interval between them has its justification in a region unfamiliar to a European ear. Like two raindrops falling, tap–tap, then the silence; tap–tap, and silence. On and on. On and on. Soon everything—the ruins, the landscape, the rocks, the hazy plains of the hot sky populated with afternoon clouds—all seemed absorbed into these two notes that repeated, and repeated, and went on, and were going on still when I climbed down the hill. . . . [16]

This is what she identifies elsewhere as 'real remembering', that is, for a moment, 'being back in the experience itself', on and on, absorbing the landscape.

So taken with the memory was Lessing that she went on to write a play introduced by the two musical notes she remembered with such intensity, although that turned out to have little to do with memory, but instead was a piece of self-syled agitprop involving a mine strike on the Rand, with characters in 'cartoon kaffir' masks, which she rather unrealistically hoped would reach local audiences, including the people who had created the 'African' musical notes that had impressed her so much. Not surprisingly, the play was found unsuitable by her London Communist Party comrades, and although Brecht liked it, he said he could not produce it since he was already being criticised by the Party for 'expressionism and formalism' and 'similar vices'.[17] Not for the first time Lessing's idea was prescient: the South African 'protest theatre' of the 1970s and 1980s used masks with great success, for example in Mtwa/Ngema/Simon's *Woza Albert!* (1981). But then, there is a constant element of dissent, if not protest, in her work that has led her to take a stand on many issues of the time, from apartheid to nuclear disarmament, from sexual politics to religious faith. In that sense, she belongs to the Left generation of the 1950s and 1960s who took their cue from Jean-Paul Sartre's definition of the writer's responsibility to society, although characteristically, as Margaret Drabble has well expressed it, if 'ideologies' have tried to 'swallow her up', she has always 'shaken herself free and moved on'.[18]

One reason for the settler-colonial assumption that Zimbabwe was created by people from the north was that it has long been well known that there were once many kingdoms to the north, and remnants of those kingdoms, from Benin and Asante to the Moorish states of North Africa, still litter the continent, as the landscape of *Mara and Dann* reminds us, without naming them.[19] In that respect, the narrative of *Mara and Dann* could as well have been situated in the present or even the past, as much as in the future. It is as if Lessing is viewing the many histories of the continent through an inverted telescope, reducing its societies, states, and peoples to pawns in some cosmic game, in which the future is condemned to repeat the past, and all any individual can do is join the unending struggle to survive, as Africa's ignorant armies clash by night.

The novel provides a few uplifting, even comic moments within this grim vision, however: such as when we learn that oral tradition has preserved Flaubert's novel as the tale of a certain 'Mam Bova, who hated her husband, tried to seduce a handsome youth, who rejected her, so she took poison and died'; or the story of 'Mam Bedfly . . . a young slave girl, in love with a sailor from across the sea [who], feeling abandoned . . . killed herself'—moments that suggest the frailty of earlier, canonical models of young women, while promoting the potential of cultural memory, albeit in fragmented form, to survive.[20] Lessing's Mara is made of tougher stuff than Mam Bova and Mam Bedfly, and wants to grasp this potential, indeed to retrieve all the histories of the world which, now that the archives have crumbled, are taught to a group of young people called 'Memories'. But when Mara expresses a wish to be trained as a Memory herself, she is told that she must first learn about practical things;[21] which means in effect how to endure a bizarre menagerie from the author's dream factory—mutated reptiles, vicious rapists, slave traders, and various menacing and alas racially defined types. Without the sharp awareness of recognisable, individual lives evident in her earlier work, the familiar issues of colonialism and female fulfilment, although they are there, remain without much purchase in reality.

What we have in *Mara and Dann* is a particular kind of nostalgia—not just for the past, although that is there, as Lessing confirmed in a radio interview in which she said writing the book had brought back memories of her childhood, and in particular the relationship with her little brother Harry,[22] but a nostalgia *for the future*, a future in which the continent of Africa becomes the centre of the world, a place where new life may spring after the global catastrophes anticipated in so much of her writing.

To understand this kind of nostalgia it is helpful to consider once again what Svetlana Boym has to say in *The Future of Nostalgia*. As we have seen in Chapter 1, exploring the range of nostalgia in the present day world, Boym—herself a Russian emigré—identifies what she sees as both the negative, past-fixated aspect of nostalgia, and its more positive, creatively reflective side. Particularly relevant here is her idea that the latter form of nostalgia may also be understood as, paradoxically, looking ahead, to the future. According to Boym,

> Creative nostalgia reveals the fantasies of the age, and it is in those fantasies and potentialities that the future is born. One is nostalgic not for the past the way it was, but for the past the way it could have been. It is this past perfect that one strives to realize in the future.[23]

Strictly speaking, the way the past *could* have been is the past conditional, not the past perfect. But one can see what Boym means: she is talking about recreating the past *as if* it were perfect. Boym's reflections were prompted by a return on her part to European cities such as Moscow and Berlin, rather than any rural, much less colonial, outpost. Nonetheless, her remarks are suggestive, prompting an understanding of where *Mara and Dann* is going, although not why it ultimately fails to convince: because Lessing's fantasy of the future perfect lacks sufficient awareness of its conditionality in the imperfect past—or present. Nostalgia, like memory in general, is a function of both unconscious remembering and conscious recall; and conscious recall might have provided the textures of reality that make some of her other futurist fantasies more effective—such as the darkly visionary *Memoirs of a Survivor* (1974), an 'attempt at an autobiography',[24] with a strange, uncanny, yet credible family at its centre distinctly reminiscent of her own.

As Lessing remarks in her actual autobiography, 'memory is a careless and lazy organ', and 'Telling the truth or not telling it, and how much, is a lesser problem than the one of shifting perspectives, for you see your life differently at different stages, like climbing a mountain while the landscape changes with every turn in the path'.[25] If she still seems to herself a lone figure in the landscape, she has come to realise that the landscape of the past keeps changing, provoking the search for ever new perspectives upon it. Few in the 1950s would have predicted the end of colonial status for Rhodesia, for example: even fewer the ending of apartheid. But perhaps when landscapes of the mind and actual landscapes infiltrate each other in people's dreams of a future, that future can become a reality: who really knows how change comes about? For Lessing, in order to change, or even merely survive, we have first to understand how different aspects of our individual experience fit into the general, or collective experience; and for her, this means reviewing her Southern African past from one perspective to another, so as to turn it into—the past perfect.

The pressing urge to find some such vision is what lies behind those 'moments' of nostalgia, as the young protagonist of *Martha Quest* herself calls them, whenever she senses she is on the brink of some revelation. The first of such moments, when Martha is sixteen, finds her overwhelmed by feelings of loss. Half-blinded and turned inward by an eye infection, she reflects on how terrible her birth-month October is:

> Terrible because so beautiful, and the beauty springs from the loaded heat, the dust, the tension . . . She sat there all day, and felt the waves of heat and perfume break across her in shock after shock of shuddering nostalgia. But nostalgia for what? She sat and sniffed painfully at the weighted air, as if it were dealing her blows like an invisible enemy.[26]

Later, this sense of embattled, nostalgic solitude reinforces Martha's need for 'something that had never existed, an "ecstasy", in short'—which, when

it arrives, she understands as 'the gift of her solitary childhood on the veld
... a sense of ... separate things interacting and finally becoming one, but
greater'. While her youthful friends seem 'drenched' in the 'nostalgic golden
light' of illusory good fellowship that for them includes even the black waiters
they humiliate, *she* dreams of a 'four-gated dignified city where white and
black and brown lived as equals, and there was no hatred or violence'.[27]

It is a vision that challenges the petty lives around her, and, as the movement of Martha's life away from the farm towards the suburbs, marriage, and motherhood proceeds, it is a vision which keeps challenging her too, until she leaves Rhodesia for fulfilment abroad, in the longed-for country of her ancestry. When her father talks to her about England, prompted by a daughter aware that he does not share her 'aching' after the farm she no longer lives on, he

> did not once mention the African farm on which he had lived for all those years. Martha listened, circling her stomach with her forearms, while with one half of her mind she saw a boy running wild across an English farm, fifty years before, and ran with him, tasting faint and exquisite dews, feeling long lush English grass around her ankles. With the other, she was indulging in the forbidden pleasure of nostalgia. The pang of lost happiness was so acute it shortened her breath. Then she asked herself if there was any moment of her childhood she would choose to live again, and she could only reply that no, there was not. If she burrowed back under the mist of illusion, she had felt a determination to continue, a curiosity perhaps, an intention to endure, but no delight. Yet that uncomfortable antagonistic childhood had over it a shimmering haze of beauty, it tugged at her to return.[28]

This captures well the ambivalence of her nostalgia, prompted by her sense of the falsity of her father's recall, of how his stock memories of a green and pleasant England are allowed to dislodge the realties of his own farm 'in Africa', a place which, for her, despite her resistance to the fond illusions of her remembered childhood, generates the feeling of lost happiness so acute it causes her to gasp, and which continues to tug at her to return.

Inevitably that is not how metropolitan London turns out—grey, fogbound, and gripped by postwar anxieties as we come to see it through Martha's eyes in the opening pages of *The Four-Gated City* (1969). All through the writing career that follows, and not just in that immense final novel of the series which all these moments anticipate, expressions of melancholy and yearning continue, yearning for a place as part of a whole—shifting, distant, and indefinable as that seems to be.

The Golden Notebook—published in 1962, some seven years before *The Four-Gated City*—is a turning point in this struggle towards illumination. The novel is set in 1957, and retrospectively narrated by means of an outer, omniscient voice, and lengthy extracts from 'notebooks' recording events going back a decade or more. Its structure was a radical departure from the kind of tame, provincial fiction that dominated metropolitan English literary life at the time, in both method and content. It is structured as a series of stages, each reflecting upon the tangled memories that the heroine, Anna Wulf, is caught up in, including those of life in wartime Rhodesia when, like Lessing herself, she was part of a communist group. The common thread is a frustrated need for wholeness. When Anna talks to her Jungian therapist Mrs Marks, she explains:

> You talk about individuation. So far what it has meant to me is this: that the individual recognizes one part after another of his earlier life as an aspect of the general human experience. When he can say: What I did then, What I felt then, is only the reflection of that great archetypal dream, or epic story, or stage in history, then he is free, because he has separated himself from the experience, or fitted it like a piece of mosaic into a very old pattern, and by the act of setting it into place, is free of the individual pain of it.[29]

Hence the pain of the present, the pain of being this woman in the present, can only be resolved for her through an understanding of the totality—which, however, as *The Golden Notebook* demonstrates by means of its reflexive narrative structure as well as its internal commentary, cannot yet, or perhaps ever, be grasped. Recalling her struggle to create its structure, Lessing remarked

> The novel had a framework made by thinking. The thought was that to divide off and compartmentalize living was dangerous and led to nothing but trouble. Old, young; black, white; men, women; capitalism, socialism: these great dichotomies undo us, force us into unreal categorization, make us look for what separates us rather than what we have in common. That was the thought, which made the shape or pattern of *The Golden Notebook*. But the emotions were stronger than the thought. . . . [30]

Which was, she added, what made the novel a failure on her terms, despite the feeling that she was in the grip of 'of discovery, of revelation' when she wrote it—a revelation which had little to do with the Women's Movement that took the book up.[31]

But this is why nostalgia is so important a theme: the longing remains, and that in itself has a value, as Roberta Rubinstein has suggested in a perceptive analysis of the central character Anna Wulf's struggles to find a 'true' perspective within the romanticised memories of her upbringing.[32] Anna wants to resist what she calls the 'terrible lying nostalgia' of her Rhodesian novel *Frontiers of War*—a sensationalised, self-deceiving account of her wartime memories—which she has used profitably to launch herself as a writer, just as

Lessing did with *The Grass is Singing*, also about an interracial relationship and what used to be called 'the colour problem'. One of the incidents she recalls as she retraces the experiences upon which she based her 'African' novel and the entangled lives of all those—the youthful RAF officers, the Marxist refugee, the staff of the Mashopi Hotel—whom she has she thinks falsified into fiction, details her passionate lovemaking with Paul, a sardonic but sexually inexperienced young Oxford man. Their encounter out in the veld is described with what at first might seem like Lawrentian breathlessness, yet in context it is finely and feelingly told, a memory of 'being happy' and at the same time 'appalled because it had come out of so much ugliness and unhappiness'. The two lovers sit on the top of a small kopje and await the dawn.

> And now we could see that the rock we sat on was at the mouth of a small cave, and the flat rock wall at its back was covered with Bushman paintings. They were fresh and glowing even in this faint light, but badly chipped. All this part of the country was covered with these paintings, but most were ruined because white oafs threw stones at them, not knowing their value. Paul looked at the little coloured figures of men and animals, all cracked and scarred, and said, 'A fitting commentary to it all, dear Anna, though I'd be hard put to find the right words to explain why, in my present state.'[33]

If this is 'lying nostalgia', a weak or overly subjective vision of the past, then Lessing has it both ways: it is both moving in itself, as the tender, loving moment we have just witnessed between the two, and, in the longer perspective the other Notebooks and the larger narrative creates, moving as an indication of the smallness and brevity of human life set against the perspective of 'Africa', represented here by the prehistoric Bushman figures stoned by the 'white oafs'.

The negative view of remembering is overtaken for Lessing herself through her own subsequent experiences, in particular her several returns home, each of which complicates her personal sense of nostalgia, as she struggles temporarily to place her individual pain within the larger pattern. Thus, for example, reflecting on her 1988 visit to an independent Zimbabwe, when she went back to the old farm, fearing to find a confirmation of her sense of 'Isolation. Being excluded', once again alone in a bleak landscape, she discovered instead a place of beauty and magnificence: 'No wonder this myth-country still tugged and pulled', she reflected; 'what a privilege, what a blessing' to have been brought up there. And if things *have* changed, 'Well, every day there are more people everywhere in the world in mourning for trees, forest, bush, rivers, animals, lost landscapes . . . you could say this is an established part of the human mind, a layer of grief always deepening and darkening'.[34]

Nostalgically generalising her own state of mind, Lessing identifies the source of her fictions in terms of memories of loss, always deepening and darkening, intermittently intercepted by the urge to connect it all within some overarching vision. It is a state of mind with which anyone living at a distance from his or her homeland can almost too easily identify: creating a desire to return again to the lives of those unwitting, almost forgotten players on the Southern African landscape, the Turners, the Quests, the Gales, and in particular the young white girl of 'The Old Chief Mshlanga'. Reflecting upon this desire and its limitations leads me to propose that, through these colonial figures, it is possible to see Lessing connecting the past with the present in a way that creates an ironic gap between the myths of Africa, and the realities. With the irony, there comes an implicit ethical demand to go beyond a reductionist, sentimental nostalgia stuck in stereotyped versions of the past, of 'Africa' as a reservoir for self-indulgence.

This is the kind of nostalgia Lessing herself criticised in the *New Statesman* review referred to earlier, written when—still very much engaged in writing her 'African' fictions—she was asked to review Laurens van der Post's book about his search for the 'real' Africa embodied in the Bushmen of the Kalahari:

> An African once said to me that beyond the white man's more obvious crimes in Africa there was the unforgivable one that 'Even the best of you use Africa as a peg to hang your egos on.' To this crime Mr. van der Post is open. So are all the rest of us.[35]

Later she was to justify her own urge to narrate her Rhodesian experiences by observing that 'more and more I realize I was part of an extraordinary time, the end of the British Empire in Africa, and the bit I was involved with was the occupation of a country that lasted exactly ninety years'.[36] Lessing's awareness of the dangers of colonial fantasising about the African soul, combined with her strong sense of the sociopolitical realities of her corner of Africa, enable her to distance herself from the limitations of personal nostalgia to the extent of acknowledging her own complicity as a white writer 'using' Africa. This acknowledgement is not enough for some. As we will see, she has been roundly criticised for drawing on European cultural memories and their implicit racism in her African work.

The Grass is Singing, Out of Africa, and the Other

For instance, there is Eve Bertelsen, who attacked *The Grass is Singing* in 1991 for its dubious reliance upon 'an idea of nature and consequently Africa' as 'an earlier, and ergo hostile form of life, antipathetic to the white man's civilizing endeavours'. In an account implicitly echoing J. M. Coetzee's critique of white colonial writing, Bertelsen argues that it is not only from the mouths of the overtly racist characters or the internal monologues of the mad Mary Turner that the word 'savage' is used about black people, but the narrator herself 'blithely invokes "the savage mind," "the savage sun," "the savage heat," and "the savage and antagonistic bush"', cumulating with Moses' act of murder envisaged as 'the bush aveng[ing] itself,' in a so-called triumph of 'darkness'.[37]

But is Lessing's indictment of racist colonial society in the novel really undermined by the impact of its pervasive imagery, the imagery of a Manichean vision of the land and its peoples? Perhaps this captures how the novel has been read—as she says it was—by Bertelsen's South African students. But what her argument misses is the countervailing irony of the situation the novel presents: of the white farmer Turner who in fact loves the land, which he wants to make more fertile, while remaining callous towards its people; and of his wife Mary, oppressed by the bush, ignorant of the lives of the Africans, yet pathetically yearning for the physical freedoms they represent and which, through her breakdown, she finally experiences.

Like so many Lessing women, Mary Turner depends on her relationship with a man to give her an identity, and can only move towards a new inner self, through dream, telepathy, breakdown, or madness—which helps explain Lessing's later move towards supra-realist strategies. But for Mary it is too late for freedom from the dominant ideology: her position as a woman, trying to make the house comfortable, to teach the servant the right way to make tea, shows the domestic sphere as both isolating and imprisoning; and in the dream of her death, the bush comes in, 'conquering the farm, sending its outriders to cover the good red soil with plants and grass; the bush knew she was going to die!'[38] This is Mary's, not the author's viewpoint. But what about her murderer?

I am reluctant to accuse Lessing of failing to convey the thoughts and feelings of the black man Moses as well. Yes, he is almost entirely presented from the outside, and as Lessing herself said in an earlier (1984) interview with Bertelsen, for a long time she thought it a pity she

> ever wrote Moses like that, because he was less of a person than a symbol. But it was the only way I could write him at that time, since I'd never met Africans excepting the servants or politically, in a certain complicated way. But now I've changed my mind again. I think it was the right way to write Moses, because if I'd made him too individual it would've unbalanced the book. I think I was right to make him a bit unknown.[39]

Lessing's dilemma is the vexed one of all white settler writings, viewed from a postcolonial perspective. How much is it possible to represent the Other? Or, to reframe the question in a way that at least allows for the power of the imagination: how much of those whose experiences one is excluded from by the situation in which one is brought up is it possible to find in oneself? The urge to rewrite the colonial past as a result of the promptings of creative nostalgia poses an acute challenge, which Lessing cannot always meet—as she realises, struggling with new kinds of narrative, while circling back to the ancient and, she clearly hopes, universal fundamentals of storytelling, variously embodied in myth, legend, or fantasy.

In some colonial writers, the urge to develop their memories away from history and towards the mythic and archetypal proves irresistible. Van der Post is one example, although the results are not always predictable (see Chapter 3). So, too, is Alan Paton, whose *Cry the Beloved Country* came out in 1948, a mere two years before *The Grass is Singing*, and which was written out of the author's homesickness while abroad. While raising awareness of the South African racial 'problem'—summed up in the grim warning of one black character 'that one day when they turn to loving they will find we are turned to hating'— Paton's novel reflected a nostalgic, Christian vision of neo-feudal ruralism that contradicted the real social problems of migrant labour at its centre.[40]

Although written by an outsider in the continent, Karen Blixen's 'African' writing provides an instructive parallel to the work of these Southern Africans. In 1931 the collapse of the international coffee market forced Blixen to return to Denmark after seventeen years running a farm in British East Africa. Her farm had proved a failure, but the poignant narrative of her time there that she wrote in the following years was a success. Its title echoed Pliny's famous saying, and *Out of Africa* (1937) became a classic account of a way of life that was soon to disappear. Part of the reason for the book's success was the sympathetic clarity with which the author recalled the peoples and the landscape of interwar East Africa, which she, too, generalised into 'Africa'. Her success was also because of her abiding sense of loss, of the disappearance of an Edenic world with its own beauty and rhythms, which chimed in well with her European readers' sense of the imminent destruction of their own world, or at least, post World War II, its fragility. 'Now, looking back on my life in Africa,' she wrote, 'I feel that it might altogether be described as the existence of a person who had come from a rushed and noisy world, into a still country'.[41]

Towards the end, when Blixen's farm goes bankrupt and she has to sell it to a foreign firm that plans to divide it up for residential development, she reflects upon the determination of her farm squatters to stay together on their own land:

> It is more than the land that you take away from the people, whose native land you take. It is their past as well, their roots and their identity. If you take away the things that they have been used to see, and will be expecting to see, you may, in a way, as well take their eyes.[42]

Land, and the landscape, are central to her view of things, from the famous, dream-like opening, 'I had a farm in Africa, at the foot of the Ngong Hills', to her final departure, when it seemed as if nature itself was aware of her forthcoming departure long before she was herself: 'The hills, the forests, plains and rivers, the wind, all knew that we were to part'. Until then, she had felt at one with the landscape. 'Now the country disengaged itself from me, and stood back a little, in order that I should see it whole.'[43]

It was not only the colonised who are blinded by the loss of their land, their roots, their identity. Colonial settlement almost always involved the displacement of the original inhabitants; and the settlers' investment in their new homes usually blinded them to the impact upon those who thereby lost their homes, although they, too, like the Lessings, very often experienced a yearning for the place they had left behind. Blixen does not refer to her own yearning for home; but having left Denmark years before, it seems as if her own sense of dislocation enabled her to reach a deep understanding of the impact of dislocation upon the 'native' inhabitants. Throughout her memoir, she attempts to position herself between the indigenous inhabitants and the (largely British) white settlers—whose racial prejudice and banality she thoroughly despises, and whose laws have turned the 'natives' into temporary residents in their own country. The Masai inspired a particular interest:

> The Masai when they were moved from their old country, north of the railway line, to the present Masai Reserve, took with them the names of their hills, plains, and rivers; and gave them to the hills, plains, and rivers in the new country. It is a bewildering thing to the traveller. The Masai were carrying their cut roots with them as a medicine, and were trying, in exile, to keep their past by a formula.[44]

The Masai fit the almost feudal view of society that she brought with her as Baroness Blixen-Finecke, her name when she first arrived in Kenya in 1914 with her new husband Bror. Yet if she sees the Masai as aristocratic in respect of their bearing and hauteur (the image of Lessing's 'light-stepping youth' comes to mind), 'their weapons and finery as much a part of their being as are a stag's antlers', she also sees them as peasants, comparable to the 'peasants of Umbria', in no way like 'the bourgeoisie of all classes', whom she associates with pettiness.[45] The sense of loss in being dislocated from their landscape 'applies in a higher degree to the primitive people than the civilized, and animals again will wander a long way, and go through danger and sufferings, to recover their lost identity, in the surroundings that they know'.[46]

There is a tension throughout Blixen's book between this totalising, essentialising discourse about 'primitive' or 'native' or 'African' people on the one hand, and on the other an increasingly deep understanding and appreciation of the diversity of the peoples she encountered, including the Masai, the Kikuyu, and Somali, whose customs and to some extent languages she got to know intimately, with the result that she was given recognition and respect by those who served her, or whom she encountered on her farm. Her biographer Judith Thurman reports her cook on the farm saying that the people 'reciprocated her love, and strangers came to her for refuge when they had been mistreated elsewhere'. The old women on her farm gave her a Kikuya feminine honorific meaning 'the one who pays attention'.[47]

An attempt to represent this aspect of Blixen's life was made by the 1985 Hollywood movie version of her story, *Out of Africa*, directed by Sydney Pollack, in which Blixen was played by a coolly superior Meryl Streep, her husband by a scene-stealing Klaus Maria Brandauer, her lover and the game hunter in tune with the wilderness by Robert Redford. If the black people in the film are granted some dignity in their dependence, they remain distinctly marginal to the romantic-melodramatic lives of the white protagonists represented by these assorted stars, while 'Africa' plays the familiar role of a *National Geographic* setting—colourful, exotic, and embalmed in a time out of history, despite or perhaps because of carefully researched period manners, clothing, motorcars, and aeroplanes. As Ruth Mayer remarked, in Pollack's *Out of Africa*, 'history gains the status of a style', confirming Fredric Jameson's definition of the 'nostalgia film', conveying 'pastness' through the attributes of fashion.[48] Absent is the complex sense, conveyed in Blixen's autobiographical memoir, of a colonial settlement out of key with the needs of both colonisers and colonised, and riven by the clash between northern European aristocratic attitudes and the local African worldviews which in some respects they resemble.

Blixen's own longing for a past world of natural order and hierarchy does enable her to engage with the longing of others for what they have lost, and wish to retain. What she does not remark, despite her antagonism towards the colonial authorities, is the ironic fact of how common this phenomenon has been among colonisers—naming the land they encountered after their remembered, familiar towns and cities, their 'hills, plains, and rivers'. And more than that: bringing with them their 'cut roots' in the form of everything from food and vegetation to language and ideology. As the impact of colonialism has receded, with the growth of new nations and the reinvigoration of the old, so the process has been considerably reversed, with renaming or in effect re-indigenisation a widespread phenomenon. That, too, relies on recalling the past, although it is not a simple matter: where the Blixen farm once stood is now a suburb of Nairobi, named Karen, after the Danish Baroness. It is particularly popular with expatriates.

'The Old Chief Mshlanga'

If the later, white colonial writer Lessing could overcome the dilemma of how to manage the regressive, primitivist tendencies of her own nostalgia, it is because in her case there was an early awareness of the potential of modernity, of how society may change, and even advance. What is surprising and impressive is that it did not require a long career of writing for this to emerge. To reinforce the point, I'd like now to turn to 'The Old Chief Mshlanga', the first words of which are also the first words of the first volume of *Collected African Stories*.

The opening certainly strikes a poignant note: 'They were good, the years of ranging the bush over her father's farm which, like every white farm, was largely unused . . . ' This is clearly more than simple, sentimental nostalgia, as the immediate hint of the profligacy of colonial possession suggests, a hint to be taken up later, when the whole issue of land ownership moves towards the centre of the tale, and the process of exploitation is delineated in a way that takes readers through the screens of what may well be an initially unfamiliar time and place towards an understanding that puts its foreignness into a perspective which connects us to it. By 'us', I mean the reader who can compare the situation outlined in the tale with others analogous to it, for example that of the lonely heroine of Nadine Gordimer's semi-fictionalised early self in *The Lying Days*, published in 1953, two years after the first appearance of 'The Old Chief Mshlanga'. Gordimer, whose early fiction remains in some respects equally as impressive as Lessing's, represents Helen Shaw as remaining imprisoned in her narcissistic whiteness, whereas Lessing's farm girl develops a more questioning perspective. At first the girl sings 'Out flew the web and floated wide, the mirror cracked from side to side'; she is a latter-day Lady of Shalott imprisoned in the castle of her isolated consciousness, unable to see the gaunt and violent landscape for what it is—any more than she can perceive the black people on the farm as anything but an amorphous mass, changing like the seasons, existing to serve whites like herself, the 'Nkosikaas', or chieftainness, as they are obliged to call her.[49]

The shift from omniscient to first-person narrator after the first two pages of the story, however, enables the reader to question and subvert this isolated white consciousness, at the same time as we are drawn into the girl's point of view when she goes on to explore her father's farm. When she encounters the old chief of the title and his attendants, they do not give way to her, but meet her with a dignity that makes the chief her equal, or, as she realizes, 'more than an equal, for he showed courtesy, and I showed none'. She begins to read explorers' accounts of the Old Chief's Country, as it used to be called, prompting a first sense of colonial usurpation, the land and its people becoming to her like a very old, intimate dance, 'whose steps I could not learn'. 'But I thought: this is my heritage too; I was bred here; it is my country as well as the black man's country',[50] a settler cliché, yet deeply felt by Lessing, as is evident from her account of her very first (1956) return home, where she wrote that 'a country also belongs to those who feel at home in it. Perhaps it may be that the love of Africa the country will be strong enough to link people who hate each other now. Perhaps'.[51] Referring here to the continent as a country reveals how far the discourse of settler nostalgia has infected her own language; and yet it is a hope that inhabitants of the subcontinent continue to wish for.

If the aim at this stage of 'The Old Chief Mshlanga' is to show that there is room for everyone, given mutual respect, this is not what emerges in the treatment of the 'natives' in the girl's house, especially in the way her mother treats the chief's son, who is their cook. This behaviour is repeated in most of the stories, and, alas, anyone who even now visits Southern Africa may find it replicated, just as Lessing's own return visits have confirmed, despite the transformations of the countries of the region into more, or less, workable democracies—less, in the case of Zimbabwe, where the unresolved issue of land ownership has helped turn the country into a starving tyranny, with land turned over to wealthy black politicians and resentful veterans of the civil war, few of whom know or care about farming. Peter Godwin's recent family memoir, *When a Crocodile Eats the Sun* (2007), vividly testifies to the impact of the Mugabe regime upon white farmers and black farm workers alike. But what Godwin seems to forget, and his black former compatriots can not, is that when the first pioneers arrived in the 1890s, the land was already populated with cattle farmers who were forced to make way for the settlers who assumed it was there for the taking. The very idea of land ownership was foreign to the local people. The first pioneers were in fact more interested in what lay beneath the land, that is, gold, which had been discovered on the Rand; but failing to find enough to justify commercial exploitation—although some went on dreaming of El Dorado[52]—they were granted land by the colonising authority, Rhodes' British South Africa Company, the tribal authorities never receiving any compensation.

It is all there in Lessing's short story, in the way the remembered incidents connect the contemporary to the historical, while containing the germ of future developments in the region. Behind 'The Old Chief Mshlanga' lies the major determining act of colonial rule in the area, the Land Apportionment Act of 1930, and an act analogous to the earlier Natives Land Act of 1913 in South Africa, equally designed to ensure that land ownership by local Africans was limited to demarcated reserves.[53] The effect of both acts was to transform Blacks who lived outside those reserves into wage or tenant labourers for white farmers, who thought they could therefore live the Arcadian fantasy that beckoned to the poor or frustrated from Britain—people like Lessing's father, a mutilated First World War veteran and bank clerk obsessed with memories of the conflict, and of the England he left behind for a hoped-for freer life in the colony. But his freedom, qualified by personal inadequacy and bad luck, was, like the supposed freedom of the settlers generally, at the cost of those they displaced or who—as the legal term so tellingly puts it—were 'alienated' from the land.

Alienation is what the emptiness of the landscape betokens: hence, for example, the moment of paralysing fear and loneliness the girl in 'The Old Chief Mshlanga' experiences when she ventures beyond the farm's boundaries. On one level it is the archetypal experience of the white incomer familiar from her reading—and from ours too, from *Heart of Darkness* or *Passage to India*:

> I had read of this feeling, how the bigness and silence of Africa, under the ancient sun, grows dense and takes shape in the mind, till even the birds seem to call menacingly, and a deadly spirit comes out of the trees,

and the rocks. You move warily, as if your passing disturbs something old and evil, something dark and big and angry that might suddenly rear and strike from behind.[54]

One has only to read of life in the rural areas of colonial Rhodesia from the local African perspective, as in Tsitsi Dangarembga's autobiographical *Nervous Conditions* (1988), to realise how homely that could be, despite the poverty and deprivation, for people who did *not* feel alone in the landscape. Even in the postcolonial Zimbabwean countryside under the present regime, depicted for example in Ian Holding's chilling novel *Unfeeling*, about a traumatised white boy whose parents are murdered and their farm 'liberated', the landscape is—to the boy's surprise—peopled, and far from empty, if nonetheless sinister and threatening to him.[55]

In 'The Old Chief Mshlanga' the menace arises within the white girl herself, in her isolation from the life, and from the long ancestral memories, the histories, around her. Like so many characters in earlier colonial fictions, from India as from Africa, the girl's lack of comprehension becomes an experience of nature as the site of obscure threat. Nevertheless, Lessing edges us beyond the stereotyped relationship between settler and landscape towards a broader understanding. When the girl reaches the old chief's kraal, she realises she has no reason to be there, and nothing to say to him or his people; and as she walks home, feeling excluded, she experiences yet again 'a queer hostility in the landscape, a cold, hard, sullen indomitability that walked with me, as strong as a wall, as intangible as smoke; it seemed to say to me: you walk here as a destroyer'. But Lessing does not leave it at that: 'I went slowly homewards, with an empty heart: I had learned that if one cannot call a country to heel like a dog, neither can one dismiss the past with a smile in an easy gush of feeling, saying: I could not help it, I am also a victim'.[56]

This suggests the strong context in which all Lessing's 'African' fictions ask to be read, and indeed how they should be read, in the postcolonial present: that is to say, with an awareness that there are no easy apologies or justifications for the historical injustice; nor, as we now know, will redress be easy. Individual and cultural memories may intersect; but, they can also diverge, leading to conflict about who precisely has a just claim on the future. Today, opposition to Zimbabwe's ruler comes from the whole spectrum of the country's people, educated business elite, black workers, black as well as white farmers, old white liberals and conservatives alike. As Lessing observes 'The land issue had always rankled, not least because during the War of Liberation [Mugabe] had promised land "to every man, woman and child"', and now his campaign of forcible acquisition was 'ruining' his country.[57]

Lessing's early fictional writing invites us to contemplate both the narrow and the broader perspectives invoked by her memories. When the girl sees the old chief again, after her father has confiscated the village's goats for trampling down one of his crops, it is to witness the chief's humiliation before white power, which leads to his and his villagers' removal to a distant 'native reserve'. But not before he has said to her father, in his own language, that all the land, this land the whites call theirs, is his land, and belongs to his people. Later, when she revisits the site where the village had been, at first she thinks that there is nothing there, it is empty; however, there is: any settler lucky enough to be 'allotted' the valley, would find suddenly, in the middle of a field, the mealies growing fifteen feet tall, 'and wonder what unsuspected vein of richness he had struck'.[58]

Most critics assume the last words are the girl's: to my reading, the *focus* is hers, but the irony is the author-narrator's, which provides a balance between sympathetic identification and detachment, marking this out as a moment of critically reflective nostalgia, that casts its light across all the succeeding stories of white efforts to relate to black people, whose inability or refusal to respond compounds the mutual tragedy of their situation.

If I seem to have spent overmuch time on one short story, this is not only because of what I consider its exemplary brilliance in relation to my chosen theme, but also because of my general sense that the short story remains an underrated form, especially in the context of postcolonial studies, despite its debt to both ancient, oral traditions and modernist strivings—a debt particularly apparent in Southern Africa, where writers as varied as H. C. Bosman, Dan Jacobson, Bessie Head, Yvonne Vera, Luis Bernardo Honwana, and Ivan Vladislavic, as well as Lessing and of course Gordimer, have flourished. All these writers deal with the colonial myths of white superiority, if from different perspectives, while perceiving the ironic gap between these myths and local African realities. What is distinctive about Lessing is the continuing thread of remembered loss, of creative melancholy, which surfaces in the early work, and which continues throughout her career, as she reiterates the necessity for individuals to realise they are part of some collective spirit, defined in more than materialist terms.

Nostalgia for the Absolute

In her 1971 Preface to *The Golden Notebook*, Lessing remarked that the only intelligent criticism the book received when it came out was from people who were, or had been, Marxists. This might seem surprising from an author who had famously discarded Marxism well before then. But: 'They saw what I was trying to do', she said.

> Marxism looks at things as a whole and in relation to each other—or tries to, but its limitations are not the point for the moment. A person who has been influenced by Marxism takes it for granted that an event in Siberia will affect one in Botswana. I think it is possible that Marxism was the first attempt, for our time, outside the formal religions, at a world-mind, a world ethic. It went wrong, could not prevent itself from dividing and

sub-dividing, like all the other religions, into smaller and smaller chapels, sects and creeds. But it was an attempt.[59]

It is important to recall that, as Lessing pointed out more recently, the book was written in the late 1950s, after Khrushchev's 20th Congress speech in Moscow acknowledging for the first time some of Stalin's crimes, thereby placing a depth-charge beneath the Left worldwide; and 'I wanted to capture the flavour of 1956 and later, and I think I did that . . . Everything was cracking up'.[60]

Throughout her life Lessing has been drawn to world systems—first Communism, in wartime Rhodesia, then in 1960s London the anti-psychiatry of R. D. Laing, and then Sufi mysticism, for her an all-encompassing religion 'beyond religion'.[61] According to George Steiner, Western culture has devised three great mythologies to explain its history, nature, and future after the collapse of formal religion—the Marxist promise, now cruelly bankrupt, the Freudian programme of liberation, only partially fulfilled, and Lévi-Strauss's structuralist anthropology, a punitive and illusory science, Steiner calls it. As a result of this threefold loss, there has been a surge of interest in the irrational, the pseudo-primitive, the fifth sense, and the occult, beneath all of which one may detect what he calls 'a nostalgia for the absolute'.[62]

This is what underlies Lessing's pursuit of transcendence, it seems to me, going beyond even the 'past perfect'. Having moved from the margins of the British empire to its centre where, although she has become a metropolitan figure, apparently at home in the restless urban swirl, she reflects a continuing sense of rootlessness, and a yearning for home—not literally, but in terms of redefining the self through a series of imaginative constructions which, however, may damagingly rely on 'the irrational, the pseudo-primitive, the fifth sense, and the occult', for all that she insists that she rejects such aberrations in favour of her chosen, post-Marxist path, Sufism. Having moved from the margins to the centre, she yearns to redefine the self through imaginative constructions which rely on the irrational and the occult. This may be the price of belonging to an imagined community of postcolonials, restlessly reflective individuals who keep questioning their origins, even as they yearn after them. And perhaps this takes her closer to the ambivalent vision of older colonials such as Laurens van der Post than is entirely comfortable.

I do not mean to devalue the search for alternative epistomologies that generates Lessing's remarkable journey, despite her reliance upon what I identify as a certain nostalgia for the pseudo-primitive or mythical in her writings that is a feature of many colonial and postcolonial representations of Africa. The telling comparison might be with Bessie Head who, through many uprootings and a life in exile in Botswana, engaged in a lifelong search for an identity as an African or, as she once put it, 'a New African'.[63] For Head, as for Lessing, it is *A Question of Power* (1974), the title of her visionary account of life for a tormented single mother in a small Southern African village. In it, the mythologizing of Africa is made to function as a complex source of strength for its prophetic heroine who, as she falls asleep at the conclusion of her long, nightmarish spiritual journey, places 'one soft hand over her land. It was a gesture of belonging'.[64]

For Doris Lessing, the search goes on. Every new novel or story represents another attempt to go beyond past fixtures and towards future new identities—embracing, while recognising or acknowledging, a relationship with the past, with her African myth. Hence all the narrative experiments that followed *The Golden Notebook*, attempts to inscribe, or better, reinscribe, 'the great archetypal dream, or epic story, or stage in history', reachable by means of earlier, pre-novel forms, such as that deployed in the African adventure of *Mara and Dann*. Every new novel or story represents another attempt to go beyond past fixtures and towards future new identities. Just as there are many kinds of nostalgia, there are also many kinds of fiction, as Lessing has so ably demonstrated.

In the next chapter, the work of German expatriate writer W. G. Sebald is considered, broadening the perspective in which postcolonial nostalgias are understood, while linking the European (and not simply British) colonial empires and their pasts with the trauma of the Holocaust and its aftermath. Remembering in the present is not easily categorised according to boxes labelled 'colonial' or 'postcolonial', although these labels do help to suggest linkages, and reveal what seems to have been hidden.

5 Recalling the Hidden Ends of Empire
W. G. Sebald

> What India is for the British Empire, Russia will be for us.
>
> Adolf Hitler, speaking in 1941[1]

> Whenever you hear anyone abuse the Jews, pay attention, because he is talking about you.
>
> quoted by Frantz Fanon, *Black Skin, White Masks*, 1962[2]

Hidden Connections

The work of German expatriate writer W. G. Sebald is not much studied by postcolonial theorists or critics.[3] But the issues his work raises concerning the literary mediation of the hidden endings of empire, including the ending of the Nazi empire, are highly pertinent. Sebald's work expresses a preoccupation with memory, nostalgia, and exile grounded in a deep knowledge of the multiple histories, including colonial histories, that continue to haunt us in the present. And by 'us' here I mean not only the first readers of Sebald, that is to say Europeans, but also all those touched in one way or another by the grip of empire, and its various ends.

It is worth reminding ourselves that the history of the world from the 1880s to the present is a history of empires, and the ending of empires. During this period a relatively small number of empires governed nearly all of the world, and then they came to an end, as the two superpowers took over, one of which, the Russian, finally fell apart in the 1990s, leaving us where we are now—with the United States, an empire in denial if not in decline.[4] As a result, the memories of earlier empires are everywhere. These memories can be, and often are, hidden or ignored, sometimes for good reason: uncovering the horrors of earlier times may do nothing to help the victims, or even the survivors, for whom forgetting may be more helpful.

What I want to do in this chapter is pursue some of those hidden memories of empire, while acknowledging the ethical and aesthetic difficulties involved. My focus will be on W. G. Sebald, whose unique prose searches out the unexpected affinities between empires as they have died or dissolved, affinities he is led to by the workings of nostalgia.

Nostalgic recall in a postcolonial Europe may seem the last resort of a scoundrel. But, as Sartre observed on reading Fanon's *Wretched of the Earth*, 'we in Europe too are being decolonized . . . the settler which is in every one of us is being savagely rooted out'.[5] Exploring the roots of European nostalgias is a part of that process of out-rooting. Sartre was of course thinking of France in the context of Algeria; and what he says is obviously relevant to Britain as well. But it applies also to Germans in their relationship to Germany's African empire, as was demonstrated by the fierce reaction, for example, to the 2004 Berlin exhibition, '*Namibia-Deutschland: eine geteilte Geschichte*', which was timed to coincide with the centenary of the Herero war in German South West Africa, an event many Germans felt should have been left firmly in the past.[6] They were in effect refusing any connection between the hidden or forgotten ends of German imperialism and the whole appalling project of the Third Reich, the ending of which is still with us, as countless books and films demonstrate—including books such as Bernhard Schlink's *The Reader* (*Der Vorleser*, 1995, 1997), which was later turned into a film (2008).

The Reader (both book and film) is a seductive example of how nostalgic tugging at the secret threads of the past brings with it problems of guilt and bad faith. The first-person narrative account of a German schoolboy drawn into a troubled relationship with an older woman who was once a Nazi raises these problems, although without resolving them—indeed the film version glosses most of this over.[7] As Eva Hoffman points out, for all that Schlink's novel is problematic, it points to the 'crucial dilemma' of the German second generation, of having to hate those whom you love, part of the 'collective psychobiography' of that generation in the aftermath of the collective crime of the Third Reich, including the perception of their parents as chilly and distant, and of sudden realisations of rottenness in the state in which they grew up.[8]

A moment's reflection suggests that guilt and bad faith are not exclusive to the memories of the Nazi empire. Ex-colonials often wish to remember imperial glories, while forgetting the connection between such glories and the death and destruction wreaked upon subject populations. Postcolonial theorists and critics have of course drawn attention to this; yet there is nonetheless a surprising lack of awareness of the connections between empires, and our common inheritance of the problems of remembering and forgetting suggested by these connections. It seems to be forgotten that the British Empire was only one among many, even if at its apogee it was the largest empire the world had seen. There are deep, if sometimes barely visible connections and affiliations across as well as within empires. Ironically, given the common perception of nostalgia as a facile glossing of the past, its promptings can be shown to bring these hidden ends once more back into focus, enabling a better understanding of the past in the present.

Imperialism and the Holocaust

I should say at this point that postcolonial theory *has* developed a way of acknowledging the complex interrelatedness of the multiple strands of empire, if not the specific strand I am interested in here. Edward Said's 'contrapuntal reading' of many mainstream English and French literary texts in *Culture and Imperialism* (1993) demonstrated how an apparently simple model of cultural resistance to imperialism could be fruitfully complicated so as to refigure past histories in terms of overlap and interconnection. And as Bill Ashcroft later argued, the imperial dynamic should be understood as 'intermittent and rhizomic', rather than 'monolithic' and 'vertical'.[9] Both Said and Ashcroft were in effect acknowledging the importance of reading with an awareness of the complex and hidden nature of allusions to empire, and the need to seek them out, although the point remains that neither cared to notice German colonial empires. And yet the connection of German imperialism to the development of Nazi ambitions, the results of which have done so much to shape the world we have lived in for the last half century and more, has an unavoidable significance for anyone concerned with the postcolonial mapping of the world.

German colonial history is a lot shorter than the 400-year history of the British Empire, having its roots in the 1870s, when the Second Reich was declared, and Bismarck brought his newly consolidated nation into the process of imperial bargaining, better known as the Scramble for Africa; formally the Second Reich lasted for only thirty years (1884–1914), although its impact upon international relations was profound. Moreover, the general process of which German imperialism was a part may be seen to have anticipated the Third Reich. As Hannah Arendt put it in her classic account of *The Origins of Totalitarianism*, nineteenth-century imperialism prepared the stage for the horrors of the Holocaust. Race as 'a principle of the body politic', she wrote, and bureaucracy as 'a principle of foreign domination' were the new devices for running societies and ruling foreign peoples that were 'discovered during the first decades of imperialism'. And both discoveries were 'actually made on the Dark Continent'.[10]

According to Robert Eaglestone, this is an area of study that still needs 'much work', as the impact of the Holocaust gets 'projected backwards in time'. The writings Eaglestone himself refers to are persuasive. According to Victor Klemperer's war diaries, for example, the first term Klemperer recognised as specifically National Socialist was the word 'Strafexpedition' (punitive raid), a term embodying a brutal contempt for people 'in any way different'; 'it sounded so colonial', wrote Klemperer, that when you heard it 'you could see the encircled Negro village'. According to historian Ulrich Herbert the Holocaust reflected 'the policies pursued by Germany and the other great powers in their (especially African) colonies and the long tradition of planning for a German, quasi-colonial Hinterland in eastern and south-eastern Europe'.¹¹ No wonder it should strike Wibke Bruhns, retracing her family's story from the times of the Kaiser to Hitler, that exports to Grodno and its hinterland in the East during World War I, 'cheap penknives and the like', resemble 'the export economy to the new African colonies', or that the notorious Order of 6 June 1941 should command the 'Germanisation of the East by the introduction of Germans and the original inhabitants to be treated like Red Indians', followed by mass executions, deportations, and starvation.¹² As Elizabeth Harvey reminds us, the *'Drang nach Osten'* which became the colonisation of wartime Poland with ethnic German re-settlers (*'Umsiedler'*) became 'an instrument of genocidal warfare'.¹³

It is difficult to avoid the conclusion that the tradition of imperial control was in effect a tradition of genocide, although that term was only invented in 1944, becoming widely known as a result of the Nuremberg trials. Each genocide has its unique character, and I am not about to suggest otherwise; rather, it can be said that genocide in the heart of darkness not only preceded but prepared the way for industrial-scale genocide in the heart of Europe. Kurtz's 'Exterminate all the brutes' was the implication of Belgian policy in the Congo basin, as Conrad's *Heart of Darkness* (one of Sebald's key intertexts) suggested in 1899, merely a few years before the Germans were attempting to exterminate the indigenous peoples of their South West African colony. As Sven Lindqvist points out, this was all happening during Hitler's childhood, when the European view that the 'inferior races' were condemned to extinction was commonplace. ¹⁴ What Hitler wished to create when he sought *Lebensraum* was a European continental version of the British Empire, one empire providing a model for another, as he on one occasion made explicit (see epigraph above). And what Hitler desired arose out of a common view of German racial superiority. Wibke Bruhns' account of her officer grandfather's attitudes suggest they were typical even of the relatively wealthy and cultivated class sometimes assumed to be above the racism of the lower middle class represented by the Nazi Party's earlier and more fervent followers.¹⁵

The ending of one empire, German, British, French, or Belgian, does not mean that its ends have ended—indeed, according to some, the empires of the past have been replaced by one global Empire that is breeding its own ending.¹⁶ In any case, memory provides one link in the chain, which German historians in particular have been pursuing with increasing intensity, driven by a sense of culpability towards their own past. At the same time, despite the undoubtedly vicious suppression of indigenous peoples in the colonies that chronologically preceded the rise of Nazism, a note of caution needs to be struck. If, as I am arguing, on one level the connection between 'Windhoek and Auschwitz' should be made, on another, it is not so easy to specify precisely and historically.¹⁷

But this leaves the way open for the artist and the writer, that is to say, those who *represent* remembering, and who thereby explore the potential for connection and affiliation: among whom Sebald stands as a key figure. Sebald challenges collective amnesia, linking the history and representation of colonial oppression with the forgetfulness of the Germans regarding the Third Reich. Sebald lacked direct personal experience of what happened in his country or abroad; what he had were not so much his own memories, but the memories of those he knew or encountered, in person or through their writings, memories which ultimately go back centuries. For him, as for many Germans growing up during or just after World War II, nostalgic memories of home and family have had to confront the issue of parental guilt or complicity; nor does he forget that for those who lost their families, anger, frustration, even a numbness in the face of the ultimate darkness, might at times override any urge to remember, much less succumb to nostalgia.

But as I have been suggesting, nostalgia can and should be much more than simply a passive longing for bygone times, it should be mediated by historical awareness; and Sebald takes us on a journey that involves a critical acknowledgment of the meanings of the past, especially past traumas as they are often secretly connected, the ends of endings.

Of course this is difficult territory. Everyone is familiar with Adorno's remark that it is impossible to write poetry after Auschwitz, or indeed about Auschwitz; but this is a view that no longer stands, as Adorno himself came to recognise.[18] The work of Paul Celan, for example, who lost his parents in the Holocaust, suggests that the abyss *can* be faced in art and literature. Writing out of direct personal experience, Celan left the unspeakable unspoken, while creating nonetheless 'a sort of homecoming' on the other side of humankind.[19] What poems such as his 'Todesfuge' ('Death Fugue', 1952) established was that it was a question of *how* the artist or writer exploited their terrible material, not whether or not to deal with it at all. The fact that he wrote in German, the language that George Steiner once described as a language of 'dissimulation and deliberate forgetting', so infected with 'bestialities' and falsehood that only 'the most drastic truth can cleanse it', makes Sebald's achievement all the more impressive.[20]

For Sebald, an art of indirection and allusion, rather than direct, realistic representation provides an ethically as well as aesthetically acceptable form for recalling the endings in and of imperial pasts. We might well feel that this recollection should exclude nostalgia, insofar as that brings back the inhuman, the unspeakable. But, again, it depends upon the nature of the nostalgia and the understandings it brings with it: in particular, whether or not a critical negotiation or dialogue between present and past is initiated by the return to past histories—what Sebald once referred to as a 'retrospective learning process'.[21]

As this implies, the moral dimension of revisiting the past is what counts. Edgar Reisz's lengthy television series *Heimat*, which appeared in Germany from 1984 onwards, is a case in point. Despite seeming initially like just another of the mass of 1950s films that evoked a German homeland untroubled by bombs, refugees, or guilt,[22] Reisz's *Heimat* depicted familiar rural characters indirectly yet inevitably involved with the large-scale events of the rise and collapse of the Reich, thereby re-establishing a link between ordinary German folk and their past to ensure what had been forgotten *was* remembered, and indeed debated, so that German audiences' sense of who they were in relation to their past was re-forged, without doing that past an injustice.[23] A more recent film, Michael Haneke's *Das Weisse Band* (2009, 'The White Ribbon'), took things a stage further, depicting an idyllic German village in the months leading to the outbreak of World War I through the retrospective vision of an older narrator who recalls how a society based on power and authority corrupts absolutely, leaving the audience to draw the connections with Fascism as well as Nazism, and indeed other forms of absolutist ideology at the heart of the last century.

W. G. Sebald

Sebald's own *Heimat* was the small Bavarian alpine town of Wertach im Allgäu, where he was born during the last days of the Third Reich on 18 May 1944. His father joined the army in 1929, later becoming an officer in the Wehrmacht who was captured by the Allies and who returned from prisoner-of-war camp in 1947, remaining thereafter a detached, silent figure. Until he was 12, Sebald was brought up mainly by his grandfather. When an interviewer once remarked to Sebald that his mother, then in her eighties, could probably no longer remember the war years, he replied 'quickly', speaking of his parents' generation: 'They could remember if they wanted to'.[24] German silence about the past in the immediate post-war period is understandable; but it was a silence that eventually had to be broken. Nobel Prize-winning author Günter Grass was among those who broke it, although when Grass's autobiographical book *Peeling the Onion* came out in 2006, it emerged that this fierce critic of post-war amnesia had himself been a member of the Waffen-SS during the closing years of the war.

Sebald belonged to the younger generation, for whom the German conspiracy of silence had obscured how people like his own working-class family had benefited from the post-war economic miracle. And as he remarked in 2001:

> Until I was 16 or 17 I had heard practically nothing about the history that preceded 1945. Only when we were 17 were we confronted with a documentary film of the opening of the Belsen camp. There it was, and we somehow had to get our minds around it—which of course we didn't. It was in the afternoon, with a football match afterwards. So it took years to find out what had happened. In the mid-60s, I could not conceive that these events had happened only a few years back.[25]

Realising more fully what had happened before and during the war, even in small backwaters like Wertach, Sebald grew disillusioned with his country and went into self-exile in England, where he lived for most of the time until his untimely death in a car accident in 2001. He first left his protected home environment to study German literature at Freiburg University, and then moved to Switzerland, before departing to become a language assistant at Manchester University in 1966. He returned to Switzerland as a schoolteacher, before leaving for Manchester once more. He went on to pursue an academic career in England and published critical studies of modern German language writers like Peter Weiss, Gottfried Keller, and Franz Kafka; he eventually became Professor of European Literature at the University of East Anglia in Norwich—where, in his mid forties, he began writing in his native German the books which, published in English, soon gave him an international reputation.

That reputation rests, for the most part, on *The Emigrants* (1996), *The Rings of Saturn* (1998), *Vertigo* (1999), and *Austerlitz* (2001), in the order of their English publication. All his writing tries to show that the question of memory provides, as he put it, the 'moral backbone of literature'.[26] His meditations on time, memory, and place go back far beyond the present, yet always return to it, taking in surprisingly vast realms of literary and historical space along the way. Unlike Proust, with whom he is sometimes compared, the workings of involuntary memory are less important for him than the determined pursuit of documents, diaries, records, books, and photographs that constitute public as well as private memory. Journeying is at the centre of his writing, generated by a form of nostalgia figured as a desire to return to a home that is, however, also the source of suffering, destruction, and ending. For Sebald, the past is our constant company, a past tending always towards the end or loss of power. That loss leads to yearning, or *Sehnsucht*, an emotion with deep roots in German art and literature, and which is not necessarily a negative or destructive emotion, but one which may and can, in hands such as Sebald's, provide a stimulus to understanding, and who knows, even change.

Sebald's books are littered with images—photos, drawings, newspaper clippings, maps—that simultaneously evoke the material survivals of the past, and the ephemerality of those survivals. These images, and their often apparently random, captionless placing in his texts, highlight the importance of the visual in all memory work;[27] but it is an importance all the more telling in that for Sebald, as for many others, it was the visual record of the Holocaust that reverberated through memory, conjuring up a sense of horror, shame, and guilt. He rarely uses such explicit images, and when he does—a newspaper photograph of corpses in the wood at Bergen Belsen in *The Rings of Saturn*, for example—the resultant shock for the reader is all the more powerful (60–61). More generally he evokes the traces or vestiges of the past as a means of acknowledgement, or witness: or, more often, elegiac remembrance. His model is the émigré German Jewish artist, Max Ferber, who appears in the final story of *The Emigrants*, and whose art is an art of traces, tending towards dust or nothingness, and yet which survives through the act of creation, the telling, the writing.

The Emigrants

The Emigrants is in many respects the exemplary Sebald narrative: it views memory and migration through the prism of a pervasive yet challenging nostalgia, prompted by a sense of endings, many of which remain enigmatic. It consists of a series of connected, increasingly complex, first-person narratives or *Erzählungen* as the German subtitle has it, revolving around four twentieth-century exiled Germans of Jewish descent who long consciously or unconsciously to return to their homelands. For various reasons to do with the rise and collapse of the Nazi empire, this return is blocked, their homes are lost, their stories have in a sense already ended. Through overlapping and intertwined narrative lines that engage with history, fiction, biography, and memoir, while displaying photographs, sketches, maps, newspaper clippings, and even a boat ticket, the stories show how post-war memory loss, its 'lagoons of oblivion' (174),[28] may be plumbed in the quest for the connections between earlier selves and identities, including, obliquely, those associated with the colonial empires.

In the first and shortest story, titled like the rest after its central character, Dr Henry Selwyn, the narrator arrives in Norfolk to search for somewhere to live, just as Sebald himself did. He finds his prospective landlord lying on the grass beside the house: 'an old man, his head propped on his arm . . . altogether absorbed in contemplation of the patch of earth immediately before his eyes' (5), like an ancient image of melancholy. Dr Selwyn lives a hermit-like existence in an old priory near Norwich, similar to the Sebalds' first residence. One day the retired doctor calls on the narrator to ask if he is ever homesick. 'I could not think of any adequate reply,' he says, 'but Dr Selwyn, after a pause for thought, confessed (no other word will do) that in recent years he had been beset with homesickness more and more'(18). The apparently clumsy locution emphasises Selwyn's increasingly deranged manner. When the narrator asks where it is he feels drawn back to, Selwyn replies that at the age of seven he had left a village in Grodno in Lithuania with his family. This revelation has been prompted by a nostalgia which turns out to be fatal. The young Selwyn migrated to London in 1899 and, after anglicising his name from Hersch Seweryn in 'a kind of second confirmation' (20), went on to study medicine, eventually becoming a colonial army surgeon in India. While there, he bought the heavy hunting rifle which, a few weeks after this conversation with the narrator, he uses to shoot himself.

The narrator reflects that at the time he learnt this he felt no great shock, 'But certain things, as I am becoming increasingly aware, have a way of returning unexpectedly, often after a lengthy absence' (23). This cautious prose hides a moral caution on the author's part. At first it seems to be not so much longing or *Sehnsucht*, but chance association or involuntary memory of the Proustian kind that brings about these returns. Thus, travelling across Switzerland many years later, 'as I recall, or perhaps merely imagine, the memory of Dr Selwyn returned to me for the first time in a long while' (23). But the permeability of the boundary between memory and imagination has been prompted by a Swiss newspaper article about the discovery of the remains of a mountain guide released from a glacier after seventy-two years, the guide Selwyn had met on a tour of the Alps in 1913, in whose company, he had said, he never felt better in his life (14). That life had become increasingly narrow during and after World War II, 'a blinding bad time for me,' Selwyn confided, 'about which I could not say a thing, even if I wanted to' (21).

Selwyn's suppressed wartime memories are never released; but his unexpected return to the narrator's imagination has released another memory—of the doctor's nostalgia for the time of supreme companionship with the guide whose remains have been freed by the slow movement of the glacier. 'And so', the narrator observes, in a phrase that resonates throughout Sebald's work, 'they are ever returning to us, the dead' (23). Nature has its own ends, which include bringing back the dead to human consciousness. 'I had to go beyond my very fond memories of him and discover the story I did not know' (28), continues the narrator, later shouldering the burden of Bereyter's past, unspoken and unknown though most of it is. And that is also the nearest we come to an end for Selwyn's incomplete story. The unhappy tale of his attempted assimilation into British culture, including (the India reference) its empire, suggests that surviving the ends of empire is only possible or even desirable through the remembering of others, but it is a process that goes beyond the merely human scale, becoming ultimately unreachable, inconceivable.

The theme of the return of the dead through chance event, involuntary memory but also nostalgic recall, is reinforced by the second tale of *The Emigrants*, which opens with the photograph of a set of curving railway tracks from ground level, and the words: 'In January 1984, the news reached me from S, that on the evening of the 30th of December, a week after his seventy-fourth birthday, Paul Bereyter, who had been my teacher at primary school, had put an end to his life' (27). This news sends the narrator—whose biography is once again interwoven with Sebald's—back to his hometown S in southern Germany, where he tries to reconstruct his teacher's life from a series of photographs which make him feel 'as if the dead were coming back, or as if we were on the point of joining them' (46). The photographs are shown him by Mme Landau, a friend of Bereyter's and herself a migrant from Germany, who reveals how the teacher was forced out of his post, and his family proscribed, because they were part Jewish, adding that she did not expect the narrator to be aware of 'the meanness and treachery' to which they were exposed 'in a miserable hole such as S then was, and such as it still is despite all the so-called progress; it does not surprise me at all,' she continues, 'since that is inherent in the whole wretched sequence of events' (50).

That wretched sequence of events includes Bereyter's return to S after the war, having avoided deportation—ironically enough, since he is part Jewish—by being called up to serve in the Wehrmacht. What moved 'and even forced' him to return, according to Mme Landau,

> was the fact that he was a German to the marrow, profoundly attached to his native land in the foothills of the Alps, and even to that miserable place S as well, which in fact he loathed and, deep within himself ... would have been pleased to see destroyed and obliterated, together with the townspeople, whom he found so utterly repugnant. (57)

Bereyter's nostalgia is not just ambivalent, it is divided against itself, since he is most alienated when he is most at home. It is a division he cannot live with, and so, on his final visit home, he lies down in front of a train. Mme Landau relates that she had an 'uncanny' premonition of this end, because 'Railways had always meant a great deal to him—perhaps he felt they were headed for death' (61). What the reader infers from this, and from her remark that Bereyter's end was 'the very image and symbol' of a 'German tragedy', is the railway's emblematic relation to the Final Solution for German Jews.[29] The railways provided the logistics for imperial control over large populations whether wanted or unwanted from the nineteenth century onwards; and where they ended was in a sense where the concentration camps began. They feature throughout Sebald's work, notably in *Austerlitz*, whose eponymous protagonist searches for his true—Jewish—identity by pursuing the railway tracks leading back to central Europe and the extermination camps where his parents died.

The third narrative of *The Emigrants*, 'Ambros Adelwarth', brings us yet nearer to the narrator's and indeed also Sebald's own life, since it involves the author's great-uncle, an émigré to the United States, and his great-uncle's companion, Cosmo Solomon. Migration, madness, silence, and ending reflect the tendency of this, like the other three narratives, towards what John Zilcosky has called a pattern of 'terrifying homecomings'.[30] For Sebald's densely interwoven narrative trails, going away always involves coming back again. During a series of disorienting travels recorded in Ambros's pocket diary, he and Cosmo find themselves in Constantinople in 1913—a key date for Sebald, perhaps because it suggests that last moment before the cataclysmic developments of the succeeding century. Every walk brings Ambros and Cosmo alarm and surprise: 'you turn down a gloomy back street that narrows and narrows until you think you are trapped, whereupon you take one last desperate turn round a corner and find yourself suddenly gazing from a vantage point across the vastest of panoramas', an experience heightened when they turn a corner in the densely populated Jewish quarter and meet an unexpected view of distant mountains, including 'the snowy summit of Olympus'; and 'For one awful heartbeat I imagine myself in Switzerland or at home again'(131).

But Ambros' Ithaca is not in Switzerland or Germany, much less Odysseus' Greece; it is in upstate New York, to which he migrates, becoming majordomo to the wealthy, yet increasingly secluded Solomon family, whose downward trajectory into depression, paralysis, and death he repeats in person, losing his memories as death approaches. 'Memory', the narrator's great-uncle reflects in a concluding postscript, 'often strikes me as a kind of dumbness. It makes one's head heavy and giddy, as if one were not looking back down the receding perspectives of time but rather down on the earth from a great height' (145).

Vertigo and Loss

This sensation was the controlling metaphor of Sebald's first prose work, *Vertigo*, entitled in the original German '*Schwindel. Gefühle*' [sic], a deconstruction of the usual phrase '*Schwindelgefühle*', so as to emphasise the associations of '*Schwindel*', suggesting dizziness or vertigo but also deception, hence the double uncertainty of his '*Gefühle*' or feelings. The uncertainty of perspective in the way memory connects us with history brings feelings of sickness, nausea—and a sense of bereavement. In *Vertigo* apparently random accounts of Stendhal crossing the Alps, Casanova's Venetian jailbreak, and Franz Kafka's visit to Verona become interwoven with the author-narrator's return home in the final, ironically titled section, '*Il ritorno in patria*', in which, no Ulysses, the narrator returns to 'W', recognisably Sebald's village home. This return brings with it the unsettling discovery that home seems less real than in his many dreams of it, indeed it has become 'more remote than any other place I could conceive of',[31] despite an inrush of childhood memories, memories that simultaneously bring an irremediable sense of loss.

If loss seems irremediable, that is partly because of how certain memories, the memories of the exterminated, have been denied, as they were in Sebald's village, and by the willed amnesia of his parents' generation. This is why *The Emigrants* is centrally about the experiences of Jews, not remembered by the narrator, but remembered by those he remembers. Their stories of endings are lost in the grim abyss of time, and are only partially recoverable through the traces that can still be written or rewritten, a process described elsewhere by Sebald as an art of 'palimpsests . . . They are written over and over again, until I feel that a kind of metaphysical meaning can be read through the writing'.[32] Desire for a meaning beyond the everyday reflects a nostalgia that involves more than a yearning to recall people and places, but for transcendence.

Yet Sebald's nostalgia always begins with places and people; it is doggedly humane, as when his narrator discovers the artist Ferber, amidst the decaying outskirts of Manchester, 'the city from which industrialization had spread across the entire world' (156), and which is now a post-industrial, post-imperial city of immigrants—'leaving aside the poor Irish . . . chiefly Germans and Jews' (191), who have been replaced by people like the Maasai chieftain who cooks in the café he frequents, the Wadi Halfa (163). The overlapping migrations produced by successive empires are never-ending, while the empires themselves are always ending, sinking into a twilight like that which envelops Manchester as it appears when the narrator and Ferber first meet and the artist gives him a 'cursory' account of his life (161).

The metropolis is evidently a place of emptiness and loss, of past greatness and power. Why is Ferber there? How did he get there? In a structural echo of the Selwyn narrative, it is many years later that the narrator chances across a review of one of Ferber's paintings and learns that in May 1939, the fifteen-year-old Ferber fled Munich for London, while his German Jewish parents were murdered by the Nazis. Prompted by this knowledge to return to Manchester and seek Ferber out, the narrator hears Ferber recall his first impressions of the city in 1945:

> The most impressive thing, of course ... were all the chimneys that towered above the plain and the flat maze of housing, as far as the eye could see. Almost every one of those chimneys ... has now been demolished or taken out of use. But at that time there were still thousands of them, belching out smoke by day and night ... I can no longer say exactly what thoughts the sight of Manchester prompted in me then, but I believe I felt I had found my destiny. (168–69)

Ironically, the city reminded Ferber 'of everything I was trying to forget', his birthplace at the heart of an empire, because here at the heart of another empire he has found a home 'to serve under the chimney' (192). The extermination camps are after all not far away.

Ferber hands the narrator a brown paper package containing photographs and his mother's handwritten memoirs of her early years in Steinach and Bad Kissingen, where three hundred years of Jewish culture once existed, memoirs which now seemed to Ferber

> like one of those evil German fairy tales in which, once you are under the spell, you have to carry on to the finish, till your heart breaks, with whatever work you have begun—in this case, the remembering, writing and reading. (192–93)

The narrator travels to Bad Kissingen to explore Ferber's origins for himself, so as to recall and write what we now read, thereby affirming the survival of these hidden ends of the Nazi empire, which however survive only as long as the spell lasts and the narrator pursues them.

The fragility of memory is debilitating: 'I felt increasingly that the mental impoverishment and lack of memory that marked the Germans, and the efficiency with which they had cleaned everything up, were beginning to affect my head and my nerves' (225). The narrator's anxiety about doing justice to the story of Ferber's family leads to doubt about 'the entire questionable business of writing' (230). Nonetheless, his book lies before us. Nor does its existence deny the possibility of writing: Sebald's kind of postmodernism—if it really is that—involves a dizzying plurality of perspectives, not a denial of any perspective at all, nor of the reality of experience.

106 *Postcolonial Nostalgias*

Thus it was in Manchester, where his landlord was a Jewish refugee, that the young Sebald apparently realised for the first time that the 'historical events' he had heard about 'had happened to real people':

> You could grow up in Germany in the postwar years without ever meeting a Jewish person. There were small communities in Frankfurt or Berlin, but in a provincial town in south Germany Jewish people didn't exist. The subsequent realisation was that they had been in all those places, as doctors, cinema ushers, owners of garages, but they had disappeared—or had been disappeared. So it was a process of successive phases of realisation.[33]

Successive 'phases of realisation' are what Sebald's narrator takes us through as, prompted by nostalgia, he encounters the memories of others: memories that provoke moments of paralysing doubt, as he becomes aware of the hidden connections they reveal.

The Rings of Saturn, Conrad, and the Congo

The Rings of Saturn, ostensibly the record of a year-long walking tour through coastal East Anglia begun in 1992, opens with such a moment: the narrator has been laid low by a 'paralysing horror' at the 'traces of destruction, reaching far back into the remote past' (3)[34] that he had come across during his tour. Supine in a Norwich hospital, he begins to conceive 'these pages' (4–5); when he finally assembles his notes a year after his discharge, reflections on deceased scholarly friends lead to reflections on Flaubert, Dürer's *Melancholia,* and Sir Thomas Browne's *Urn Burial—*a discourse on sepulchral urns from a Norfolk field. Of these multiple intertexts, the neo-Platonist Browne's 1658 work is especially resonant: an encyclopaedic collection of ruminations on ruins, graves, decay, and the destructive forces of nature 'deploying', as the narrator remarks,

> a vast repertoire of quotations and the names of authorities who had gone before, creating complex metaphors and analogies, and constructing labyrinthine sentences that sometimes extend over one or two pages, sentences that resemble processions or a funeral cortège in their sheer ceremonial lavishness. (19)

Not unlike Sebald's own manner, then, reflecting an inevitably futile urge to encompass known history, which in *The Rings of Saturn* involves interweaving such apparently random phenomena as the life cycle of the herring, early English colonial forays into Imperial China, and the history of the silk industry, circling back, finally, to the Third Reich again, that—it is hard to believe—inaugurated a new era of silk cultivation in Germany involving measures to 'monitor productivity and selection, including extermination to prevent racial degeneration' (293-94).

Sebald's irony plays over encounters with fading East Anglian coastal towns, worn-out industries, and dying or extinct local personalities, while revealing the interconnectedness of imperial ends. It is not only the landscape of Suffolk that betokens imperial decay: so too do the great houses that once depended upon imperial exploitation, houses such as Somerleyton, a medieval manor rebuilt to resemble 'an oriental palace in a fairy tale' (35) by the mid-Victorian industrialist Morton Peto. Peto's massive fortune derived from colonial railway building, a vital element in Britain's imperial ascendancy, an achievement as dated as the trophies, from African masks to hand-coloured engravings of Boer War battles, which adorn the walls and which are said to resemble the contents of a pawnbroker's or an auctioneer's (35-36).

For Sebald, the ending of one empire is related to that of every other—a chance encounter brings memories of bombers flying over Somerleyton on their mission to destroy the Third Reich. This connectedness is an aspect of his global, even cosmic vision, although the nearer, human history of destruction touches us more than the universal forces to which he alludes from time to time: the second epigraph to the novel refers to the tidal forces that destroyed the moons of Saturn, forces echoed in accounts of the collapse of the East Anglian coastline. But Sebald's concern with memory, and specifically with the memories of empire, is signalled, too—by the first epigraph to *The Rings of Saturn*, extracted from a letter by Joseph Conrad to his distant cousin Marguerite Poradowska, dated 23-25 March 1890, in which Conrad says one must forgive those unhappy souls who have chosen to make 'le pèlerinage à pied' along the shore, observing without comprehending 'l'horreur de la lutte, la joie de vaincre ni le profonde désespoir des vaincus'.

These Conradian echoes pervade *The Rings of Saturn*, which in the original German was subtitled *'eine Wallfahrt'* or pilgrimage. When the narrator's pilgrimage touches the East Anglian shoreline at Lowestoft, he discovers that this is where the coaster arrived on which ordinary seaman Józef Korzeniowski served in 1878, twelve years before signing up with the Sociêtê Anonyme Belge pour le Commerce du Haut-Congo. Thereafter the long voyage began in which 'the madness of the whole colonial enterprise' was gradually borne in upon Conrad (117), whose vision in *Heart of Darkness* of successive empires resembling brief lights upon the desolate landscape of time chimes closely with Sebald's view of 'human civilization' as 'no more than a strange luminescence growing more intense by the hour, of which no one can say when it will begin to wane and when it will fade away' (170). The urge to control, exploit, and destroy the subjects of empire is what commands Sebald's attention, and an entire chapter of the ten-chapter sequence of *The Rings of Saturn* is devoted to the horrors of imperial penetration into Africa witnessed by Conrad—and by Roger Casement, 'the only man of integrity' among the Europeans Conrad encountered in Africa, the rest having been 'corrupted partly by the tropical climate and partly by their own rapaciousness and greed' (104).

Sebald goes on to provide a detailed account of Conrad's upbringing and early years, derived largely from *A Personal Record* (1912), and an objective correlative for his own sense of himself as the displaced, homesick foreigner seeking a new identity in Britain. ('Homesickness', we are told, corroded Conrad's mother's soul, and was in part the cause of her death in exile (107).) Sebald imagines the fortnight Conrad spent in Lowestoft, where

> Doubtless he rented a room and made whatever enquiries were necessary for his plans. In the evenings, when the darkness settled upon the sea, he will have strolled along the esplanade, a twenty-one-year-old foreigner alone among the English. I can see him, for instance, standing out on the pier, where a brass band is playing the overture from *Tannhäuser* as a night-time serenade. And as he walks homeward past those who remain to listen, with a gentle breeze coming off the water, he is intrigued by the ease with which he is absorbing a hitherto quite unfamiliar language, a language he will one day employ to write the novels that will win him worldwide acclaim, whilst for now it fills him with an altogether new sense of purpose and confidence. (113–14)

For Sebald's Conrad to hear the overture from Wagner's turning point opera of high romantic nostalgia in this dreamlike moment is wonderfully ironic, given Conrad's youthful yearnings for travel and adventure; and for the future author to hear it as he walks 'homeward' highlights the uncertainties about what that word means for the narrator as well as for Conrad, whose 'new sense of purpose and confidence' anticipates as Sebald must have felt or hoped his own future, but which also led Conrad to embark upon the voyage which brought a profound realisation of 'the madness of the whole colonial enterprise' (117), a realisation which thereby becomes the narrator's as well. The appeal of Wagner's Germanic mythmaking to the Nazis adds a further layer of ironic prolepsis.

The 'white patch' on the map of Africa over which the young Conrad had pored for many hours as he tried to escape the uncertainties of exile brought about by his father's radical beliefs had become by the time he arrived in the Congo colony 'a place of darkness'. 'And the fact is', Sebald's narrator adds, 'that in the entire history of colonialism, most of it not yet written, there is scarcely a darker chapter than the one termed *The Opening of the Congo* (118). Sebald details the familiar facts, of how Leopold II 'proclaimed that the friends of humanity could pursue no nobler end' than to 'open up this last part of our earth' hitherto 'untouched by the blessings of civilisation' (118). As the narrator points out, those blessings involved 'legendary profits' and the eradication by forced labour, mutilation, murder, and illness of almost all the indigenous people from an area of land Leopold had made his personal possession, an area a hundred times the size of Belgium. 'Every year from 1890 to 1900, an estimated five hundred thousand of these nameless victims, nowhere mentioned in the annual reports, lost their lives. During the same period, the value of shares in the Compagnie du Chemin de fer du Congo rose from 320 Belgian francs to 2,850' (119).

Sebald does not give his source. But it is easy enough to confirm the validity of such details, for instance from Adam Hochschild's well-researched book *King Leopold's Ghost: A Story of Greed, Terror and Heroism in Colonial Africa*, which came out the same year as the English translation of *The Rings of Saturn*. One of Hochschild's heroes is the English shipping clerk E. D. Morel, who noticed that when the company's ships arrived in Antwerp from the new colony, they were filled with immensely valuable cargoes of rubber and ivory, yet when they sailed back, they carried nothing but soldiers, military supplies, and firearms. Abandoning his job, Morel became Leopold's scourge, and with the help of Roger Casement, at the time British consul in Boma, created a cause that would unite the world in ending the Belgian king's Congo venture—at least until the Belgian government took over and, while mitigating some of the worst excesses of Leopold's company officials, saw to it that the treasure-house of minerals in the Congo continued to support a vast network of exploitation, brutality, and hypocrisy, a network in which the original players have today been replaced by indigenous politicians, businessmen, and warlords. As Hochschild points out, the Congo 'offers a striking example of the politics of forgetting'.[35]

For Sebald, it offers a striking example of the importance of the politics of remembering. It has been argued that Conrad's novella represents a kind of 'modernist nostalgia' that is complicit with 'imperialist nostalgia', through lamenting the loss of the 'pristine condition of primitiveness that inspired the civilizing mission in the first place', a lament expressed in Conrad's infamous 'improved specimen' passage, which depicts in patronising terms a local African who has taken on some features of European civilisation.[36] But Sebald's remembering of Conrad guides us towards seeing how such passages should be contextualised, in terms of the realities of twentieth-century genocide. Far from suggesting nostalgia for the primitive past, Conrad's novella presents what is 'primitive' in the supposedly civilised and civilising present, when an idealist such as Kurtz ends up behind a row of shrunken heads on poles, which takes us quite far from his own (and in contemporary terms, progressive) view that some features of empire were redeemable, if its instruments behaved decently.

Conrad himself tried to forget what he had experienced and written about, and the guilt of his mere presence in the Congo which, as Sebald notes, his own travails did not absolve him from (120). But having written *Heart of Darkness* so as in his own words to push experience 'a little (and only very little) beyond the facts of the case for the ... purpose of bringing it home' to his readers,[37] Conrad may be forgiven for trying to forget what he saw and felt there. In any case, *Heart of Darkness* asks to be read less as a direct representation of conditions in the Congo in 1890 than as an expression, in Ian Watt's words, 'of the essence of the social and historical reality' as Conrad's memory and imagination recreated it.[38] This is why, for example, *Heart of Darkness* does not mention Casement, whom Conrad met shortly after landing, since that would have interfered with what he wished to show of the stark polarity between coloniser and colonised and its impact upon his complicit narrator Marlow.

As Sebald's narrative reminds us, the first news of 'the nature and extent of the crimes committed' in the Congo came to public attention as a result of Roger Casement's 1903 memorandum to the British Foreign Secretary, in which he gave an exact account of the merciless exploitation of its peoples, including the severing of hands and feet as an 'everyday' means of punishment (127). When Casement was transferred to South America some years later, probably to get him out of the way, he began to expose conditions there, too, where whole tribes were once again being wiped out, as a result of the 'imperialist mentality' (128). 'It was only to be expected that in due course he should hit upon the Irish question', espousing the cause of what he called 'the white Indians of Ireland' (129). Casement's prosecution and subsequent execution in 1916 for treason, after an ill-fated attempt to engage German support for the Irish republican movement during World War I, might have been overturned were it not for the publication of the so-called Black Diaries that revealed his promiscuous homosexual life. Two pages from the Diaries in facsimile interrupt Sebald's text, as if to interrupt the calm flow of the narrative with this lone voice of conscience, whose sexuality displeased those he supported as well as those he opposed. But, according to Sebald's narrator, Casement's homosexuality 'sensitized' him 'to the continuing oppression, exploitation, enslavement and destruction, across the borders of social class and race, of those who were furthest from the centres of power' (134).

Thus the ends of empire connect coloniser and colonised as power ebbs away from the centre like the tides on the Suffolk coast. As if awakened by Casement's ghostly presence, the narrator's memories move on in the next section to Ireland, and the collapse of the great houses with their once-dominant families, become 'refugees' themselves, 'prisoners in their own homes' (210, 217), after the civil war. Both victims and architects of empire, the Irish are no more exempt from the cycles of decline and destruction than anyone else. What *Rings of Saturn* offers is a remembering that challenges facile oppositions; and yet, there are moments when the reader feels like exclaiming: 'oh no, not again!' Wandering among the remains of the wartime installations littered about the Orford estuary on the Suffolk coast, the narrator immediately thinks of 'the remains of our own civilization after its extinction in some future catastrophe' (237). But what he sees are merely the remains of past war, their collapse an indication of lack of use, which should prompt at least some sense of relief.

Melancholy and *Austerlitz*

André Aciman has gone a step further than this, labelling Sebald's themes 'ultimately sterile' because they are about 'how relative meaning is, and about how inadequate all literary constructs are destined to remain'.[39] But this relative inadequacy is the point: literary constructs alone cannot assuage our increasing awareness of human if not also natural destructiveness, which the writer finds himself obliged to recall on his pilgrimages through time and place—and which are prompted, one cannot help suspecting when confronted by moments of excessive, Schopenhauerian melancholy, by a profound sense of guilt, the felt burden of the memories of earlier generations. Nor does Sebald avoid the occasional joke at his apparently terminally depressed narrator's expense—as, for example, when the narrator suggests that the 'dark secret' of the Congo colony seems to be borne within the Belgian people, to the extent that it has stunted their growth: 'At all events, I well recall that on my first visit to Brussels in December 1964 I encountered more hunchbacks and lunatics than normally in a whole year' (122–23).

More seriously, however, it is hard not to accept his impression of the 'ever more bombastic buildings' of the capital of Belgium, erected over 'a hecatomb of black bodies' (122), an impression amplified by the opening of *Austerlitz*, when the narrator finds Austerlitz the eponymous protagonist in the *Salle des pas perdus* in Antwerp Centraal Station, one of many projects (says Austerlitz, an architectural historian) constructed under the patronage of Leopold II as a result of the success of 'little' Belgium's colonial enterprises in Africa.[40] This is the architecture of the power-crazed, the architecture of Fascists and Nazis like Albert Speer, on whose plans Elias Canetti commented that, 'for all their evocation of eternity and their enormous size, their design contained within itself the idea of a style of building that revealed all its grandiose aspirations only in a state of destruction'. Thus, 'Only from its ruins does the end of the Thousand-Year Reich that intended to usurp the future become conceivable'.[41] For Sebald, it was no coincidence that the SS ran quarries next to the concentration camps.[42]

Sebald's sensibility responds to what he has witnessed travelling away from home—a home that becomes almost mythical, serving as the source of both yearning and despair, because of the horrors which pass it by and yet with which it is complicit. Like Austerlitz, he is plagued by the angst of the past. But Austerlitz's anxieties and subsequent breakdown are brought about by the gradual realisation that his preoccupation with accumulating knowledge about the past as an architectural historian had served 'as a substitute or compensatory memory', enabling him to close his eyes and ears to the occasional emergence of some 'dangerous' piece of information about his personal past (198).

Imprisoned in a past he tries obsessively to understand and reconstruct, Austerlitz—whose name itself evokes a deep European history—experiences the extreme physical symptoms of anxiety prompted by memories of being a child suddenly cast out of his familiar surroundings. The home he yearns for he does not know, yet he discovers he has lost it through the Holocaust, having been saved from extermination by one of the *Kindertransporten*, and taken to a second home, in Wales. But there he has been brought up in ignorance of his origins by a childless couple in an atmosphere of bullying, narrow Calvinism, making it for him an unhomely home, while his true home is among the German Jewish lost. In this, he resembles the protagonists of *The Emigrants*. Like them, Austerlitz cannot ultimately recover his past, his origins, the *Heimat* of nostalgic yearning; it is an ever-receding signifier, hence his repeated attacks of anxiety and depression as he wanders the night-time streets of the metropolis, or seeks out railway stations and forts.

Prompted by the uncanny familiarity of the name of a ship called *Prague* on a radio programme about the *Kindertransporten*, Austerlitz develops a pressing interest in his own recent past, rather than the distant past of buildings on which he has built a career; and he pursues traces of his family to Terezín (Theresianstad), represented in a cynically staged Nazi propaganda film as an unreal city of people unknowingly en route to annihilation. The description of the ghetto by means of a description of the film created to deceive the world about what the Nazis were doing to the Jews of occupied Europe functions as part of the protagonist's search for an authentic trace of his unknown mother, rather than bearing witness to the creation of the ghetto and the deaths of its inhabitants, all of which is simply taken as given.

What the Terezín pseudo-documentary does is remind us of what totalitarian regimes everywhere have tried to do: control knowledge, and access to knowledge. As Tzvetan Todorov points out, the Soviets produced 'a similar sort of film about the Solovki islands', another 'transparent fabrication' of happiness which, he argues, lingers in 'remote corners of the world'. This is why 'the humblest act of recollection' has been 'assimilated to antitotalitarian resistance'. But this may lead to simplistic oppositions, for example between remembering and forgetting; whereas the two opposing terms are 'destruction' and 'preservation', 'memory can only ever be the result of their interaction'; hence, memory is always partial; paradoxically, memory is a partial forgetting 'that is indispensable to making sense of the past'.[43]

If Austerlitz strains to catch a glimpse of his mother in the Terezín film, it is only to discover that the four-second segment of a woman's face that he thinks is hers is someone else's. It is *'Schwindel. Gefühle'* again. Frustration meets him in Paris, too, where the trail of his father runs out between the new Bibliothèque National and the Gare d'Austerlitz, formerly the site of a warehouse complex containing goods stolen from Jews sent to the gas chambers. Thus the desire to know who he is, and where his home is, leads to an awareness of destruction and genocide, the dizzying abyss behind modern history and identity, as well as the struggle for preservation, symbolised by the great library of France. For Austerlitz, nostalgia as the search for a lost home and family leads to—nothingness. As every day passes, a piece of time disappears, never to be found again—except that his imagination reiterates past images until they seem almost real, as real as the living, who become for him interchangeable with the dead.

When Sebald published a book on Austrian authors he called it *Unheimliche Heimat* (1991) or Unhomely Homeland. 'Unheimliche' also means uncanny, and it is often through the uncanny return of repressed memories that the present everyday of *Austerlitz* is radically disturbed, and past atrocity recalled. Looking back, Sebald remembered growing up in

> quite an idyllic environment, at the same time the most horrendous things had happened in other parts of Europe. While I was sitting in my pushchair and being wheeled through the flowering meadows by my mother, the Jews of Corfu were being deported on a four-week trek to Poland. It is the simultaneity of a blissful childhood and those horrific events that now strikes me as incomprehensible. I now know that these things cast a very long shadow over my life.[44]

The tension between the nostalgically remembered, idyllic childhood on the one hand, and the later knowledge of what was happening in the world, is what drives Sebald's writing, creating an uneasy sense of the past as the source of endless layers of destructive human impulse that will and indeed must be remembered for survival in the present. How far memory may function as a redemptive instrument is left open, just as the nature of time remains an enigma. His writings reveal an inability to shake off the traumas consequent upon past imperial designs of mastery over the stranger, the Other, within and beyond Europe. Nor should we expect him to manage that.

Fragments against the Ruins

As John Beck observed of *The Rings of Saturn*, if everything in Sebald's writings appears to confirm a view of history as 'a story of universal decomposition', 'the sinister spiral of decay and deterioration' taking in 'individual lives, towns, empires, geographies, universes, theories of representation, time and history', the narrator can at least 'walk through and read the signs'.[45] Sebald's texts create a space of reading and hence understanding, and so suggest the importance of overcoming contemporary amnesia through the remembering that may be and often is instigated by nostalgia, and as a result is always (in Todorov's terms), partial. As T. S. Eliot's narrator remarked in that other great modern document of despair, *The Wasteland*: 'These fragments I have shored against my ruins'. Yet, like Eliot's, Sebald's journeying tends towards an inner, even spiritual dimension, glimpsed through the various masks or personae he creates.

Sebald's search for enlightenment is always grounded in real people and places encountered or read about, experiences which, through hidden echoes and connections, blur the boundary between the found and the made, fact and fiction, history and memory. This can lead to problems: when one of those 'real people', Susie Bechhöfer, discovered that Sebald's *Austerlitz* was in part based on her life story as one of the 10,000 Jewish children rescued by the *Kindertransporten*, she felt she had been robbed of her past; but Sebald, who 'didn't want to make use' of the full horror of what happened to her, admitted 'I haven't the right. I try to keep at a distance and never invade'.[46] He is fully aware of the dangers of what he is trying to do, representing the European Jewish past as a German. As he remarked in his last interview, writing about

> the incarceration and systematic extermination of whole peoples and groups in society . . . particularly for people of German origin, is fraught with dangers and difficulties . . . you could not write directly about the horror of persecution in its ultimate forms, because no one could bear to look at these things without losing their sanity. So you would have to approach it from an angle, and by intimating to the reader that these subjects are constant company, their presence shades every inflection of every sentence one writes.[47]

This sense of every line being infused with the past creates his characteristically formal, mesmeric quality, a way of writing that draws the reader ever deeper into a labyrinth, the end of which is almost always something appalling, and from which it is difficult to look away.

But for Sebald it is imperative that we look down into the past, into those pasts in which no single imperial venture stands alone, rather it contributes to the overlapping and interconnected growth and decay of world civilisations. The bureaucratic control over people exercised by the imperial ventures that preceded Nazism provided a way of destroying them. His writings are inevitably haunted by the extreme events, the catastrophes of the past, while avoiding any direct account of the horrific events themselves. The deep affiliations between large historical changes such as the ends of empire and individual histories are often obscure and indefinable, and can only be determined by means of indirection and implication; and, to understand the ends in the sense of both the dissolutions and the purposes of empire is to try to come to terms with the existence of remembering and forgetting. These endings are a matter of both the everyday and the extreme in human history and behaviour: of the ease with which racism and fascism link arms and yet remain often inexplicable. Nostalgia has a role in this, although at times it lies within the hidden springs of being and behaviour, an aspect of hidden, secret or apparently unknown longings, pursuing which may but does not inevitably shed light upon the present.

It is clear from its origins that nostalgia implies the draw of a past that involves pain, if only because the past is forever lost, irretrievable. The fact that the past experience or place is a locus of suffering in Sebald's work does not deter him; and this applies even when, given the choice, he might prefer to pass over it in silence. Or indeed, when there is an ethical imperative to forget, rather than remember, if we are to 'move on' as individuals or a society, from events as terrible as slavery or genocide. But, as many of those who have tried to wrestle with the ruptures in time and value represented by, for example, the Holocaust, have argued, admitting atrocity into discourse is part of an ongoing quest for insight that cannot nor should not be denied.

In conclusion, then, the end of Sebald's work is to create an awareness of complicity with the histories of earlier generations, and a deeper understanding of the connectedness of hidden imperial ends. He is aware of the risk involved in taking on the identities of those who suffered. Haunted by the multiple pasts of individuals and societies, he provides a unique template for remembering histories that are mislaid or forgotten, by means of the nostalgic yearnings and hidden, involuntary memories of travellers, migrants, and exiles like himself.

The next chapter returns to Africa, and to the work of two writers who have left their former colonial homeland, and for whom nostalgia functions as the generative source of a profound critique of it. Within such diasporic consciousnesses, memory takes on the experience of multiple histories of migration and movement, connecting migrant authorial selves and their remembered childhoods. National revival in the postcolonial state has led to the reconstruction of collective identities through commemoration and memorialisation, a context in which the realist novel has been found well suited to rewriting the recent past, including the violence of civil conflict and mass killing. But writing back, even while drawing on earlier, 'traditional' cultural forms, has been transformed by a new generation of authors, such as Chimamanda Ngozi Adichie.

6 Remembering 'Bitter Histories'
From Achebe to Adichie

> The elephant has fallen
> Can we remember the date.
>
> Christopher Okigbo, 'Elegy for Slit-Drum', 1964[1]

> The literature of exile, more abundant than ever, is, for the most part, a literature concerned with the loss of childhood.
>
> Jean Starobinski, 'The Idea of Nostalgia'. 1966[2]

> The writer of fiction can be and must be the pathfinder.
>
> Ngugi wa Thiong'o, *Decolonising the Mind*, 1986[3]

A New Voice, a New Negotiation with the Past

In a television programme to celebrate the 50th anniversary of the publication of Chinua Achebe's *Things Fall Apart*, the Nigerian novelist Chimamanda Ngozi Adichie said she and Achebe 'share a nostalgia for something better [and] we wish we didn't have the bitter history we have'.[4] Adichie was not yet born when Achebe's novel came out, yet the two Nigerian writers are linked by their longings for the future, and despair over the past, of their country. When independence arrived for Nigeria, it could have been offered, in Wole Soyinka's words, 'as a model of tolerance, but [it] has suffered, in the intervening period, a spate of religion-motivated violence on an unprecedented scale, and is fast becoming only another volatile zone of distrust, unease and tension'.[5] A land of immense resources, human and material, post-independence Nigeria is now 'a sorry spectacle'.[6] As a result, many writers have left the country, including Achebe, Soyinka, and Adichie, while remaining active in Nigerian literary and cultural life.

In this chapter I look at two novels by Chimamanda Ngozi Adichie in terms of their consciously nostalgic recall of the post-independence past of the nation; at the same time, I shall recall the founding work of Nigeria's most well-known author, Chinua Achebe. Achebe's *Things Fall Apart* (1958) is the most widely read and influential work of African fiction, to the extent that it may be said to have engendered a new canon of postcolonial writing, focusing upon the revaluation of 'traditional' or indigenous cultures. This has had a profound impact upon what one might call Adichie's writerly project, to revalue her own and her country's past while remembering the conflicts of that past in the present. The result goes beyond what Achille Mbembe refers to as the 'endless' struggle to achieve a balance between 'total identification' with 'traditional' African life on the one hand, and 'merging with, and subsequent loss in, modernity' on the other.[7] If she does seek such a balance, Adichie also represents a new, feminist voice in search of healing for the post-independence generation.

Adichie wrote her two novels from abroad, whereas Achebe originally wrote from within Nigeria, drawing on family memories to revalue his country's past and challenge colonialist views, thereafter providing a chronicle of its descent into autocratic rule in *Man of the People* (1966) and *Anthills of the Savannah* (1987), novels written during increasingly extended stays in North America—which became his permanent residence after a disabling car accident in 1990. Adichie also draws on family memories while living in the United States, to represent both individual and collective struggles in the present era, an era beset by ethnic, religious, and national differences. In effect, she exploits Achebe's inheritance so as to open up a new negotiation with the past of her country, witnessed from abroad. This she does through her two prize-winning novels, *Purple Hibiscus* (2004) and *Half of a Yellow Sun* (2006)—the former won the Commonwealth Writers' Best First Book prize, the latter the women-only Orange Prize for Fiction. The short stories in her more recent book, *The Thing Around Your Neck* (2009), are also relevant, confirming an interest in representing the present condition of Nigerians, many of them living or trying to live abroad. In all these writings the politics of memory interact with the politics of difference and diaspora to produce a rich new take on postcolonial nostalgia.

Without focusing upon nostalgia as such, postcolonial theory has always had a broad interest in memory as an aspect of history, fostering alternative or oppositional versions of the past, with the aim of redefining the present in ways that encourage the imagining of a future free from colonial and neo-colonial oppressions. The first step for the colonised struggling to find a voice and an identity has always been to reclaim their history from colonial ignorance and devaluation. Colonialism, said Fanon, was a systematic negation of the other person, denying their humanity, and forcing them to ask themselves 'In reality, who am I?'[8]—a question that cannot be answered without reconstructing individual as well as collective pasts, and the relationship between them, a process that is always complex and incomplete, involving many different levels, practices and experiences, but one in which memory is the key. We do not know who we are without memory.

And if, as Frederick Cooper suggests, the term 'identity' is ill-suited to perform analytical work, being 'riddled with ambiguity, riven with contradictory meanings, and encumbered by reifying connotations',[9] then this is precisely why we attend to writers and artists, whose special territory is ambiguity and contradiction, if not reification. And perhaps especially those postcolonial writers whose texts, as we read them now, gather around themselves the excess of signification generated by ambiguity, contradiction, irony, and paradox, for all that they might at first seem naively realist—an accusation sometimes aimed at Achebe, whose aesthetic has been undervalued from the beginning.[10]

This aesthetic, an aesthetic of return to a real or imagined homeland, is likely to involve realist narrative, although that is far from being as simple a formula as it may sound. This is because, as Tim Woods has pointed out, for African literatures history and memory 'are not merely literary tropes—they are the crucial sites where postcolonial national and cultural identities are being formed and contested'.[11] Today, the unprecedented access of elite Africans to political and cultural mobility generated by global modernity means that through diasporic consciousnesses, memory takes on the experience of multiple histories of migration and movement, while fragmented subject positions demand their own space, as they shift between migrant authorial selves and remembered childhoods. It has certainly been the case in many postcolonial countries, in Africa and beyond, where national revival has been motivated by an urge to reconstruct collective identities through commemoration and memorialisation, that narrative in general, and the realist novel in particular, have been found well suited to satisfy the continuing urge to rewrite the past. This has led to a writing back into the past, even while looking ahead to the future, typically in the African context drawing on earlier, 'traditional' cultural forms in order to validate those forms in the present.

The process is patently more than a matter of simple nostalgic harking-back. Anglophone African writers such as Achebe (or Amos Tutuola, or Wole Soyinka, or Ngugi wa Thiong'o) have embedded oral narrative elements in their work to recuperate earlier, pre-colonial traditions and create an African tradition for Africans. So too did their Francophone predecessors, such as Léopold Senghor (or Birago Diop, or Cheikh Hamidou Kane, or Camara Laye). The Négritude movement Senghor helped to create was highly criticised for its essentialism—not least by Fanon, who attacked as dangerous fantasy the movement's tendency to idealise the pre-colonial past. But it was an essentialism produced by the utopian tendency in postcolonial memory work in general, the result of the fact that it so often involves a looking back to look forward. When South African President Thabo Mbeki began his call for an African Renaissance in Tokyo in 1998,[12] he was engaging an analogous set of feelings, redefining a European concept within the context of a decolonised continent, in order to set in motion a new, home-grown politics of remembering, one result of which was to grant the San a new desert homeland (see Chapter 3 above).

This kind of conscious, politically inspired nostalgia demands close scrutiny as much as any other kind. Nostalgia is never innocent, whoever invokes it, least of all when it is indulged by those who have benefited from past structures of oppression such as, notoriously, those former colonisers (or their descendants) who yearn for the supposedly pristine landscapes of earlier times, seemingly free of the disturbing images of indigenous people, as depicted in the protagonist of Nadine Gordimer's *The Conservationist* (1974), which showed how the nostalgic desire of the urbanite Mehring for an old-style colonial farm could only be achieved at the cost of the death of the Africans who work it, symbolised in the figure of a Black labourer's corpse disinterred at the end of the novel by a storm from the Mozambique Channel. As Gordimer's prescient novel implied, debates about the politics of remembering revealed that imagining the past by inventing narratives to put in the mouths of those silenced or forgotten by the dominant histories of the present is not simply a matter of replacing the white, male-dominated constructions of the past through accounts written 'from the erstwhile margins'.[13] What is needed is the opening up of a negotiation with the past by those who have been colonised, in which nostalgia may play a key role, but a nostalgia redefined to include a self-aware harking-back that includes the individual and his/her national identity; and nowadays, in an increasingly mobile and mobilised world, this means also reaching beyond, towards what one might call the *transnational* space.

Beyond Female Empowerment

Calling for this kind of negotiation between present and past is not entirely new. Fanon's teacher and fellow Martinican Aimé Césaire pursued a vision of collective, transnational Black identity in *Cahier d'un retour au pays natal* (*Notebook of a Return to my Native Land*, 1939, many revisions). A poignant account of the search for an identity free of colonial taint, *Cahier* had its critical edge, implicit in a linguistic inventiveness incorporating Martinican colloquialisms within its high literary French, and which recalled the desolate poverty of the author's Antillean home even while revelling in its sensual detail. Césaire identified with his Black ancestors, but in a way that also involved identifying with the rejected and abused everywhere—'je serais un homme-juif / un homme-cafre / un homme-hindou-de-Calcutta / un homme-de-Harlem-qui-ne-vote-pas' ('I shall be a Jew-man / a kaffir-man / a Hindu-from-Calcutta-man / a man-from-Harlem-who-does-not-vote').[14] Césaire's humanism refused mere assimilation to historically compromised national identities.

Whatever one might think of Césaire's negotiation with the multiple legacies of colonialism, in terms of the search for transnational, transcultural connections it reflects an aspect of Négritude that has taken on new force in recent years, especially since Paul Gilroy's *The Black Atlantic: Modernity and Double Consciousness* appeared in 1993. Gilroy emphasised the historical realities of the African diaspora, while criticising the racial essentialism of those who, like Césaire's co-founder, the more conservative Senghor, posited a pre-colonial, nostalgic African golden age as a way of creating a new pride in Black identities. But the most problematic aspect of Négritude from today's perspective is less its struggle to find a 'return' to an ancestral 'homeland' than its silence about gender issues. Apart from a tendency to idealise the Black Mother, women were either invisible or simply sidelined, seriously if not fatally compromising the projected search for an 'authentic' Black identity. In the present, postcolonial context the voices of Black women must be attended to, voices still too often excluded from the creation, or remembering of identities in the postcolonial era.

Thus, as several critics have pointed out, the writings of West African Anglophone and Francophone authors such as Flora Nwapa, Efua Sutherland, Ama Ata Aidoo, and Mariama Bâ have depicted women as empowered, independent agents; and even when they have chosen pre-colonial or 'traditional' settings so as to defend 'African' values in terms familiar from Senghor or Achebe, they depict women as more varied than the stereotyped African mother figure.[15] According to Mariama Bâ, 'We no longer accept the nostalgic praise to the African Mother who, in his anxiety, man can confuse with Mother Africa. Within African literature, room must be made for women'.[16] Women like, say, Tsitsi Dangarembga, whose *Nervous Conditions* (1988) centred on the struggles of a teenage Zimbabwean girl chafing under male authority, before finally departing the country.

Although there are comparable elements in her work, Adichie's writing represents a step beyond this paradigm of African female empowerment, reflecting the violent dislocations in space and time characteristic of the diasporic realities of the globalised world with which she is familiar, even as she does not forget the longing for home and wholeness on an individual, social, and even spiritual level. The result is a complex aesthetic, in which modern, predominantly realist representations of the past in all its remembered, everyday textures are at times shot through with intimations of deeper, spiritual realities.[17]

From *Things Fall Apart* to *Purple Hibiscus*

Shuttling backward and forwards between her old home in Nigeria and her new one in the United States, Chimamanda Adichie writes as one of those postcolonial 'exiles or emigrants or expatriates' who, as I referred to earlier (in Chapter 1), Salman Rushdie claims are 'haunted by some sense of loss, some urge to reclaim, to look back' towards their origins, out of which they create 'imaginary homelands'. These are fictional versions of the past of their country, distorted as they may be by subjective recollection, but as valuable as if they were unflawed.[18] As Adichie admitted to another expatriate postcolonial writer, Michael Ondaatje, she was in her senior year in college in the United States when writing *Purple Hibiscus*,

> and very homesick, very nostalgic. I really wanted to sort of reinvent Nigeria in this book, which I think I did. If I'd written the book in Nigeria, it would have been very different . . . I drew a lot of the mood of the book from my sense of being homesick and nostalgic. When I'm homesick, I'm given to idealizing things and suddenly the rains smell like perfume and that sort of thing.[19]

Wistful longings for her home and family while she lived and studied abroad were to be transformed into a profound analysis of her country's recent history of division and violence on a multitude of levels in *Purple Hibiscus*.

Reimagining the past of the individual as a child growing up in a post-independence Nigeria under military rule, questioning through her protagonist's perceptions of family dynamics the divisions and corruption of Nigerian society at large—all this will seem a long way from what Achebe's classic *Things Fall Apart* began to do by invoking a vision of pre-colonial order and dignity so as to reassert the culture, history, and humanity of African peoples 'othered' by colonial ideology. Yet there are important continuities, not least in terms of the common focus upon family memory. *Things Fall Apart* retrieved the memory of Achebe's ancestors and his ancestral Igbo home. Opening a series of lectures at Harvard University in 1998 with what he said was one of his earliest childhood memories, Achebe recalled the family's return home to Ogidi when he was five, that is, in the 1930s, after his father had retired from a lifetime of Christian evangelism (his grandfather continued to follow traditional Igbo practices). Ogidi was also where his father had helped to found the Anglican church at the turn of the century; it was one of those hundreds of towns 'which were in reality ministates that cherished their individual identity but also, in a generic way, perceived themselves as Igbo people'.[20] The expression of their Igbo identity appeared in markets, marriages, funerals, music, and dance; for the Igbo, every single human being was a unique creation of 'chi', or the presence of God. Suspicious and argumentative, says Achebe, the Igbo lived in a world of continuing struggle, with anarchy a close neighbour, brought home to them as a result of the depredations of the Atlantic slave trade followed by the arrival of the British. He was prompted to write, he said, by the crossing of his path as a young student with the path of the author of *Mister Johnson*, Joyce Cary, 'and such crossings may sometimes leave their footmarks, faint or loud, on memory. And if they do, they should be acknowledged'.[21]

The massive popularity of *Things Fall Apart*, within as well as far beyond Nigeria, suggests how far and wide those footmarks have echoed. As Achebe said a few years after its publication, he wrote to 'help my society regain its belief in itself and put away the complexes of the years of denigration and self-denigration';[22] a project fit for many other African colonials, such as his Kenyan contemporary Ngugi wa Thiong'o, whose first novel, *The River Between* (1965) established the legend of land being given to the Kikuyu people, before it was alienated by the colonisers—in outline, the pattern underlying all his succeeding novels. *Things Fall Apart* represents a more singular, individualist remembering than Ngugi's, whose socialist, anti-colonial agenda dominates his work. Yet Achebe recognised the perils of a false nostalgia, displayed for example in what he called Camera Laye's 'too sweet' fictional memoir *L'enfant noir* (1953; *The African Child/The Dark Child*, 1954). 'We cannot pretend that our past was one long, technicolour idyll,' said Achebe. 'We have to admit that like other people's pasts ours had its good as well as its bad sides'.[23] Nonetheless *Things Fall Apart* was 'an act of atonement with my past, the ritual return and homage of a prodigal son',[24] words that touch many whose colonial inheritance involves a complicit experience which can be explained only partially in terms of the broad politics of anti-colonialism, and which reflects the strength and importance of the intimate, personal, and moral dimension of that inheritance.

Achebe's inheritance has been empowering for many African writers who have followed in his footprints, among whom Adichie is perhaps the most notable recent example.

> Reading Achebe gave me permission to write about my world. He transported me to a past that was both familiar and unfamiliar, a past I imagined my great grandfather lived. Looking back, I realize that what he did for me at the time was validate my history, make it seem worthy in some way.[25]

Unlike the older generation of Nigerian writers such as Achebe, who grew up within a still colonised country as it moved gradually and relatively smoothly towards independence during the 1950s, Adichie, who was born in 1977 in the Igbo town of Enugu, and grew up in the Eastern Nigerian university town of Nsukka (where Achebe once taught), found herself in an independent Nigeria subject to increasingly corrupt and brutal military rule. In fact it was not until 1999, with the election of President Olusegun Obasango, that thirty-three years of military rule came to an end; and the road since then has been extremely bumpy, with questionable elections, large-scale corruption, and religious riots marring the path.

As Elleker Boehmer has pointed out, Adichie's work is 'stamped with numerous filiative gestures towards Achebe', most explicitly in *Purple Hibiscus*.[26] The novel opens with the author placing herself within the tradition of postcolonial African writing inaugurated by *Things Fall Apart* over fifty years before its appearance: in a direct, if ironic echo of Achebe's novel's title, *Purple Hibiscus* begins 'Things started to fall apart at home when my brother, Jaja, did not go to communion and Papa flung his heavy missal across the room and broke the figurines on the étagère' (3). Again, such a scene of middle-class domestic discord might at first seem an immense distance from the world of *Things Fall Apart*, which opens with the words: 'Okonkwo was well known throughout the nine villages and even beyond', words that take the reader immediately into the Igbo clan world of pre-colonial west Africa, so as to begin the novel's challenge to Western constructions of Africa as a site of the primitive, violent, and heathen. Achebe's novel creates a sympathetic understanding of how much is lost or forgotten through the arrival of European civilisation via its missionary precursors, despite the violence that is shown to attend traditional Igbo society. That violence is most powerfully revealed when Okonkwo, terrified he will seem weak, cuts down his foster son Ikemefuna when he learns that the boy must be sacrificed to the clan to prevent war with their neighbours—an act that turns his own son Nwoye against him, and prepares the way for Nwoye's eventual conversion to the white man's religion.

It is no coincidence that the ill-fated Ikemefuna is closely associated with the oral, folk tale traditions of the clan that pervade Achebe's narrative— his favourite story is that in which 'the ant holds court in splendor and the sands dance forever'. The arrival of the white missionaries, in the words of Obierika, Okonkwo's far-seeing friend, 'put[s] a knife on the things that held us together and now we have fallen apart'.[27] By the time we hear these words, however, we have come to appreciate Igbo society as a human world with its own integrity, culture, and values, a world in which, as Abiola Irele has well said,

> Achebe's depiction of the prescribed pattern of social gestures and modes of comportment creates an overwhelming impression of a collective existence that unfolds in ceremonial terms, punctuated as it is by a train of activities that enhance the ordinary course of life and serve therefore as privileged moments in a more or less unending celebration of a social compact that is remarkably potent and is in any case fully functional on its own terms.[28]

This is what makes the last lines of the novel so disturbing, with the realisation that the story of this ceremonial, fully functional society will be turned into a few dismissive lines of British colonial history.

> The story of this man who had killed a messenger and hanged himself would make interesting reading. One could almost write a whole chapter on him. Perhaps not a whole chapter but a reasonable paragraph, at any rate. There was so much else to include, and one must be firm in cutting out details. He had already chosen the title of the book, after much thought: *The Pacification of the Primitive Tribes of the Lower Niger*.

By a clever twist of narrative perspective, Achebe both recapitulates the process of cultural denigration his book was designed to challenge, and pre-empts the outsider viewpoint that denies its validity.

Postcolonial Modernity and the Challenge to 'Traditional' Patriarchy

If Adichie's *Purple Hibiscus* alludes to *Things Fall Apart* while proposing a different direction and a different challenge, it, too, is ultimately about religious and cultural clash. Of course, it deals with a later historical stage, when the blossoming of the hibiscus flowers of the novel's title provide just a faint hint of hope in an independent Nigeria torn apart by increasingly corrupt and incompetent rule. By following the Achebean strategy of taking us inside the everyday life and rituals of Nigerian society, the narrative invites readers to appreciate its human reality, which cannot merely be dismissed as the country was being—and still sometimes is—dismissed for its poor external image. Moreover, while Achebe's novel is ultimately—as Sam Durrant has well expressed it—'elegiac, melancholic, inconsolable' in the face of the catastrophic collapse of the clan at its centre,[29] Adichie's novel suggests the potential for a more liberated life emerging out of the remembered trauma of a military coup for the young woman at its centre, Kambili Achike.

Purple Hibiscus focuses closely on the internal dynamics of 1970s Igbo family life as seen through the eyes of its young protagonist—naive, often silent, yet imperceptibly maturing as she witnesses the complex forces that impact upon their lives. Adichie provides a sensitive, slowly evolving account of Kambili's physical and emotional awakening under the religious oppression of her wealthy, charismatic Catholic father Eugene, rather than, as in Achebe's novel, attempting to define the larger social dynamics of a traditional Igbo society about to collapse under the external pressures of the colonial encounter, and to depict the awakening of Okonkwo's son to an awareness of those pressures that leads to his adoption of the new religion. Unlike Achebe's novel, which is told from the point of view of an all-knowing, if sympathetic narrator, whose discourse is imbued to a large extent with the proverbial, masculinist language of oral tradition, Adichie's narrative is conveyed through the perspective of the modern young Igbo girl who, if she may be in some respects an alter ego for the author, is more importantly a strategic mediator of Adichie's remembered experiences that enables a critique of 1970s Nigeria as part of an exploration of modern African identities.

This difference is very much the point of *Purple Hibiscus*: harking back to the pre-colonial past of the grandparents' generation, as Achebe's novel does, was about reinstating that past as a source of identity for the new nation constructing itself, a land with its own dignified, if—with retrospective irony—fatally flawed way of life; whereas Adichie's novel returns to the time of her own childhood in an independent Nigeria dominated by military rule and the suppression of individual liberties, a time when Achebe's earlier agenda had been overtaken by the concerns of Nigerians struggling to make their way in a society beset by new, postcolonial uncertainties. The colonial inheritance continues, although its manifestations within the country present themselves as part of the make-up of present-day Nigerians—most obviously, in Eugene's mission-inherited religiosity, which has become a means of dominating and controlling his family. At one point Eugene, a staunch upholder of his Catholic faith and, like Achebe's Okonkwo an admired 'Big Man' in the community, punishes his daughter and her brother for their disobedience in visiting their 'heathen' grandfather by pouring boiling water over their feet because they have, he says, 'walked in sin' (194).

The cruelty of this action, comparable to the punishments Okonkwo metes out to members of his family, is given added weight and immediacy in Adichie's novel by the context of personal detail that textures the narrative. Adichie described *Purple Hibiscus* as a novel about the remembered 'tiny wonders' of Nsukka, 'the small, slow town where I grew up, where chicken is a delicacy, where your neighbour is a witch and responsible for all your illnesses, where young girls want to put on weight and people raise free-range goats that eat the flowers in the yard next door'.[30] The nostalgic tone is unmistakeable, as is the humorous address to modernity implicit in that word 'free-range'. It is no surprise to learn that the novel was written at a time of the author's intense loneliness and homesickness during her final year of college abroad, after four years out of Nigeria. Yet, as episodes like the father's punishment of his children show, the form that her recall takes is not uncritical—far from it. Adichie's position as a diasporic subject has produced the necessary detachment towards her own personal background that enables her to confront and begin to deal with her country's bitter history, not ignore it in favour of a soft-focus return to adolescent girlhood wonders, tempting as that might at first have been.

Eugene's violence towards his family connects with and reflects the larger violence generated by different belief-systems in a society that has yet to find a means of containing them. The novel is clearly structured around the growing clash of religious belief within the family and, implicitly, the entire community: its four sections are titled 'Breaking Gods—Palm Sunday'; 'Speaking with Our Spirits—Before Palm Sunday'; 'The Pieces of Gods—After Palm Sunday'; and 'A Different Silence—The Present'. The split titles and the disjunctive time scheme of the novel reflect the disjuncture between nostalgia for 'traditional' or 'heathen' belief, and the apparently progressive Christian faith which divides the generations as it divides the larger society, creating a discord that reaches all levels, with sometimes comic results. When the white British missionary Father Benedict (who insists on Latin for the liturgy) addresses his 'native' congregation (as he calls them), he refers to 'the Pope, papa, and Jesus—in that order', according to Kambili (4). Her father, who is a soft-drinks factory owner, is the financial mainstay of the local church, and enforces a regime of constant vigilance within his family, insisting they listen to the 'Ave Maria' on the car cassette player when they travel (31).

Adichie, herself a Catholic, is not attacking any specific religion; rather, it is the local, contemporary manifestation of the spiritual she brings into her sights. There is, she avers, 'a wave of very materialistic fundamentalist Christianity in Nigeria', the sort in which 'sleek and rich' pastors tell you 'that God wants you to have Mercedes-Benz', while at the same time being 'anti-woman and anti-truth'.[31] It is as if the new religion that first arrives in the world of *Things Fall Apart* in the person of the tolerant, sympathetic missionary Mr Brown has re-emerged in the fiery faith promoted by his zealous successor the Reverend Smith. As their names suggest, for all its realist pretensions—crucial to the overall aims of the novel—*Things Fall Apart* engaged a symbolic level of discourse as well, something which later critics of it began to note as the tide of discourse analysis and poststructural criticism reached its height, and realism fell out of favour.[32]

Adichie's work is unquestionably realist, although this is not to say she writes the closed, monolithic narratives of stereotypically realist fiction. Her writing is open to a variety of voices, languages, and textures, more evident in her second novel than the first which, nevertheless, adopts a singular narrative persona that notices what the reader will understand as symbolic—hence the title. Adichie's almost mute, repressed yet observant young narrator is the major achievement of the novel. At first a bookish 'backyard snob' (52), stammering and unsure of how or when to express her own mixed feelings about the people and events surrounding her—love and fear for her charismatic father, affection and uncomprehending disregard for her passive mother—Kambili gradually learns to decipher what is happening around her, eventually finding a voice for herself. Adichie lovingly presents the small details of Igbo family life through her narrator's questioning eyes, while implicitly suggesting how those details reflect upon and connect with the competing ideologies of her society. Thus, when Kambili and her brother Jaja first visit their grandfather Papa-Nnukwu, despite knowing the visit to the 'heathen' old man will meet with their father's disapproval, they refuse the old man's offer of enamel bowlfuls of 'flaky fufu and watery soup'. 'It was custom to ask', the girl-narrator informs us, 'but Papa-Nnukwu expected us to say no—his eyes twinkled with mischief' (64).

It is a complex moment, in which past indigenous custom seems to resist present, postcolonial modernity. Yet the continuing vitality of Papa-Nnukwu, for all his heathen ways, aligns him with that other family figure of alternative, yet in her case modern belief, Eugene's widowed sister Aunty Ifeoma, a lecturer at Nsukka University who brings up her three children in a happy, noisy household. In the understated symbolism of the novel, it is she who is associated through her tiny garden with the flowering of the purple flowers of the title, 'fragrant with the undertones of freedom' (16). And it is she who tells Kambili off for proudly using her father's term for her grandfather, that is, 'pagan': 'Your Papa-Nnukwu is not a pagan, he is a traditionalist' (81).

The word is given depth by the way in which Papa-Nnukwu's behaviour resonates with memories of the old Igbo religion. He refuses to be bullied by Eugene, who tries to make him throw away 'the chi in the thatch shrine in his yard', absurdly offering to build the old man a house, buy him a car, and hire him a driver if he will renounce his faith (61). But the old man's shrine is sacred, and when Kambili and her brother Jaja see a rooster walk into it on their short visit, she realises it is where 'Papa-Nnukwu's god was, where Papa said Jaja and I were never to go near' (66). Ironically, to Kambili's Catholic eyes 'It looked like the grotto behind St Agnes, the one dedicated to Our Lady of Lourdes' (67). In a further irony, she recalls her deceased maternal grandfather who, by contrast, was 'very light-skinned . . . one of the reasons the missionaries had liked him'; he always spoke English, could quote the articles of Vatican I, and helped win many converts before he died (67–68). Papa-Nnukwu is deeply religious too, but in his own way, which is the way of the old 'pagans'. This is emphasised by the scene in which Aunty Ifeoma invites Kambili to witness him talking to 'the gods or the ancestors', his Igbo words flowing into each other. When he is finished, and has blessed the family, including a prayer to ask for 'the curse' on his son Eugene to be lifted, he rises before them, his body 'like the bark of the gnarled gmelina tree in our backyard'. Kamibili does not look away 'though it was sinful to look upon another person's nakedness'. The old man departs, smiling, but 'I never smiled after we said the rosary back home' (167–69). No wonder he prompts a 'longing for something I knew I would never have' in Kambili (165). That is, nostalgia for the earlier form of belief, across the divide between 'traditional' African life and alienated modernity.

Yet Adichie presents no simplistic polarisation of the old faith and the new, or the secular and the spiritual. Her aim seems to be to suggest a more syncretic religion, as Brenda Cooper has observed, in a persuasive account of the novel that emphasises its pointed intermingling of Igbo words, songs, and rituals with Catholic spirituality.[33] As the narrative proceeds, Kambili learns to appreciate Aunty Ifeoma's view of Papa-Nnukwu, as well as her aunt's values more generally, while continuing to worship her father for his strength, his generosity to the people of the town, and his belief in a 'renewed democracy' for Nigeria (25), expressed through his financial support for a radical newspaper, the *Independent*. This newspaper is, as Aunt Ifeoma says, one place where the truth is told, which is why the editor is killed by a parcel bomb not long after the military takeover. Despite Eugene's opposition to the military—clearly dangerous—and his support for freedom, he remains an appalling bully, smashing his wife's china figurines and abusing her with repeated beatings, one of which causes her to miscarry. Her silent acquiescence in his violence, witnessed by the children too young to understand why she does not condemn him, turns in the end to resistance, even vengeance, when she dispatches her husband by poisoning him, and, somewhat improbably, allows her son Jaja to go to prison instead for the deed. The china figurines that her husband smashed in the opening scene of the novel are in effect her small gods, representing the longings of women for their own space and belief structures—structures drawn from an imagined, sacred past denied by men's rampant urge to dominate.[34]

It is central to the novel's purpose to show Eugene as an image of the very dictatorship he opposes, loved as well as feared and hated. When the villagers speak of her father's achievements, Kambili is suffused with pride. But the tears he sheds after punishing his daughter, who has to be hospitalised as a result of the burnt feet episode, are reminiscent of the tears of the tyrant in Auden's 'Epitaph on a Tyrant', written at the time of the rise of fascism in Europe, which concludes: 'when he laughed, respectable senators burst with laughter / And when he cried, the little children died in the streets'. The point is, tyranny is local, and ordinary, and when the fate of a whole country is dependent upon a frail human being, the destruction he causes may well not even be intended. The rioting of students at the university of Nsukka when Kambili visits her aunt is but a small local symptom of the larger unrest in the country; so too are the futile attempts of the police to intimidate the aunt by searching her house, while the country's slide into near-chaos has already been suggested by news of striking doctors and the lack of fuel.

If nostalgic recall has partly motivated the close interweaving of the small domestic concerns of Adichie's heroine as she grows into troubled womanhood with the difficult evolution of her society, then it is also evident that creating a traumatised, almost mute yet inwardly articulate girl at the centre of the narrative has enabled the author to maintain a critical distance that takes us towards understandings well beyond the usual limitations of a coming-of-age story. This much may be gauged from the following account of the first appearance of a young Catholic priest whom Kambili meets at her aunt's house in Nsukka, and whom she falls in love with. Father Amadi, whom it seems to Kambili 'almost sacrilegious' to call Father (because that implicitly acknowledges her physical attraction to him, as well as, on another level, questioning her loyalty to her own father),

> had a singer's voice, a voice that had the same effect on my ears that Mama working Pears baby oil into my hair had on my scalp. I did not fully comprehend his English-laced Igbo sentences at dinner because my ears followed the sound and not the sense of his speech. He nodded as he chewed his yam and greens, and he did not speak until he had swallowed a mouthful and sipped some water. He was at home in Aunty Ifeoma's house; he knew which chair had a protruding nail and could pull a thread off your clothes. "I thought I knocked that nail in," he said, then talked about football with Obiora [her aunt's son], the journalist the government had just arrested with Amaka [her aunt's daughter], the Catholic women's organization with Aunty Ifeoma, and the neighbourhood video game with Chima [her aunt's younger son]. (135)

The author's awareness that writing about serious subjects demands a light touch reveals her distance and control. This in turn enables her to show how football, women's organisations, video games, and a journalist's arrest are all part of the confusing texture of everyday life Kambili has to negotiate to create an identity for herself, a mix of cultural and linguistic pointers to a society in postcolonial flux.

We cannot fail to notice how the young priest—his youthfulness suggestive of the future, by contrast with the elderly Papa-Nnukwu—engages fully with the world around him, using a hybrid linguistic register representative of a culturally inclusive brand of Catholicism. Similarly part of everyday life are the small acts of rebellion that the family carries out against 'the Big Men in Abuja' (243), although Kambili's father's support for his independent newspaper is crushed when its editor is murdered—'Defiance', as Aunty Ifeomo remarks, 'is like marijuana—it is not a bad thing when it is used right'. This is after she explains the aptness of Kambili's brother's nickname Jaja, because it is the same as that of a king who defied the British, and who ended up in exile for not selling out to the coloniser (144). Yet, ironically, it is exile that beckons this family, as the only way to avoid further harassment by the authorities. Their departure is an escape for the wealthy, talented elite, however, something unavailable to those whose lives we are protected from visualising by the choice of narrator. But Adichie's achievement is to have turned nostalgia for her childhood into an indictment of independent, postcolonial Nigeria, challenging traditional, patriarchal views, without relying on simplistic assumptions about her community's continuing investment in tradition, or indeed in patriarchy.

An Act of Remembering

As Helen Dunmore argued in a review of *Half of a Yellow Sun*, Adichie returns again and again to the idea of belonging, 'and how do cultures create networks of belonging and exclusion'.[35] Having gained remarkable success with her first novel, the writer turned to a key moment in Nigeria's post-independence history for her next, a hugely ambitious, indeed epic work about the struggle over national and individual identity. The title refers to the flag of Biafra, and to the Nigeria-Biafra War of 1967–70, a defining historical moment for the nation, when the ethnic tensions always present as a result of the colonial carve-up of the country burst into a catastrophic civil war in which more than a million (nobody is sure how many) people died, as the Muslim-dominated forces of the North laid siege to the predominantly Christian Igbo of the South—who had attempted to secede after the widespread massacre of their people. Why were the Igbo attacked? According to Achebe:

> The origin of the national resentment of the Igbo is as old as Nigeria and quite as complicated. But it can be summarized thus: The Igbo culture being receptive to change, individualistic and highly competitive, gave the

> Igbo man an unquestioned advantage over his compatriots in securing credentials for advancement in Nigerian colonial society. Unlike the Hausa/Fulani he was unhindered by a wary religion and unlike the Yoruba unhampered by traditional hierarchies. This kind of creature fearing nor God nor man, was custom-made to grasp the opportunities, such as they were, of the white man's dispensation . . . Had the Igbo been a minor ethnic group of a few hundred thousand, their menace might have been easily and quietly contained. But they ran in their millions! . . . this kind of success can carry a deadly penalty: the danger of *hubris*, over-weening pride and thoughtlessness, which invites envy and hatred . . . He is accused of unduly favouring his kindred and running to their defence at all times . . . pan-Igbo solidarity is a figment of the Nigerian imagination. It has never existed except briefly, and for a unique reason, during the Civil War.[36]

Achebe's calm prose hides the desperation he felt at the ethnic tensions that erupted during the 1960s, when his own home was destroyed by a bombing raid, and a cousin killed in the mayhem. Like many writers at the time, Achebe tried to intervene in the conflict—Soyinka was imprisoned for two years for attempting to take over a radio station, an experience recorded in a prison diary and a poetic sequence, *A Shuttle in the Crypt* (1971), and Christopher Okigbo, the poet who became a major in the Biafran army, died in a battle near Nsukka, but not before writing the last, extraordinary poems in *Labyrinths* (1971). For these and other writers, Biafra stood for 'true' independence, that is, without the divisions of the colonial past and neo-colonial present, as they saw it.[37] The defeat of the breakaway region and the ending of the war, in which many external powers aided the different factions (and the former colonial power Britain supported Nigeria), left a country ravaged and bitter.

For Adichie, whose novel demonstrates vividly the source of the bitterness which pervaded Nigerian society in the aftermath of the war, *Half of a Yellow Sun* is a reminder of what happened, and how it came about. Above all, it defies the silence which fell upon this aspect of the country's recent past. Adichie's motivation for writing the novel was multiple, but her concern to overcome forgetting is manifest in what she has said about it:

> I wrote this novel because I wanted to write about love and war, because I grew up in the shadow of Biafra, because I lost both grandfathers in the Nigeria-Biafra war, because I wanted to engage with my history in order to make sense of the present, because many of the issues that led to the war remain unresolved in Nigeria today . . . I don't ever want to forget.[38]

Hence her novel

> is not an act of closure, it is an act of remembering. I don't believe in the concept of closure. I think that the traumas we have experienced remain an indelible part of who we are; we carry it with us always.[39]

Less directly a product of nostalgia, yet insisting on the need to remember and not to forget the terrible events of the recent past of the nation, in which members of her own immediate family were killed, Adichie's novel represents the latest reflection on a war that has prompted many Nigerian writers into print;[40] including Okigbo (who features in the novel as Okeoma), Flora Nwapa, whose *Never Again* (1975) drew on the civil war, and, again, Achebe, whose title story in the 1972 collection *Girls at War* directly inspired Adichie. Achebe's *Christmas in Biafra and Other Poems* (1973) also provided the novel's epigraph:

> Today I see it still–
> Dry, wire-thin in sun and dust of the dry months–
> Headstone on tiny debris of passionate courage. ('Mango Seedling')

Adichie sets up more than a mere headstone as a memorial to the 'passionate courage' of those who were caught up in the war. With 433 closely written and densely plotted pages including numerous vividly realised characters, dramatic crises, and unexpected twists and turns, *Half of a Yellow Sun* is a massive undertaking, interweaving private and public lives to create in effect a new genre of African writing—what John Marx has called 'failed-state fiction'.[41]

As Marx points out, Adichie's novel stretches the form of the domestic romance to accommodate civil war, and through its emphasis upon the intellectual life of the university-educated figures at its centre—more than merely representatives of their class or ethnicity—it equips the reader to adopt a distanced and historically informed perspective upon the crisis that beset Nigeria. True as far as it goes, this is perhaps to turn the novel into something of an intellectual exercise, a *roman à thèse*, doing less than justice to the impact of the traumatic events at its centre. Nor does this view do justice to the range of characters and their experiences, which include much more than the debates of its elite—significant though these are—as a result of the author's deployment of different voices and perspectives, and her focus upon (sometimes horrific) detail.

Delving into the past not so much of her own, but of her parents' generation, involved Adichie in recording the memories of others, memories she represents through the multiple filters of not just one but a trio of narrators, whose lives intersect and whose backgrounds and personalities motivate the narrative. Firstly and most engagingly, the narrative begins from the point of view of Ugwu, a teenage houseboy fresh from a rural village (based on memories of a houseboy in Adichie's family home), who longs to please his master Odenigbo, a bumptious, left-wing lecturer at the university in Nsukka (where Adichie's father was a professor). Odenigbo's sympathies lead him to foster the boy's education, exposing him to, amongst other things, the standard texts of a colonial-inspired education, including, bizarrely yet characteristically, *The Great Chain of Being* and *The Norman Impact upon England* (6).

Ironically, however, the newly educated Ugwu ends up a willing conscript in the Biafran army, where his skills include becoming an expert in planting mines—or *ogbunigwe* as they are called. He is an example of what has become alarmingly familiar in Africa's many conflicts, from Biafra to the Congo, from Chad to Sierra Leone—the child soldier.[42] Challenging the sympathies his narrative arouse in the reader, Ugwu takes part in an explicitly described gang rape, before nearly dying in a failed attack and being returned to his master—transformed, it seems, by his experiences. His master Odenigbo is in love with Olanna, a beautiful, London-educated woman who is nevertheless close to traditional belief and who seeks consolation from the *dibia* or spirit doctor. She is a kindly woman, eventually Odenigbo's wife and the adopter of his love-child, Baby. Olanna is the second narrator, and she too survives the war, after many tribulations, including an affair with Mohammed, a wealthy and attractive Hausa neighbour to her Igbo relatives in Kano in the north, who becomes a murderous Jihadist as ethnic tensions break out. The third narrator is Richard, a naive, idealistic Englishman who falls in love with early Igbo art and with Kainene, Olanna's sharply self-possessed twin sister, a businesswoman who turns to brokering military contracts on behalf of Biafra during the war, and whose eventual fate remains unknown—as was the fate of many, after the war.[43]

The Englishman's nostalgic, outsider anti-colonialism fuels his desire for Kainene, as it does for an understanding of the Igbo past. This prompts him to try to write a history informing the reader of the historical sources of the Biafran conflict—or so it appears, when extracts from the book-within-the book, called *The world was silent when we died*, emerge from time to time in the text, without explanation—until the very end, when, in a surprising last twist, the true author is identified as Ugwu, who thereby effectively takes over the telling of his country's bitter history from the well-meaning former coloniser whom the reader has been led to believe was writing it. To emphasise the point, when Ugwu finds himself in a defunct school classroom towards the end of the novel, he comes across a copy of the *Narrative of the Life of Frederick Douglass, An American Slave: Written by Himself*, which he reads out aloud, and which influences his decision to write a 'big book' that he thinks he will call 'Narrative of the Life of a Country' (360, 424). This is clearly intended to mark the return of authorship to the new generation of Africans, influenced by Black cultural achievement and history across the nations. It also suggests the self-creation of an identity that is public or collective, or at least larger than the individual.

Yet the interruption of the main text by extracts from what is to become Ugwu's 'book' in sections at the end of several chapters in a different typeface and a variety of styles makes for a kind of interference that lessens the impact of the realist narrative, highlighting the fact that the book is at times slackly written, including an excess of—nostalgically remembered?—detail that at times overwhelms the plot. However, accepting that the narrative is attempting to persuade us that the remembered textures of everyday life—as in *Purple Hibiscus*—signal attachments both personal and cultural, we can accept that the plethora of detail serves its purpose. Further, the metanarrative extracts do provide historical perspective, and to begin with at least they are embedded within an explanatory context. When Richard drafts an article about the refugee problem created by the first massacres, his closing paragraph is given within the text, in italics. The extract begins

It is imperative to remember that the first time the Igbo people were massacred, albeit on a much smaller scale than what has recently occurred, was in 1945. That carnage was precipitated by the British colonial government when it blamed the Igbo people for the national strike, banned Igbo-published newspapers, and generally encouraged anti-Igbo sentiment. The notion of the recent killings being the product of 'age-old' hatred is therefore misleading. . . . (166)

Ironically, the overseas editor to whom Richard sends his report is not interested, the press having apparently already been inundated with 'stories of violence from Africa, and this one was particularly bland and pedantic' (167).

Adichie's purpose is here obvious: providing the reader with one source for the conflict that challenges old and continuing Western stereotypes of Africa, calling into question the role of earlier colonial policies and practices, while at the same time encouraging the reader to understand that this is at least one version of the sources of the bitter civil strife that has broken out, but it is not the whole story which by the end we understand will be written. A later extract, in another typeface again, with the heading 'The Book: The World Was Silent When We Died', follows Richard's narrative but without explanation. It begins 'He writes about the world that remained silent while Biafrans died. He argues that Britain inspired this silence . . . ' (258). We assume 'he' is Richard because his narrative immediately precedes this, until much later we learn it is the reformed and self-educated Ugwu.

Adichie's strength lies not with such devices, however appropriate the intention, but with those realist specifics which bring home to readers within and beyond Nigeria the traumas of the war, while recalling its origins. The importance of the reminder to Nigerians, and their sense of identity in the present, is evident in the response of one local critic, who remarked that *Half of a Yellow Sun* showed how 'the democratization of the country can only be achieved through an honest engagement with "matters arising"' from the country's recent tragic past.[44] Yet recalling that past represents a massive challenge, especially perhaps for a writer who has not experienced the war herself; on the other hand, Adichie researched her family's memories, and those of surviving witnesses, which enabled her to create the convincing detail with which the brutal realities of the time are depicted. Of course detailing the violence carries with it the danger that far from enabling us to enter into and understand how and why it is taking place, we will be pushed towards the familiar, dismissive image of Africa as the failed continent against which Richard's text, and the book-within-the-book, are supposed to work.

There are many examples of the sudden eruption of violence, but one will suffice to demonstrate the problem created by their depiction. When Richard's plane touches down in Kano en route to Nsukka from a visit home he engages in friendly conversation with a young Igbo customs officer called Nnaemeka. Suddenly three wild-eyed soldiers burst in: '*Ina nyamiri!* Where are the Igbo people? Who is Igbo here? Where are the infidels?' yells one of them, waving his rifle around. Nnaemeka is accused of being Igbo, which he denies. The soldiers command him to say 'Allahu Akbar', but he will not, because he knows his accent will give him away; and so, in front of a horrified crowd, he is shot. The soldiers then turn on the bartender, who has been shouting a prayer in Igbo, and shoot him too. Their bullets shatter the bottles behind him so that, sick with fear, Richard notices that the room smells 'of whisky and Campari and gin' (151–53). The action is visualised with an awful, detailed clarity. But when the first rifle goes off, it is said to blow Nnaemeka's chest into 'a splattering red mass', an image that is unnecessary, blurring the effect, reducing its impact, and bringing to mind what Mahmood Mamdani (writing about Darfur), has called 'the pornography of violence' in representations of Africa.[45]

And yet, arguably, such details provide the novel with a sense of *witnessing* what has happened, rather than merely remembering or recording it. The issue it not unique to Africa: the burden of representing the unrepresentable is familiar from attempts to write the mid-twentieth-century Jewish experience, referred to by Odenigbo in a typically heated, alcohol-fuelled discussion about the making of history (50–51). As Nicola King has pointed out, for many Holocaust survivors 'it has proved impossible to assimilate the traumatic past into a present which would enable the subject to construct a coherent narrative of the self'.[46] Adichie herself is not a direct survivor of the trauma of Biafra, but her parents are, which perhaps has made it easier for her to develop a narrative that enables a negotiation of the bitter past by translating their memories and those of their generation into fiction for her generation. As she remarked in a recent interview, 'Nigerians of my generation know very little of our history, [the novel] is a book about my grandfather but also a book about our history, I want my Nigerian readers to go and ask their parents about it'.[47]

Assembling the fragments of memory brings a recognition that no single, coherent narrative self *can* be constructed out of them—hence the multiple narratives of the novel, which indeed vary considerably in intensity and conviction. Only Ugwu seems in the end to provide any kind of continuous focus—Ugwu, whom the author describes as 'for me the soul of this book', and who was based on two houseboys, one described to her by her mother, the other whom she remembered and who disappeared during the war.[48] The focus on Ugwu is maintained by means of a brilliant interweaving of his story with the remembered textures of everyday life, of acknowledged yet fictionally transformed nostalgia, as in *Purple Hibiscus*. This is in part a matter of a deft use of language, of 'translating' Ugwu's Igbo thoughts into straightforward, educated English, while his speech is halting; it is also, again, a matter of how the narrative engages with the everyday lived experience of the people at its centre.

Again, as in *Purple Hibiscus*, food as the material as well as ceremonial basis for life features throughout *Half of a Yellow Sun*, drawing the reader into a sympathetic engagement with and understanding of even the most violent and extreme events. The appalling events leading up to and during the war are given due weight—but so, too, are the everyday experiences of those who live through them, to the extent that we come away with an almost Brechtian sense of the absurd 'normality' of war, and consequent 'abnormality' of peace. Thus the novel opens with an establishing, comical account of Ugwu's devoted creativity in his master Odenigbo's kitchen, serving his guests with jollof rice and chicken boiled in herbs as they argue about the nature of Igbo identity and whether or not it existed before the white man, which makes all the more convincing the way it ends, with distressing scenes of starving refugees fighting over scraps of food while bombs fall in the distance, the Odenigbos' baby developing kwashiorkor, and the war finally grinding to a halt.

With the apparent restoration of what seems a kind of normality, the survivors Olanna, Odenigbo, Ugwu, Richard, and the Baby return to Nsukka, only to find themselves forced to learn what this 'normality' means: they are made to lie on the floor of their half-destroyed house by two federal Nigerian soldiers who search the house 'for any materials that would threaten the unity of Nigeria' as one of them puts it, before they help themselves to Ugwu's special dish of jollof rice.[49] After they have left, Olanna pours the rest of the rice into the dustbin. Her gesture does not symbolise a disposal of the past, rather, an attempt to spurn present humiliations. She had prayed as she lay on the floor that the soldiers would not find her Biafran pounds which, after they have left, she takes out and burns. 'You're burning memory,' says Odenigbo disapprovingly.

> 'I am not', she replies. She would not place her memory on things that strangers could barge in and take away. 'My memory is inside me.' (432)

The points to take from this are that people survive; things do not. And with people, within them, memory, including nostalgia, survives, which in this postcolonial context has enabled a sympathetic re-imagining of some of the worst events a society has to live through, creating the faint hope that lessons might have been learnt, and the cycles of oppression will one day be broken. The novel recalls the memories of those who went through war in Nigeria, but it also—as Rob Nixon has remarked—'honors the memory of a war largely forgotten outside Nigeria'.[50]

Reworking Nostalgia

Yet it is important to notice how open the view of history is that emerges from the novel. Adichie is too subtle to suggest any simple, deterministic account, as the debate about history at Odenigbo's house early on in the novel makes clear. After dismissing Hegel's view of Africa as not worth debate, the host turns to the current trial of Eichmann in Israel, with its (ironically timely) reminder of the Holocaust, suggesting that if people had 'cared more about Africa' that terrible event might not have happened. Challenged to explain, he continues: 'It's self-evident, starting with the Herero people . . . Don't you see? They started their race studies with the Herero, and concluded with the Jews.' The others are not convinced. Okeomo half-seriously turns the discussion round by remarking that World War II was 'a bad thing that was also good, as our people say', because 'My father's brother fought in Burma and came back filled with one burning question: How come nobody told him before that the white man was not immortal?' Everyone laughs, and yet there was 'something habitual about it', Olanna thinks (50–51). Her thought clarifies the clichéd element in the group's simplistic anti-colonial sentiments, while allowing the reader to acknowledge the relevance of an African perspective upon a familiar European history, and the links between different histories, societies, and nations. Retrospectively the tiredness of the group's debates suggests, too, the inability of the country's elite to anticipate or understand the larger movement of their own history, about to break out into a civil conflict in which they are to play a key role.

If the Biafran secession seems at times to become part of an inevitable cycle of history, the novel's structure encourages a view that history is less easily grasped, understood, or imagined than that implies. If the war appears on one level to become almost part of everyday life, it also represents a rupture: when the abnormal becomes normal, the normal becomes abnormal. The overall narrative structure is designed to create a sense of history as interrupted, fractured, just as the country is fractured: the four parts are titled 'Early Sixties', followed by 'Late Sixties', later switching back to 'Early Sixties' again, before finally depicting the 'Late Sixties' again and the post-war period. The unravelling of the post-independence nation is imagined as a breakdown in perceptions of time, leading to a sense that the breakaway state represented a new present which, however, could not last. The retrospective ironies are heavy, and go beyond their immediate African context, however convincingly detailed, towards the realisation that the conditions for war—long-standing divisions and differences, inherited and dormant—are paralleled elsewhere in the collapse of empire, for instance in the 'ethnic cleansing' that broke out in the former Yugoslavia.

Such parallels are left to the reader's imagination, the book's main focus is upon Nigeria. What it demonstrates is how memory grasps history on the individual, microlevel, and for Adichie, this is by means of a reworked nostalgia refiguring a family past: not simply as a longed-for recreation, but to depict social realities as they existed for the individual as the nation appeared to collapse, old loyalties disappeared and new ones had to be forged. The personal and the domestic, and the public and historical are never as far apart as the longing subject imagines. Thus, in the second 'Early Sixties' section, after we have witnessed the brutal events of the preceding 'Late Sixties' such as the airport killings, it seems as if we are returning to the trivially domestic, the romance novel level of the plot. Yet the sudden realisation by Olanna that Odenigbo has betrayed her now carries echoes of earlier betrayals, the collapse of loyalties among the peoples of the country and their governing groups, culminating in the disastrous secession.

First we see through her eyes how Odenigbo's panicky behaviour arouses suspicions of an affair while she has been away. Suspicions confirmed, she goes outside into the backyard, where she sees a kite swoop down and take a chick from the mother hen, leaving it running uselessly around in circles, squawking. She wonders if the remaining chicks 'understood their mother's mourning dance. Then, finally she started to cry'. The symbolism is understated, but legible enough, confirmed and developed by the next scene, when Olanna visits her relatives in Kano in the north who advise her to return to Odenigbo, despite his infidelity, and on the flight home she falls into conversation with an attractive man who, unaware of her ethnic origins, tells her that the Igbo people want 'to control everything in this country', including the police, so that if you are arrested 'as long as you can say *keda* they will let you go'. 'We say *kedu* not *keda*', responds Olanna quietly. 'It means how are you.' Caught out, the man accuses her of looking like a Fulani, not an Igbo, and guiltily avoids her from then on (227).

The very means of communication and indeed identity become a threat when a nation is divided against itself. Adichie continues to assert the need to remember the past even now, as the Biafran war recedes yet further into the past. In one of the stories in *The Thing Around Your Neck*, 'Ghosts', an ageing Maths professor experiences a 'hazy nostalgia' prompted by the reappearance of an old comrade from the war whom he thought dead. But it is his wife's memory that seems real to him, rather than the war. She has been killed by the fake drugs of the new war, against endemic corruption. In the title story a lonely Nigerian girl in the United States struggles to maintain her identity until finally tugged back home by a family death. Disoriented and displaced, the Nigerians depicted in the fragmented narratives of *The Thing* yearn in vain for a sense of wholeness. The question remains: whether releasing the 'thing', the longing for home, is possible, for people dislocated by trauma and distance.[51]

Adichie has created a range of fictions that reveal how far memories of past and present trauma may threaten as well as liberate. She avoids the danger of essentialising her own culture, while exploring the troubling impact of nostalgia for the recent past in the quest for a secure sense of self in the postcolonial dispensation. She takes full advantage of her perspective as a modern diasporic writer, able to view her Nigerian homeland and its recent history of conflict from a distance, while seeking a new sense of the relevance of feminist commitment.

In the next chapter, I will look at J. G. Ballard's search for an 'inner space', the space not of an authentic, stable self, constructed out of past traces, but a shifting collage of perspectives, in which memory, nostalgia, and history participate at different levels, returning us to the present—or 'the next five minutes', as he once memorably expressed it. Ballard is chosen here as an exemplary modernist writer who acknowledges the larger movements of history in a way that does not mean simply recalling the past, but adopting new perspectives upon history, including a perspective cleansed of imperial and colonial delusions. For him, this meant finding a genre free of the blinkered, class-ridden assumptions of the familiar 'serious' English novel, inextricably entwined with declining British power, but looking towards more popular narrative genres, such as adventure, romance, and science fiction, that could be engaged to convey a sense that modern, urban civilisation was a cover for hidden, obsessive drives towards self-destruction—drives he felt were evident in past and present wars and the nuclear arms race.

7 Nostalgia for the Present
J. G. Ballard's *Empire of the Sun*

'Il faut accommoder mon histoire à l'heure' (one must accommodate the history of the hour). Montaigne, *Essais,* 1588[1]

'I wanted to write about the next five minutes. Not the last thirty years.'
J. G. Ballard, BBC Open University TV, 1991[2]

The Empires of the East

Like modernity, nostalgia is a way of thinking about time. And not only about time past, but time passing, and to come. The dynamic of memory is that its existence is always in the present, even as it struggles to reclaim the past: this means that it constantly acts as a drain on the future, which cannot be imagined without reference to the past. For a writer like J. G. Ballard, exploring the present meant imagining the future, and for many years he wrote futuristic fantasies developing the imagery and narrative conventions of science fiction; but with the publication in 1984 of *Empire of the Sun,* a compelling fusion of autobiography, fantasy, and history, it became clear that writing about the present also meant revisiting the past—but a past transformed into a narrative form that incorporated elements of science fiction, war story, popular adventure, and the traditional *Bildungsroman,* so as to enable an exploration of the psychopathology of everyday life in a postcolonial, post-nuclear world.

Since the publication in 1962 of his first major novel, *The Drowned World,* Ballard has been known as the writer of dazzlingly inventive fables about catastrophe and survival, although until the arrival of *Empire of the Sun* he was marginalised by the low status of science fiction. With *Empire of the Sun* his position altered dramatically: awarded The Guardian Fiction Prize, the James Tait Black Award, and short-listed for the Booker Prize, the book was immediately hailed as one of the best British novels about the Second World War. Gollancz's hardback edition was reprinted four times within a month of its first appearance in September 1984; in paperback hundreds of thousands have been sold worldwide. It remains his best-known work, its continuing popularity underwritten by being turned into a successful Hollywood film, directed by Steven Spielberg.

Born in Shanghai in 1930, the son of well-off British immigrants, the young Ballard's early years were profoundly affected by the Japanese invasion of the coastal areas of China in 1937, followed by the occupation of Shanghai after Pearl Harbour in 1941—'the first sustained counter-attack by the colonised East against the imperial West', he later called it[3]—which led to the internment of foreign civilians, including himself and his family. With the end of the war and release from the camp, the young Ballard came to England, his distant 'home' country, to be educated. This was a shock from which he never really recovered. He studied medicine for two years at Cambridge—which he said he forgot 'within five minutes of leaving that academic theme park', unlike his memories of Shanghai, which he 'hoarded' ever after.[4] He then worked variously as a copy-writer, a Covent Garden porter, and, after a spell with the Royal Air Force in Canada, became an editor of technical and scientific journals. His first short story was published in the science-fiction magazine *New Worlds* in 1956, but it was not until the appearance of *The Drowned World* that his work began to have any impact, mainly upon science-fiction enthusiasts, who recognised a new vision of contemporary reality in the novels and stories which then began to emerge with increasing frequency.

In Shanghai, Ballard grew up in a gaudy, violent, and cosmopolitan environment, where civil war was never far away; yet his parents and their friends in the international community pursued the absurd formalities of colonial life without a care for the future—or the past. The persistent sense of estrangement his upbringing generated remained with Ballard throughout his life, becoming increasingly evident in the radical tendency of what he wrote, all the while settled in the quiet suburban enclave of Shepperton, West London. Books such as *The Terminal Beach* (1964), *The Atrocity Exhibition* (1970), *Crash* (1973, filmed by David Cronenberg), *The Unlimited Dream Company* (1979), *The Day of Creation* (1987), *Cocaine Nights* (1996), and *Millenium People* (2003), assumed that Western civilisation was either non-existent, or little more than a fragile veneer—what Guy Debord has called a 'Society of the Spectacle'.[5] For Ballard, as for Debord, the relentless pressure of the spectacular consumption of contemporary images made the past seem non-existent, the future unimaginable—apart perhaps from 'the next five minutes'.

Yet the frequent eruption of arbitrary, even apocalyptic, violence registered throughout Ballard's work suggests that time, in the sense of history's larger and more public movements, remained pervasive—in effect a repeated acknowledgement of his traumatic wartime experiences. This is not to say that Ballard's vision is simply derived from its early origins: rather, that his personal past provided the often secret motor behind his drive to define the post-war world in terms of the domination of social, economic, and technological systems—systems that, as Andrzej Gasiorek has pointed out, 'show up the appeal to agency as a nostalgic dream'.[6] For Ballard, the individual is the meeting point of forces beyond his or her control, and if this makes it seem pointless to look back to the past, the temptation to do so remains, and has repeatedly to be overcome. Once he became fully aware of the pull of his personal past, Ballard wrote it into his present, having finally come to realise how far his views had been shaped by the clash of empires he had witnessed as a young boy. It was when he found he could no longer ignore or resist the inner clamour of his childhood that he produced *Empire of the Sun*.

In this chapter I will be looking at how Ballard negotiated his memories so as to define his past in terms of specific historical events, reliving the experiences accompanying the collapse of imperial power in East Asia which, he felt, had been ignored or sidelined by the dominant version of events in the West. Reasserting history, especially a history forgotten or ignored, was a large task, given the sense that had come to prevail among many writers, artists, and cultural commentators after the 1960s that history had in some sense disappeared, leaving—as Robert Hewison put it—a past disappearing into the endless flux of post-modernity on the one hand, or its shallow reproduction as 'heritage' on the other.[7] But 'history' is always more than a series of given facts; it is a form of representation, analogous to, yet different from, the arts, including literature, in its claims to a relationship with the world. It involves the disciplined study of the past, according to certain agreed norms which, as Hayden White and others have shown, of course includes rhetorical patterns, whereas literature engages with the aesthetic realm. Again, that too—especially in its narrative aspect—makes strong claims to engage with reality, however defined. The fuzziness of the border between these different forms of representation is obvious; what is useful here is to recall that there are always different versions of history, since it is always written in the present, each generation of historians inevitably reflecting their own times when describing the past.

Postcolonial historians (such as the Indian Subaltern Studies group) have struggled to provide their own, local histories, not so much recapturing lost pasts as rewriting the past in terms of what is relevant for their present. Through an imaginative exploration of his own memories and their relation to known but neglected or obscured pasts, Ballard shows how the writer— even one brought up nominally a member of the ruling imperial class—may redefine history in terms which challenge the accepted paradigm. Ballard's project in *Empire of the Sun* involves rewriting the present through recapturing a lost past which, despite his rejection of nostalgia, he was repeatedly drawn towards, and challenged by—as are we, his readers.

The 'Inner Space' of History

Recovering the past for Ballard meant more than simply recalling history: it meant recreating a particular version of what had been remembered, preserved, or written. And more: as Angela Carter remarked with (understandable) enthusiasm at the time of its appearance, *Empire of the Sun* was the 'great British novel about the last war for which we've had to wait forty-odd years'—great because it lacked heroics, being about a British schoolboy lost in Shanghai when the Japanese invaded, and great because it was also about 'a vast company of the doomed', with 'in the background, history working itself out'.[8] What was truly remarkable at the time was that this vast company of the doomed was mainly Asian, although the Westerners' sufferings are made plain too.

History is never far from his work; although it is often history transformed by the media onslaught of the twentieth century into dream-fragments, re-arranged to form a pattern of obsessive images glimpsed from time to time in the sensational, chaotic underworld of contemporary civilisation, evident in, for example, *The Atrocity Exhibition*. What was unique about *Empire of the Sun* is how far, in the middle of his career, Ballard produced the single work which most clearly engaged with history in the sense of a pattern of known past events, adjusting and reinscribing them according to the perspective of his own experiences, which meant from the world outside Europe. As Dipesh Chakrabarty was later to point out, the dominant historical paradigm based on a Eurocentric version of the past continues to require challenging.[9] This challenge was an essential part of Ballard's adjustment of history as he understood it should be interpreted in the present. Looking back over his life in his last, autobiographical book *Miracles of Life* (2008), he observed that

> I had always wanted to write about the war years, partly because so few people in England were aware of the Pacific war against the Japanese . . . Few novelists have waited so long to write about the most formative experiences of their lives, and I am still puzzled why I allowed so many decades to slip by. Perhaps, as I have often reflected, it took me twenty years to forget Shanghai and twenty years to remember.[10]

As this suggests, Ballard had long resisted his memories. He did not like remembering, remembering brought back the unsettling, long-submerged stream of images that, however, had already begun to surface in his work. No wonder he claimed he had 'always detested' nostalgia (161), although that is what fuelled his best novel.

The strength of his feelings was at least partly the product of contempt for the sentimental, backward-looking views of the British at home and abroad, apparent in everything from their haughty behaviour to their pseudo-Tudor buildings, in Shepperton as in Shanghai. But by the mid 1980s he could no longer forget his childhood memories, and the scenes of violence and brutality associated with that time. As he himself came to realise, when readers of his earlier work spotted echoes of the imagery of *Empire of the Sun*—the drained swimming pools, abandoned hotels, flickering newsreels, deserted runways, derelict weaponry, rusting machinery, and flooded rivers—these could all be traced back to the memories 'that I had tried to repress', but that had been 'knocking at the floorboards under my feet, and had slipped quietly into my fiction' (251).

Nostalgia is still often thought of as little more than the sentimental return to an imaginary, idyllic past, and this is also how Ballard himself tended to see it. He was scathing about what he perceived as the collective nostalgia of the British, evident in the heritage industry as in their lifestyle more generally. In a characteristic 1997 essay on 'Airports', he attacks British post-war culture's 'kitsch and nostalgia' which, he says, blinds people to the 'glamour and optimism' of places like the surroundings of Heathrow, where the 'discontinuous city' of 'the next five minutes' is displayed, the 'intricate networks' of perimeter roads, air freight depots and light industry that constitute 'the reality of our lives' could be found, not the 'mythical domain of village greens, cathedral closes and manorial vistas'.[11] Meanwhile, as he concluded in his last book, individual memory had been essential to his work: it was 'the greatest gallery in the world', the source of 'an endless archive' (248). The archive of Ballard's memories is at once a source and a construct; how far it involves nostalgia depends upon how he defines his personal archive for himself.

Despite his disdain for the nostalgic, suburban longings of post-imperial Britain, the traumas and catastrophes Ballard had witnessed as a child ensured that even his most far-fetched fantasies remain glued to the past, often on an unconscious level. What he tries to avoid as far as he can is the direct representation of the past in terms of the stock literary forms of social realism. Hence the appeal of the imaginary landscapes of science fiction, a genre allowing release from more traditional 'literary' fiction. He avoids the popular genre's stock-in-trade of space travel and planetary landscapes, preferring as his inspiration the 'classic modernism' of surrealist painting, Kafka short stories, and 'noir' films, all of which helped him to create the 'inner space' he was interested in representing (132, 215).

This 'inner space' is the space not of an authentic, stable self, constructed out of past traces; but of a shifting collage of perspectives, in which memory and history participate at different levels. Acknowledging the larger movements of history does not mean simply recalling the past; it means adopting new perspectives, including a perspective cleansed of imperial and colonial delusions. Embarking on his career as a writer, this meant finding a genre free of the blinkered, class-ridden assumptions of the traditional English novel, inextricably entwined as it seemed to be with declining British power in the world. The turn to science fiction during the 1960s, followed by the more experimental writing of the 1970s which reached its apogee in *Crash*— a fiction of self-styled 'technological porn'—showed how popular narrative forms could be engaged so as to test the limits of everyday reality, and convey the sense that modern, urban civilisation was little more than a cover for hidden, obsessive drives towards self-destruction.

Ballard's dystopic vision is never absent from his work, which is one reason why Spielberg's sympathetic film version of *Empire of the Sun* came across as surprisingly upbeat to readers familiar with the novel. The film's achievement was to bring out the visual intensity of the author's memories, but it lacked that sense of defunct imperial power and almost universal despair with which Ballard contemplated the past. Ballard had seen at close hand the workings of the racial arrogance accompanying imperialism—American as well as European and Japanese—with the result that he developed early on a clinically detached view not only of the world around him, but of himself. It is this detachment that is most striking about the tone of his work, a way of writing about even the most extreme events in a curiously affectless, and at times hallucinatory way.

Developing an armour against feeling was an important part of his survival mechanism: hence his stubborn refusal of nostalgia, while accepting the pull towards his younger self in the end. The stress of these contrary forces within sometimes became almost too much to bear. Once, when assisting Spielberg in the accurate recreation of his Shanghai childhood home in West London, he stepped out of the house to find a row of 1930s American automobiles, each with a uniformed Chinese chauffeur, lined up in the drive: 'The scene was so like the real Shanghai of my childhood I almost fainted' (257). Not long thereafter he returned to the real Shanghai for the first time, seeking out 'shrines' to his 'younger self'; but despite the 'remarkably resilient' memories 'waiting for me everywhere', Shanghai had apparently forgotten the Europeans who had created it, and was now a Chinese city (266–69). In short, its former history had come to an end. Or so it seemed.

The title of *Empire of the Sun* alone suggests the importance of historical reality for the book, as a process working independently of the individual will. The title also contains an important ambiguity: it has to do with the empire of the rising sun, the Japanese empire; and it alludes to the arrival of a vastly more destructive power, a 'second sun' (as it is called in the narrative) detonated by the Americans at Hiroshima and Nagasaki.[12] The book is also concerned with another empire, upon which it used to be said the sun never set: the British Empire. *Empire of the Sun* can be thought of as a postcolonial text, although post-imperial might be more apt, given the hints towards the end of the book that the Chinese, for the most part an almost undifferentiated mass of peasants, servants, and defeated soldiers, are a people who will emerge as a great power in the future—just as the sudden appearance of Chinese acrobats at the end of V. S. Naipaul's mordant account of collapsing postcolonial societies in *In a Free State* (1971) hints at their country's future role. Whether or not the Chinese will become the next imperialists, as they once were, Ballard leaves open. Yet the opening metaphor of tidal change in *Empire of the Sun* suggests that as one form of power ends, another will begin, in the endless, resistless movement of history.

The first reviews of the book are particularly instructive, while missing one of its most important features—its irony. A week after its publication a reviewer in *The Listener* suggested the degree of puzzlement and misunderstanding with which some viewed its take on history, while acknowledging its impact as a compelling reminder of a specific past:

> When Japan occupied Shanghai in 1937, the International Settlement, that city-state within a city imposed on China by the so-called Unequal Treaties, remained untouched; and the state of unreal immunity lasted until December 1941, when Japan attacked Pearl Harbour and Malaya.
>
> Amid the general débâcle of British power in the Far East, the occupation of the International Settlement was a minor event. Most surveys of the Pacific War make hardly any reference to it. But now J.G. Ballard, who was born in Shanghai, has given this Western city on the mudflats of the Whampoa its requiem—and a curiously dry-eyed, yet absorbing, novel it is.
>
> Ballard was 11 when the Japanese finally moved in, and he spent the rest of the war in an internment camp outside the city. This, too, is the experience of Jim, the young hero of *Empire of the Sun*, through whose eyes and limited perceptions the reader shares the collapse of Western power and the horrific events which followed ... When Japan surrenders and Jim is reunited with his exhausted parents (they have been in another camp all the time) there is no emotion. And, in a way, how could there be? This, for all its pace and clarity, is a *Boys' Own Annual* view of the world—and who would look there for pity, for a real understanding of what was going on or for an awareness of tragedy?[13]

For this reviewer, and presumably many of its first English readers, the novel is about 'a minor event' in the Pacific War, the 'collapse of Western power' in Shanghai, seen through the eyes and 'limited perceptions' of the book's young hero. If it offers an unsentimental ('dry-eyed') account of what the history books overlook, it is also crucially limited by this boyish perspective, evincing no pity, no 'real understanding of what was going on', much less a sense that what was going on was a tragedy.

Perhaps the most important point here is the reviewer's implicit recognition that *Empire of the Sun* claims to tell a story that has been overlooked, or that has not been told before. History is about perceptions of the past, and Ballard's account offers a new perception, a new history. Telling the story of a people who have been forgotten or marginalised is one of the major claims to history any text can make, as postcolonial critics and theorists have long insisted. But acknowledging the book's offer of a memorial to a forgotten people means acknowledging its emphasis upon the international community of Shanghai, not the Chinese or most challengingly, the Japanese—although the novel leaves open the question of how far those conquerors can be thought of as in any sense victims too. But the review undermines the positive impression this conveys by concluding that the book is finally limited and naive, suggesting mere schoolboy heroics. Apparently it would be more appropriate to treat the fate of the Westerners involved in the Japanese occupation of Shanghai as tragic; the end of Western imperialism is clearly no fit subject for non-tragic treatment.

And yet the reviewer began by referring to the 'so-called Unequal Treaties' which created the International Settlement in Shanghai. This refers to the Treaty of Nanking (1842), which concluded the Opium War between Britain and China by forcing—among other things—the cession of Hong Kong to the British and the opening of several ports, including Shanghai, to international trade. In succeeding years the British, followed by the French and the Americans, obtained further privileges, establishing for their subjects virtually self-governing settlements within the Chinese ports. The growing commercial power and prestige of these foreign enclaves was most obviously represented by the impressive public buildings built by the British on their section of the Shanghai Bund, including a neo-Gothic cathedral designed by Gilbert Scott, in the crypt of which Jim watches newsreels at the beginning of the novel, setting up the train of film imagery that permeates the boy's perceptions of the increasingly grotesque events that take place before his eyes, until by the end he cannot distinguish between film and reality—a condition Ballard exploits elsewhere in his fiction as a sign of our contemporary media-saturated condition.

The lack of which *The Listener* complains is a function of the kind of novel it is—supposedly akin to a *Boys' Own Annual* story. So what kind of narrative would provide a better understanding? The reviewer's answer is revealing, contrasting *Empire of the Sun* with a South African novel just out, *The Wall of the Plague* (1984; by Andre Brink), about six feverish days in the life of 'a beautiful Cape Coloured girl' exiled in Europe for breaking the apartheid laws against inter-racial sex. This fiction apparently offered the desirable alternative to Ballard's book: 'every page is dense with awareness of suffering, persecution, human inadequacy and the fragility of liberal hopes'.

But even if we were to argue that *Empire of the Sun* shows an awareness of suffering, persecution, and human inadequacy (which it does), it certainly is not very concerned with the fragility of 'liberal hopes', hence the reviewer's contradictory impressions. What seems to matter most is not so much Ballard's choice of subject, or his treatment of a 'minor event' in the Pacific war, but, rather, how the reviewer and his presumed readership's (male, white) liberal English values are handled by a work from within the unserious domain of popular realist fiction. The reviewer's remark about the lack of emotion when Jim and his parents are reunited is especially telling. In fact, the book does not show their reunion at all; what we are shown is the emotion when Jim is reunited with his surrogate parent of four years, Dr Ransome (341–42). His own parents have become shadowy figures who have their own terrible experiences to get over, and the reader is left to imagine the painful distance developed in a family so cruelly separated by events, rather than offered a potentially sentimental and in that sense nostalgic reunion scene between them.

As we have seen, *The Listener* review began by placing the novel in a specific historical context; and there is no question of the extraordinary density of historical implication in the opening pages. This is in the first place a matter of numerous clearly defined signals to the reader, from the author's own prefatic claim, before the narrative proper begins, that the book 'is based on events I observed during the Japanese occupation of Shanghai', then a map of 'Shanghai in 1941', followed by the ominous first chapter heading, 'The Eve of Pearl Harbor'. The narrative's claim to offer personal testimony, and its assertion of some relationship with an assumed, known history is clear, although whose known history it is requires some unravelling, as does the precise nature of the book's relationship to it. This is more than a matter of a 'minor event' in the Pacific War. The first page alone refers also to Dunkirk and Tobruk, Barbarossa and the Rape of Nanking: in short, to a global context. And although the opening perspective is evidently that of a young British boy, it is also that of a colonial-expatriate position.

Certainly the emphasis appears to be on defeat, for all the Allies. Dunkirk and Tobruk involved humiliating withdrawals from France and North Africa; Barbarossa was Hitler's plan for the invasion of Russia, begun in June 1941 and sweeping all before it by December; and the Rape of Nanking refers to the earlier Japanese conquest of the capital of Nationalist China. With the attack on Pearl Harbor immediately pending, the nadir of Allied power beckons. Since the end of the narrative coincides with the Japanese surrender and the successful conclusion of the Allied war effort, it seems that on one level the novel is dealing with a single, large phase in world history, involving the rise and fall of the Japanese empire, the fall and rise of the American—a global shift that coincides with the decline in power of Europe and, specifically, of Britain. And yet, registering the larger events of the time within his young expatriate's consciousness creates an oddly distanced effect, so that Western history appears as quite unreal, newsreels turned into dreams which leak into the crowded streets of the only city the protagonist knows—itself the centre of another, Asian history.

Again, this is not to deny the constant outward reference to a wide range of known events, as well as to the interpretation of them as signalling the rise and fall of empires. Following up almost any detail reinforces this sense of historical awareness in the narrative. Consider, for instance, the name of the street of Jim's home, Amherst Avenue, first mentioned in the second paragraph of the narrative, and then repeatedly alluded to. On one level it is a typical function of realist narrative to provide actual street names; but on the level of its historicity, the name suggests a further dimension: the street was named after a former British Governor-General of India, the Earl of Amherst (1773–1857), who played a key role in British attempts to open up commercial relations with China. It is the kind of detail that makes us aware of an important aspect of the way Ballard's narrative operates from the start, not noticed by early reviewers: its irony.

Ballard's irony is more than merely a matter of vivid or amusing detail—for instance, of the British drinking and partying as their time runs out in Shanghai. It is part of the larger irony of events, an irony that dominates the narrative from the beginning. 'Wars came early to Shanghai, overtaking each other like the tides that raced up the Yangtze . . . ' (11). The ironic resonance alerts us to the assumption that the reader more than any of the characters knows what has been happening, or is about to happen. But a further irony works against Western readers, in that this is also being presented from a perspective beyond the West. The ironic potential sometimes veers towards farce, although it is hard to laugh when, for example, Jim's father kneels by the radio in his pirate costume to hear that 'Hitler will be in Moscow by Christmas' (18). This does more than just anticipate the collapse of Allied power, since, as we know, Hitler did not reach Moscow. It is also ironic on other levels: 'It must be snowing in Moscow', remarks Jim's mother as she stares out at the winter sky. 'Perhaps the weather will stop them . . . '. This assumes our knowledge that it will, and did. But 'Once every century?' replies her husband. 'Even that might be too much to ask. Churchill must bring the Americans into the war'. History is full of surprises, including the possibility that it will repeat itself, as when Hitler failed against Russia, like Napoleon one hundred thirty years before him. And, of course, although Churchill was trying his utmost to 'bring the Americans into the war', it was the Japanese attack the next day, not Hitler's march against Russia, which finally ensured full-scale American entry. Meanwhile, eleven-year-old Jim stands in the doorway, 'the amah carrying his airgun like a bearer' (18).

This suggests a sense of history as a matter of repeated retrospective ironies, generated by a narrative rich in mainly anticipatory or proleptic moments, although it also leaps backwards in time, usually no further back than the beginning of the Sino-Japanese war—that is to say, 1937. This key date—referred to several times in the opening chapters (24, 32, 40, 54)—was when full-scale hostilities broke out between China and Japan, Shanghai was invaded, and, wars coming early to that city, 'the first campaigns of the Second World War took place.'[14] Nor are readers allowed to forget preceding wars, including the First World War (Avenues Foch and Joffre, named after French commanders of the 1914–18 conflict). The point of stressing the ironic overtones is to suggest that this makes for a complex engagement with the past, and with different versions of the past. As Anne Whitehead has pointed out, World War II was less amenable than World War I to tropes of memory or remembrance that crossed national frontiers, the victors, and the victims: in the context of the Pacific War in particular, memory of the events was heavily dependent not only on victory or defeat, but upon the nationality of the rememberer—American, British, Australian, or Japanese[15]—not to mention Chinese, one might add.

The sense that *Empire of the Sun* might offer some kind of requiem for a lost people, as well as a lost period, is part of what Ballard creates through his evocation of the turbulent Shanghai city setting, if not also in the manners of the expatriate community, including characters such as Mr Maxted, 'the perfect type of the Englishman who had adapted himself to Shanghai', designer of the Metropole theatre and numerous nightclubs, whose relaxed, raffish air Jim finds quite exhausting to imitate (27). And yet, 'requiem' hardly seems the right word for this—any more than it does for the barefoot beggar drumming on the side of Jim's Packard shouting, 'No mama! No papa! No whisky soda!' (13). The irony is clear: this is to be Jim's own position shortly, when he is separated from his parents in the post-invasion chaos, wandering around the deserted mock-Tudor houses on Amherst Avenue, until even the cocktail biscuits and soda water run out (chapter 7). He will then have been brought almost—but never quite—to the position of all those scurrying, desperate Chinese beggars and refugees previously observed in wide-eyed, but detached, superior wonderment from his father's chauffeur-driven car. The shock of his change in position, as well as that of the community to which he belongs, is brought sharply home when, entering the Raymonds' house, he asks for help from the two amahs dragging their former masters' furniture out, and is soundly slapped in the face: 'Jim knew that they were paying him back for something he or the Raymonds had done to them' (68), an insight developed later, when he realises that 'one day the Chinese might emerge from the mirror' (103)—as they do when the city begins to return to them (351).

Jim's fate is at least partly an index of the fate of the British community as a whole: protected by race, wealth, and the history of their position from understanding the people around them, they are involved in a charade of empire, which is about to be smacked by the reality that the power upon which their imperial certainties was based has leaked away without them realising it. Maxted's role is more apt than he could know, designing theatres and clubs rather than being a 'serious' businessman like Jim's father (27). The imagery of the first chapter, of newsreels playing to an empty cinema, of a theatre about to close, underlines the impression of a people play-acting, fulfilling a role that is no longer theirs, an impression clinched by the concluding lines:

> They were going to a party, and he would try to cheer his father and think of some way of stopping the Germans at the gates of Moscow.
> Remembering the artificial snow that Yang had described in the Shanghai film studios, Jim took his seat in the Packard. He was glad to see that Amherst Avenue was filled with the cars of Europeans leaving for their Christmas parties. All over the western suburbs people were wearing fancy dress, as if Shanghai had become a city of clowns (20).

This is hardly pathos, much less tragedy, but nearer to grotesque comedy. In another complex bit of analeptic/proleptic irony, the chauffeur's film career is alluded to: he had 'once worked as an extra in a locally made film starring

Chiang Ching, the actress who had abandoned her career to join the communist leader Mao Tse-Tung' (13), the leader of a despised group who had 'an intriguing ability to unsettle everyone' which appeals to Jim (27). Mao's future role as Chinese head of state and world leader after the communist takeover of Shanghai in 1949 does not require any explicit reference for the historical ironies to become apparent.

The Reception of *Empire of the Sun*: A Requiem?

Ballard's narrative is steeped in history at many levels, alluding to past, present, and future in public (pre-war, the war itself, and post-war developments) as well as private (Jim's own future prospects after the war) aspects. In the mid 1980s, this was not as common in fiction as it has become since, largely as a result of the inroads upon mainstream English fiction made by such prize-winning postcolonial and historically informed texts as Giles Foden's *The Last King of Scotland* (1998), *Ladysmith* (1999), and *Zanzibar* (2002), Abdulrazak Gurnah's *Paradise* (1994), and Ronan Bennett's *The Catastrophist* (1998)—all of which challenge familiar historical perceptions while dealing with crisis points in colonial history. And, nearer to Ballard's field of action, Timothy Mo's *An Insular Possession* (1986) was set during the Opium Wars of the early nineteenth century, and his *The Redundancy of Courage* (1991) was about the 1976 Indonesian annexation of East Timor.

These works, and others like them but less openly aware of empire—such as Pat Barker's *Regeneration Trilogy* (1990–95)—have engaged with history as a set of facts existing extra-textually. Popular and influential, they have inhabited a largely critical- or at least theory-free zone, excluded because of the long-standing critical assumption of the superiority of self-consciously modernist or postmodernist, metafictional novels—like Salman Rushdie's *Midnight's Children* (1981) or Julian Barnes' *A History of the World in 10½ Chapters* (1989)—over predominantly realist works, and of the presumed seriousness of novels that focus primarily upon the inner workings of the individual consciousness, a tradition established by Joyce's *Ulysses* or Woolf's *Mrs Dalloway*, rather than, say, Kipling's *Kim* or Nicholas Monsarrat's *The Cruel Sea*, or Olivia Manning's *The Levant Trilogy*, or Evelyn Waugh's *Officers and Gentlemen*—that is, works more interested in external action, public life, and war. Modernist fiction did not wholly exclude history in the larger, public sense: for example, *Mrs Dalloway* (1925) registers the presence of empire in the characterisation of Peter Walsh, who once ruled in India, and it acknowledges the recent experience of the First World War in the fatally disturbed mind of Septimus Warren Smith. But this is not the main focus, and we have to look elsewhere for fiction centrally concerned with the impact of external action and event, and especially with action and event beyond the boundaries of upper-middle-class, domestic English behaviour.[16]

Empire of the Sun as a *Boys' Own Story*?

It is in the domain of the popular subgenres of adventure, romance, and war story that fiction notably departs from the inward gaze of classic, elitist modernism. Yet, for all that they subvert the modernist focus upon small-scale, intimate relationships, at the same time these subgenres suffer from their own narrowness: in their unquestioning acceptance of—if not enthusiastic support for—prevailing ideologies of empire and gender. This limitation is most obvious in the subgeneric level to which Ballard's narrative was related by *The Listener*. And not only *The Listener*: another contemporary reviewer concluded: 'Ballard, in the finest piece of modern fiction I have read for some time, incarnates the spirits of Kim and of Barrie's Peter Pan'.[17] Is this accurate? And if so, how far does it undermine the claims of Ballard's book to seriousness?

It is important to be clear about the nature of the subgenre being brought into the frame by such remarks. What was the *Boys' Own Annual*? The original *Boys' Own Magazine* had its origins in mid-Victorian attempts to 'improve' the cheap literature available for children, to wean them from an 'unhealthy' devotion to the smugglers and highwaymen who featured in the 'penny dreadfuls' of the time. Instead, a high moral tone was adopted, and a preference for dashing, but pure, 'historical' figures such as 'The Black Prince's Page'. The *Boys' Own Annual* was of more recent vintage, offering a regular anthology of pieces from the successor to the *Boys' Own Magazine*, the *Boys' Own Paper* (first published by the Religious Tract Society in 1879 and lasting until 1967), in which upright, well-spoken lads, crammed with useful knowledge and a respect for women, fought their way against fearful odds through trackless forests and lethal swamps. Clear, fast-moving, and vigorous narrative with a sympathetic, easily identifiable central character gave these fictions immediate, sometimes lasting appeal, and not only to boys. War featured as a familiar theme, with foreign spies (usually German) a favourite challenge to patriotic impulses. Weaponry was usually described in loving detail. Non-European races were generally stereotyped as submissive children or ferocious pagans. The contribution of such writing to the public-school ethos, and hence to the ideology of imperialism, was immense. Is this then the kind of writing that *Empire of the Sun* resembles?

Certainly what one might label *Boys' Own* elements appear throughout the novel: most obviously in the presentation of the action through an eleven-year-old, English colonial, public-schoolboy's perspective, but also in the boy's fascination with aviators and aircraft, his worship of individual, heroic military endeavour, his ability to survive virtually alone against the odds, and in the emphasis upon extreme conditions, upon war. Furthermore, the focus upon Shanghai, 'this gaudy city' (the opening words) but also (the concluding words) 'this terrible city', offers the familiar excitement of the exotic, occasionally bizarre, Asian Other.

But if moments such as the opening of hostilities against the Allies in front of the Shanghai Bund (chapter 4), or the American bombing raid on Lunghua airfield (chapter 23), dramatically conveyed as they are, seem to excite a *Boys' Own* response, what of the gruesome results of conflict? Such as the 'yellow silk glove' of the British petty officer's skin, 'boiled off the flesh in an engine-room fire' (48) on the gunboat *Petrel*? Or the eyes of the dead young Belgian woman in Lunghua Camp, momentarily swivelling to fix on Jim when Dr Ransome squeezes her heart (207)? Or the 'coils of viscera strewn around the terrorist bomb victims in the Nanking Road' that Jim once saw (41), and the bayoneted Japanese pilot whose 'chipped teeth' close around the boy's finger when he tries to feed Spam to the corpse (338–39)? All this is offered in an almost clinical tone: precise, detailed, and detached.

This hardly invites an empire-building *Boys' Own* ideology; moreover, a broader, more knowing and mature perspective upon events is implied from the opening lines, when the focaliser has a moral authority beyond the boy's viewpoint: 'Wars came early to Shanghai . . . Jim had begun to dream of wars' (11). Certainly we share Jim's perspective as he watches newsreels in the cathedral crypt, worries over his schoolwork, listens to Flash Gordon, and puzzles over bridge bidding and other adult mysteries. But we are also continuously made aware of another perspective, by reported dialogue or by apparently neutral narratorial comments, occasionally even parenthesised:

> The dances and garden parties, the countless bottles of Scotch consumed in aid of the war effort (like all children, Jim was intrigued by alcohol but vaguely disapproved of it) had soon produced enough money to buy a Spitfire—probably one of those, Jim speculated, that had been shot down on its first flight, the pilot fainting in the reek of Johnny Walker. (12)

The war in Europe is incorporated into a humorous boyish fantasy on Jim's favourite subject, aerial warfare, as the narrator uses the boy's plausibly—and to the adult reader, comically—exaggerated notions of what those around him accept without question, to undermine it, by means of a distinct authorial presence.

Despite his privileged and protected status as a junior member of the expatriate community, tended by numerous watchful and obliging amahs, Jim resists the accepted viewpoint of most of the Europeans around him. Far from sharing their characteristically nostalgic, patriotism-at-a-distance, he is—unconsciously at first, and then increasingly consciously—at odds with it. The 'only nostalgia that Jim had ever known', we are told, was the 'intact memory' of the dead Japanese pilot who had sat at the controls of the rusting fighter plane he comes across on his secret expedition to Hungjao Airfield (31). His uncanny yet limited perceptions encourage a different order of sympathies and concerns from those around him. This is most obvious in his appreciation of the determination, power, and daring of the Japanese—a people looked down on by the Europeans—although he never quite attains the narrator's perspective of the Chinese 'as passive and unseeing as the furniture' to Jim as to the international community (16): yet a people who will, we are told by the end of the novel, 'punish the rest of the world, and take a frightening revenge' for their repeated defeats and humiliations (351).

The nearest Jim comes to a realisation that he and those to whom he belongs by origin and race have themselves become the 'Other' as a result of a shift in world power is revealed when he tries to make himself useful to a Chinese bandit leader in order to return to Shanghai towards the end of the novel:

> But Captain Soong did not want Jim to run any errands for him. The war had changed the Chinese people—the villagers, the wandering coolies and lost puppet soldiers looked at Europeans in a way Jim had never seen before the war, as if they no longer existed, even though the British had helped the Americans to defeat the Japanese. (320)

The complex way in which a popular-genre discourse is called into play, and yet, at the same time, called into question, is well exemplified at the outbreak of hostilities in chapter 4—a stunning action sequence told from the point of view of the boy watching in his hotel bedroom as the British gunboat *Petrel* is sunk and the neutral city invaded. It is a powerful, almost hallucinatory scene, modified by touches of humorous plausibility as the boy assumes he has begun the war with his 'confused semaphores' from the hotel window. The sense of dislocation and fear that has driven him into the self-imposed guilt typical of a young child adds to the persuasiveness of the sequence, and means that the excitement of the action—as burning pieces of the gunboat soar into the air like 'rockets in a firework display' (43), for instance—is nonetheless situated by the older narrator, ensuring that the reader is left to reflect upon the factors that have helped to bring about this particular historical moment, not merely left to enjoy the spectacle of war.

Even more important, as we watch the Japanese gunboat by the public gardens with Jim, is the authorial reflection upon the contrast between the boy's 'deep respect' for their ships and the British disparagement of them. And the information that the Japanese flagship had been built by the British and had served in the Royal Navy before being sold to the Japanese during the Russo-Japanese War in 1905 (40) is part of the continuing density of historical texture. The memory of that war, the first in which a non-European power had soundly defeated a major European power, and which began with the surprise attack by the Japanese upon the Russian navy, had long been forgotten or ignored by the West. Now this imperial presumption is shown up. The Japanese marines board the USS *Wake* (whose American officers are sound asleep in their hotel rooms), and go on to exchange words with the young British officer on the bridge of the *Petrel*,

> who dismissed the Japanese in the offhand way that Jim had seen his parents refuse to buy the Java heads and carved elephants from the dugout salesmen who surrounded the cruise ships in Singapore harbour. Were the Japanese trying to sell something to the British and Americans? Jim knew that they were wasting their time. (42)

After the Japanese have overrun Shanghai and are busy consolidating their grip, and the resources of the foreign residents' deserted houses have been exhausted, Jim cycles around the empty streets vainly attempting to give himself up, so as to secure at least some food and shelter, if not a return to his parents: 'Like his school friends, he had always despised anyone who surrendered—he accepted without question the stern morality of the Chums Annuals—but surrendering to the enemy was more difficult than it seemed' (78). The 'stern morality' of boyhood reading cannot be sustained in the face of history, in the form of these dramatically altered circumstances. The parenthetic comment alerts us to a wider cultural and historical awareness that subverts the traditional imperialist ideology of the adventure story tradition.

Empire of the Sun as Testimony

Defining the precise relationship of *Empire of the Sun* to that wider, post-imperial awareness is trickier than it seems. This is confirmed by the strong response which emerged at the time of the novel's publication from wartime survivors disputing the accuracy of Ballard's version of events, and in particular his presumed view of the British. Three weeks after that original review in *The Listener*, for example, a correspondent from Glasgow who had also been a youthful member of the international community in Shanghai, and who was duly interned in Chapei Camp near Lunghua, complained about Ballard's 'grave distortion of historical facts, since episode after episode in the book bears hardly the remotest resemblance to what happened to me'. In particular, he objected to Ballard's depiction of the low morale of the British civilian internees towards the end of the war, and the 'odious' comparison between 'the British and the American inmates', which he suspected was 'merely the fashionable national self-denigration of our own day'.[18]

In other words, not only was Ballard's history suspect: so, too, was his ideology—a view based on the assumption that *Empire of the Sun* is a simple realist narrative. Of course, nobody denied, or denies, the fact that the Japanese invaded Shanghai, or that they interned foreign civilians in nearby camps, or that they had to release the survivors when the war ended with their defeat. But there is evidently some dispute about exactly what happened when the invasion took place, how people behaved and felt in the camps, and how that can or should be interpreted in Britain forty or more years later. If *Empire of the Sun* claims to be historical in the sense that it offers personal testimony—which is how this Glaswegian correspondent certainly takes it—then how should we take the testimony of other witnesses?

When Martin Amis (a novelist much influenced by Ballard) asked how closely the book followed his own experiences, Ballard replied:

> I'm the same age as my hero, I was born in Shanghai as he was, lived in that big house as he did. I was interned in that camp but I wasn't separated from my parents—as Jim is in the book. The vast body of Jim's experiences are invented, though psychologically true. You fictionalize to reach the truth . . .
>
> In the book, I played it all down. The beating to death of the rickshaw-coolie, for instance—I wasn't 100 yards away when that happened, I was 10 feet away [227ff]. No, they were very violent times. Executions, public stranglings, disbanded soldiers wandering about, starving armies. You'd have to go to Uganda during the last days of Idi Amin, or the Congo during the civil war, or Cambodia perhaps, to get some idea of what life was like for the ordinary Chinese. . . . [19]

Ballard links the violence he witnessed with the violence of contemporary decolonised states so as to underline the historical truth of his representation. 'You fictionalize to reach the truth': this is the traditional claim of realist fiction. In so far as *Empire of the Sun* is an instance of traditional realist fiction, there is bound to be a large overlap between the world of history or document and the world of fiction; but that still leaves the problem of where the history ends and the fiction begins. It is important to recognise exactly what Ballard says: for instance, that the 'vast body' of Jim's experiences are invented, 'though psychologically true'. This helps explain the parentless boy's changing relations with a succession of mentors and father-figures in the violent, desperate world into which he has been thrust by events: from the impeccably relaxed Mr Maxted, to the louche American ex-steward Basie and his counterweight, the very English Dr Ransome. Mr Maxted's role is soon dissipated by the circumstances of life in the prisoner camp, and he dies before the end: not so Basie and Dr Ransome.

This brings us back to the opposing testimony of other camp survivors. Although Jim meets Basie and Ransome before they all end up in the camp, it is their behaviour as inmates, alongside that of their compatriots that drew down the wrath of other survivors upon Ballard's head. In his interview with Amis, Ballard does not distinguish the behaviour of different nationalities in the camp; in the novel he certainly does. In the fiction, he is trying to tell a different kind of truth. In this sense it is not so much a document, or even perhaps personal testimony; rather, as a fictional representation it is a version of history that rewrites it as well.

At first glance, the characterisation of Basie, Ransome, and the other inmates seems to represent the supremacy of the Americans and the futility of the British. But the novel offers a more complex, less stable interpretation of the shifting fortunes of imperial power, as the central section of the novel, Part II, in particular the two chapters dealing with camp life as the war nears its end, demonstrates. The camp is seen in terms of contrasting viewpoints, indeed, contrasting ways of life; and Jim's function is at least partly to bring us to some understanding of their competing claims to offer a means of survival. Part II is focused on what happens towards the end of the camp as the momentum of external events begins to accelerate, and the possibility of death through illness or summary execution becomes as strong as when the city was first invaded and the foreign civilians rounded up. There is a gap of three years between the arrival of Jim and the others at the camp in Part I, and the opening of Part II. In Part I, Jim succeeded in being interned by the Japanese to ensure his survival—an instance of his instinct for self-preservation that differentiates him from the rest of the British, a point which touches on something very basic about the novel—not only its witnessing to the atrocities of the East, but to those perpetrated upon civilians. It is a complex kind of witnessing, however, infused by Ballard's ironic historical awareness.

Degrees of atrocity are hard to measure, but the situation in which Jim, and the rest of the demoralised, poorly fed Allied civilians find themselves is in important respects different from that of other Second World War prisoners we know about: such as those who found themselves on the notorious Japanese death railway, or in the concentration camps. Nevertheless, life in Lunghua represents something central to the late-twentieth-century experience of war in that the victims are predominantly non-combatants: civilians, women, and children. And as the victory of one lot of combatants over another draws nearer, their lives are increasingly endangered. In these extreme conditions, the prisoners—and in particular, the British and the Americans whose values are represented to a degree by Dr Ransome and Basie—respond in interestingly different ways.

In chapter 25, 'The Cemetery Garden', the positive side of Dr Ransome's role is revealed, and Jim's (qualified) admiration for him seems justified. Ransome does more than offer his professional skills, although that is a lot; he has initiated a garden, ensuring a splendid growth of fresh vegetables by having human excrement added—a job Jim willingly executes, working 'with the slow but measured rhythm of the Chinese peasants he had watched as they fertilized their crops before the war' (204). Ransome's Christian charity appeals to Jim, whose parents 'were agnostics', and so he

> respected devout Christians in the same way that he respected people who were members of the Graf Zeppelin Club or shopped at the Chinese department stores, for their mastery of an exotic foreign ritual. Besides,

those who worked hardest for others, like Mrs Philips and Mrs Gilmour and Dr Ransome, often held beliefs that turned out to be correct. (206)

Such correct beliefs (all part of the boy's *education sentimentale*) are practical rather than theological, although Jim tests the theology too, by observing, for instance, the eyes of the dying for the 'flash of light when the soul left' (207).[20] When Dr Ransome is tired or angry he turns to making wax panels for the prisoners' broken window panes—work for which few are grateful. 'Still, as Jim had observed, Dr Ransome was not interested in their gratitude . . . he was preparing for the winter as if trying to convince himself that they would all be there when it arrived' (207–08). Jim is shown absorbing what he needs from the doctor, while distanced by his upbringing and recent experiences from Ransome's dispassionate altruism. The most revealing passage comes when the doctor cleans Jim's infected ankle:

> Jim submitted without protest. He had formed his only close bond in Lunghua with Dr Ransome, though he knew that in many ways the physician disapproved of him. He resented Jim for revealing an obvious truth about the war, that people were only too able to adapt to it. At times he even suspected that Jim enjoyed Latin for the wrong reasons. The brother of a games master at an English boarding school (one of those repressive institutions, so like Lunghua, for which Jim was apparently destined), he had been working up-country with Protestant missionaries. Dr Ransome was rather like a school prefect and head of rugby, though Jim was unsure how far this manner was calculated. He had noticed that the doctor could be remarkably devious when it suited him. (208–09)

On one level the doctor represents the great civilising mission of the British Empire. He has played a positive role in China and continues to do so in the camp for which, ironically, his public-school background has well prepared him. The possibility that he might share the deviousness that is the key to Basie's very different personality suggests how important it is as a quality for survival; yet he also has his own innocence, and debilitating nostalgia—suspecting that Jim enjoys his Latin lessons 'for the wrong reasons', and resenting the moral challenge implicit in the boy's use of everything he learns in order to survive and—more alarming still—even flourish in the camp. No wonder he has tried to get Jim to memorise 'a foreign field that is forever England' (167).

Basie has flourished, of course, as the reader has guessed he would from the moment we first saw him, testing Jim's gums for gold teeth to barter for provisions before trying to sell the boy himself (chapters 10–11). So when Jim admits he has stolen three tomatoes from the kitchen garden, because 'I have to give something to Basie whenever I see him', Ransome replies:

> 'I know. It's a good thing that you're friends with Basie. He's a survivor, though survivors can be dangerous. Wars exist for people like Basie.' Dr Ransome placed the tomatoes in Jim's hand. 'I want you to eat them, Jim. I'll get you something for Basie.' (212)

Do wars exist for people like Jim, too? In the succeeding chapter, 'The Lunghua Sophomores', we see Basie's response to the receipt of Dr Ransome's 'something'—condoms, in place of the vegetables he had hoped for from Jim. But before we see the Americans, a more critical view of the British is exposed.

The morale-boosting activities of the so-called Lunghua Players are shown as grotesquely irrelevant: they recruit their members from 'the snootiest families', and even totter around in a parody of a rugby game to the jeers of those fellow-prisoners 'excluded from the game because they had never learned the rules' (213–14). More damning, however, is the atmosphere of the British men's dormitory:

> The sight of so many adult men unwilling to cope with the reality of the camp always puzzled Jim, but he recovered as soon as he reached the American dormitory. He liked the Americans and approved of them in every way. Whenever he entered this enclave of irony and good humour his spirits rose . . . When they noticed him, most of them liked Jim, who in return, and out of respect for America, ran endless errands for them . . . All in all, Jim felt, the Americans were the best company, not as strange and challenging as the Japanese, but far superior to the morose and complicated British. (214–16)

Jim here registers the shift in global destiny of the warring nations endorsed by Ballard's novel. The British are trapped forlornly in their nostalgic, class-ridden decline; the Japanese remain 'strange and challenging'; while the more egalitarian and virile Americans blithely convey a sense of themselves as the superior power.

Yet these new imperialists are dangerous, too, in their way—as Jim realises when Basie asks him to move their pheasant traps further out: are the Americans testing their escape route (this turns out to be the case), or gambling on how far he can get before being shot by a sentry? 'Although they liked Jim, they were quite capable of gambling with his life. That was American humour of a most special kind' (219). Basie, 'like Dr Ransome . . . had come into the camp with nothing', but now seems almost burdened with possessions (218). Unlike Jim's other mentor, he stirs himself only to serve his own direct interest; and, unlike Dr Ransome's muscular Christian, his

> hands and cheeks were still soft and unworn, though with a pallor like that of an unhealthy woman. Moving around his cubicle, as if in his

pantry on the *SS Aurora*, he regarded Lunghua Camp in the same way he had viewed the world beyond it, a suite of cabins to be kept ready for a succession of unwary passengers. (216–17)

Basie's interest in Jim is at least partly sexual; and yet he has helped the boy to survive as much, if not more, than the apparently disinterested Dr Ransome. Whether Jim could have survived the camp without both of them is unlikely. They 'helped to make up a world' for the parentless boy (221), which is what ultimately keeps his spirit for survival alive, not some outdated notion of imperial patriotism or morality.

Heroism and Sacrifice

If, as I have been suggesting, *Empire of the Sun* reclaims a certain marginalised history by proposing at least a partially non-Western perspective upon the past, does this also involve going beyond the privileged, white male viewpoint of its central character? Jim admires Basie and Ransome, and although it is not only men that he admires—his mother and the missionary women in the camp also appear to offer values he needs to consider, while Mrs Vincent appeals to the first troubled stirrings of his adolescent sexuality—this confirms the support in the novel for the masculine discourse of classic, adventure-romance writing.

Jim's first exploration of the ruined Japanese aircraft at Hungjao seems, if not specifically *Boys' Own*, nonetheless part of a long-established masculinist discourse:

> He gazed at the instrument dials with their Japanese ideograms, at the trim wheels and undercarriage lever. Below the instrument panel he could see the breeches of the machine-guns mounted in the windshield cowling, and the interrupter gear that ran towards the propeller shaft. (31)

This kind of erudition is specific to the popular masculine genres of science fiction, films, and videogames, in which the authors are, like Ballard, thoroughly familiar with the technology of destruction. Jim thrills to the exploits of the pilots he sees, or—as here—imagines he sees; and yet his experience goes beyond mere boyish thrill:

> A potent atmosphere hovered over the cockpit, the only nostalgia that Jim had ever known, the intact memory of the pilot who had sat at its controls. Where was the pilot now? Jim pretended to work the controls, as if this sympathetic action could summon the spirit of the long-dead aviator. (31)

What begins as a familiar evocation of technological expertise, offering its presumed (male?) readership a reassuring sense of men's closeness to machinery, turns into a potent image of death in war, and of the impact of death upon the boy's consciousness. This is more than a matter of the nostalgic idealisation of the fighter-pilot, although that is part of it, it is a matter of the long-dead warrior's recalled spirit inhabiting the present with an 'intact', almost determining force.

What this suggests on the symbolic level is an idea of past wars inevitably reasserting themselves. This idea is central to the book, and suggests another way in which it registers the past, and the impact of the past upon the present. We have been prepared for the symbolic dimension to Jim's experience in the ruined aircraft by a moment in the opening chapter when he recalls seeing 'the bones of the unburied dead' of earlier battles rising to the surface of the paddy fields at Hungjao and Lunghua each spring (14); and its effect continues almost immediately after he climbs out of the aircraft at Lunghua, when he discovers an entire company of Japanese soldiers 'resting in this old battlefield, as if re-equipping itself from the dead of an earlier war, ghosts of their former comrades risen from the grave and issued with fresh uniforms and rations' (33).

There is apparently no escape from the war-ridden past: Ballard manipulates Jim's memory to take us beyond the Asian sphere of battle, so that when the Japanese take their Western internees from Shanghai to Lunghua across the flat countryside beyond the city, 'the miles of rotting trenches and rust-stained blockhouses reminded Jim of encyclopaedia illustrations of Ypres and the Somme, an immense museum of battle that no one had visited for years' (150). Clearly war and death are indissolubly linked in a continuous thread of historic memory, going back beyond Lunghua to Ypres and the Somme. The reminders of war appeal to Jim, especially the battles of the air which tug most at his imagination; but that appeal is counteracted. The spectacular air attacks on Lunghua Camp (which provide one of the most memorable sequences in Spielberg's film) leave him exhilarated; yet the other side of the spectacle is made quite clear too, the closeness of the American planes drawing Japanese fire onto the camp, killing some of the prisoners. Jim's admiration for the American Mustangs, 'the Cadillacs of air combat' (192), registers their superiority over the Japanese, but he also witnesses their terrible destructiveness as one explodes

> in a curtain wall of flaming gasoline through which Jim could see the burning figure of the American pilot still strapped to his seat. Riding the incandescent debris of his aircraft, he tore through the trees beyond the perimeter of the camp, a fragment of the sun whose light continued to flare across the surrounding fields. (193)

This reminds Jim of the perpetual nearness of his own death, while anticipating a more deadly explosive light, another 'fragment of the sun' produced by the Americans: that 'second sun' that flashes over the Nantao stadium (267).

This, we later discover, coincided with the detonation of the atomic bomb. The images coalesce in Jim's memory: 'Jim remembered the burning body of the Mustang pilot, and the soundless light that filled the stadium and seemed to dress the dead and the living in their shrouds' (276). In moments like these, *Empire of the Sun* does become a requiem for the dead—and the living, whose lives are represented as a living death.

The ambivalent power of war, which kills some as it permits others to survive, ensures some ambivalence of association; but on the symbolic level it feels as if death is the only winner. Hence the repetition of the particular image—of a dead or dying young pilot—throughout the narrative, gathering new and varied overtones until that last, uncanny moment when Jim tries to revive the dying young Japanese pilot whom he has come to think of as a kind of twin, and who seems, Lazarus-like, about to return to life (337–40). War is an essential condition of life, so that those who battle on appear in some sense already dead—the tormented Lieutenant Price, for example, with his 'dungeon pallor and bandaged hands . . . the first of the dead to rise from the grave, ready to start the next world war' (304). Repeated references to a Third World War in the concluding pages of the novel confirm this vision of history as an endless cycle of war.

Ballard's text displays modernist as well as traditional realist features: not only through its recurrent symbolism, but also in terms of its vision of history as cyclic, rather than progressive or linear. Yet the narrative always retains its grip upon psychological realism, just as it never loses its sense that history involves a 'real' and potentially remembered past world. The more bizarre or uncanny moments are entirely explicable in terms of Jim's shocked, starved, and fevered condition; and the nature of his encounter with the dying young pilot reflects at least partly the deranged state of his mind as he recalls the teaching of the missionary women, who had insisted that 'far from being a marvel', the raising of Lazarus was 'the most ordinary of events'. His growing knowledge of science (thanks to Dr Ransome) affirms their teaching in almost comic terms: 'Every day Dr Ransome brought people back from the dead by massaging their hearts' (339).

Further, by this late stage of the narrative Jim's position has long been distinct from the predominantly white, English, imperial and Christian values of his community, although not to the extent that he cannot exploit those values when under pressure. Learning of the Japanese surrender from an armed Eurasian who picks up his prized leather golf shoes, he flatly demands the shoes despite his exhausted condition, 'aware that he was once again asserting the ascendancy of the European' (276). The ideological distancing apparent in these later scenes has been potentially present from the start, when the difference between the boy's values and those of the community to which he ostensibly belongs is marked by his lack of loyalty—indeed, his apparent indifference to loyalties as such. Everything he has seen since the Japanese invasion of 1937 has made him realise that, unlike the war of the newsreels, in which it was clear which side to be on, 'In a real war no one knew which side he was on, and there were no flags or commentators or winners. In a real war there were no enemies' (14). He shares Wilfrid Owen's insight—'I am the enemy you killed, my friend' ('Strange Meeting', 1918).

Paradoxically, Jim's realisation is partly at least the product of his boyishly nostalgic idealisation of military heroism and self-sacrifice, since that was what first enabled him to view those whom others perceive as the enemy more favourably. His initial respect for the Japanese was derived from his own memory of their stoic fighting abilities against the Chinese in 1937, as well as the ancient appeal of their aura of neo-feudal power. Even before he could know about the attack upon Pearl Harbor, his identification with the Japanese made him unconsciously share their experience at this historic turning point in the war, thereby on some level remaining alienated from his own side, his own people, after the dangerous appeal of the Japanese has been undermined. Thus, when he tries to sleep in the hotel to which the remaining Europeans have withdrawn as the Japanese takeover of Shanghai becomes imminent, and he thinks again of the dead aviator's spirit, he dreams of standing 'in his flying suit on the decks of a silent carrier, ready to take his place with those lonely men from the island nation in the China Sea, borne with them across the Pacific by the spirit of the divine wind' (38).

At times, the Japanese themselves seem aware of Jim's vision of them: in Lunghua Camp, as their own position becomes less secure, they forcibly prevent the boy from continuing to identify himself with them, forbidding him to carry on wearing the youthful Private Kimura's kendo uniform, for example. But the behaviour of the camp guards in Part II, as the war grinds to an end, ensures that Jim's realisation of the darker side of Japanese militarism catches up with ours—as when he witnesses the Chinese rickshaw coolie being slowly and deliberately beaten to death by the men he once admired (227–28). Yet the appeal of apparently heroic, self-sacrificial action as such is never entirely lost: American airmen replace the Japanese as a focus for Jim's idealising fantasies, although that appeal has been qualified. We are made further aware of the multiple ironies involved when it is revealed that the airmen who dropped the atomic bombs on Hiroshima and Nagasaki thereby saved Jim's life, since otherwise he and the other remaining prisoners would have been herded together for the killing fields of the north. At the same time, the new and more deadly destructiveness of the bombs is a portent for the future.

The continuous interweaving of future as well as past perspectives counteracts the simplistic implications of war-adventure discourse: for such fictions, history is a matter of stereotyped, providential conflict, in which good overcomes evil, and established class, race, and gender positions are predictable and privileged; *Empire of the Sun* offers a challenge to such stereotyping, while relying on popular realist elements to make itself accessible. In this way, its engagement with history in our post-nuclear as well as postcolonial age is a reminder of the value of nostalgia in the present, whether it is consciously acknowledged or not.

8 Endnote

Frisch weht der Wind
Der Heimat zu
Mein Irisch Kind,
Wo weilest du?

                        Richard Wagner, *Tristan und Isolde*, 1865

And your past life a ruined church—
But let your poison be your cure.

                        Louis MacNeice, 'Thalassa', 1949[1]

The Australian poet Judith Wright remarked some time ago that 'if we reject outright the literature of nostalgia, we fail to understand something important about ourselves'; we fail to realise how we can make 'our loss into a gain'.[2] Grasping this sense of the potential of nostalgia is not easy—least of all, perhaps, in the contexts of large-scale historical change, such as those that characterise the loss or overthrow of empires. What I have been suggesting in this book is that we need to think about the nature of nostalgia in various embodiments or forms, with a view to approaching it as a process with the potential to reconnect the individual in a critical or reflective way to his or her past, and to a community. Further, I have been arguing that this process is especially significant for—although not exclusive to—people whose experiences derive from the massive uprootings generated by colonialism and its aftermaths.

Nostalgia has long been a pervasive human emotion, and remains a source of both consolation and understanding in the face of suffering, but it has been relatively neglected as a focus of study or 'theory' until recently. In the preceding chapters, I have touched on a range of nostalgic formations, mainly but not exclusively within narrative fiction: in terms of a struggle for identity, a yearning for the homeland, an idealisation of the future, a witnessing of trauma, a rewriting of bitter histories of civil conflict and mass killing, or a historicising of the present. Along the way, I have been considering the limits of nostalgia too, asking in effect: how do we judge the boundaries between sentimentality and critique, melancholy and release? The imaginative works I have been looking at offer ways of understanding these questions, if not coming to terms with or indeed answering them. Thinking through nostalgia enables us to respond to the ethical imperative that resists postmodern attempts to deny the temporal, or to transform it into a fixation upon a consumable present. This ethical imperative calls on us to recognise the demand of the Other, by which I mean all those lost or condemned by the onward march of history, but whose shades still inhabit the twilight zone, searching for signs of recognition.

The seriousness of the issues at stake has been pointed up by a number of writers, including Doris Lessing. In *The Golden Notebook* there is a key passage in which the narrator thinks back to the time about which she writes, the time of colonial Southern Rhodesia during the 1940s, when she belonged to a group who felt themselves to be apart in their knowingness, yet whose understanding of the world around them was highly partial and limited. In order to write about that time truthfully, she has to switch something off in herself:

> It is like remembering a particularly intense love affair, or a sexual obsession. And it is extraordinary how, as the nostalgia deepens the excitement, 'stories' begin to form, to breed like cells under a microscope. And yet it is so powerful, that nostalgia, that I can only write this a few sentences at a time. Nothing is more powerful than this nihilism, an angry readiness to throw everything overboard, a willingness, a longing to become part of dissolution. This emotion is one of the strongest reasons why wars continue.[3]

For Lessing here nostalgia becomes nihilism, an expression of the deepest anger as well as longing, even a kind of death-wish. This is not far from what we sense in Wagner's music, as Eliot implied by his use of Wagner in *The Waste Land*. But for Lessing's narrator, the novel she produced out of it contained 'nothing' that 'wasn't true' yet 'the emotion it came out of' was the 'lying nostalgia' of war, hence 'immoral'.[4]

It is not only difficult to capture the past directly through memory, the difficulty is compounded for writers drawn by nostalgia into evoking an apparently true, but inauthentic representation of their personal pasts. It is inauthentic because it lacks a sense of connectedness, of the relation between the writers' pasts and the pasts of those around them. The power of nostalgic representations is precisely what makes such representations compelling and attractive, and therefore worth pursuing to salvage the past. But without the element of reflexivity, of self-analysis, the past becomes a distorting fiction, lacking the crucial connection to the general experience. This is not necessarily to argue for a postmodern, metafictional style, although that has its place—as writers from Rushdie to Sebald have demonstrated—but for at least a double awareness, reflecting the power of yearning for the past, but also what that yearning obscures or ignores, as Chimamanda Adichie has so persuasively argued by means of a fictional retelling of the Biafran War in *Half of a Yellow Sun*. The traumas of history may only be overcome—if at all—by identifying with the wretched of the earth.

Lessing's narrator is properly sceptical about what attracted a film company to the novel she wrote about the earlier time. There are many films set in pre- or postcolonial environments (including a version of *The Grass is Singing* (1984)) that distort the past, sentimentalising or sensationalising the relations between the powerful and the powerless. In the preceding chapters I have mentioned several filmic rewritings or recreations of nostalgia, from the BBC TV series of van der Post's *The Lost World of the Kalahari*, to the primitivising representation of Bushman people in *The Gods Must be Crazy*; from the glossy Hollywood reworking of Karen Blixen's memoir in *Out of Africa*, to the more sympathetic, yet ultimately falsifying version of *Empire of the Sun*. The evocative German television series *Heimat* was set beside the more challenging *Das Weisse Band*, in which the narrator's yearning for a pre-war rural idyll is undermined by grim memories of small-town fascism—all the more alarming for the perpetrators of apparently random evil acts turning out to be the children who will grow up in the Nazi era.

Many more examples of media nostalgia ask for closer scrutiny, including such popular and influential works as the televised miniseries of Alex Haley's *Roots* in the mid 1970s, which exemplified the reversioning of a core story in terms of the quest to define the self in relation to longed-for real or imagined pasts. Or there was the 1984 BBCTV series *The Jewel in the Crown*, based on Paul Scott's 1966 end-of-the-Raj novel, subsequently the name of numerous restaurants, holiday firms, and the like, as the commodification of that particular set of memories and histories has proceeded within the regime of postmodernism. Fredric Jameson has written forcefully about what he anathematises as 'nostalgia film', by which he means postmodern pastiche, a mode not merely of popular versions of the past, but a mode attempting to inaugurate a new subgenre—such as two mid-1970s films dealing with guilt and complicity during World War II, *Lacombe Lucien* and *The Night Porter*. Such works, Jameson suggests, reveal how a specific historical period joins the bric-à-brac of fashion styles, automobiles, and music as a time-marker, weakening their potential for representability, and placing us in a 'nostalgic' (his scare quotes) frame of mind that makes us merely receptive to 'old photos and the distant contemplation of bygone fashions and scenes from the past'.[5] Jameson's mordant analysis is part of his broader critique of fashionable postmodernism under what he calls 'high capitalism'. I suspect he is correct in identifying how far and how quickly authenticity is lost in certain popular nostalgic developments, but I am less sure that he is right to insist on the lack of depth in all popular culture. Are old photos really so limited and limiting? And what about the films of John Ford, for example? Ford's nostalgia for the old West and Ireland is dream-like, almost hallucinatory, yet often laced with irony, so that the conservative drive of his plots is undermined—most notably in *The Searchers* (1956), a film challenging the racism that led to the genocide of native Americans implicit in his own and others' films.

But it is probably in the domain of 'high' or 'serious' modernist cinema culture that we are likely to find evidence of critical, contestatory, and even subversive possibilities. I am thinking of work such as Russian filmmaker Tarkovsky's *Nostalgia* (1983), an enigmatic and profoundly moving narrative of heightened or symbolic realism made in exile in Italy. There is a revealing account of the making of the film in Tarkovsky's *Sculpting in Time*, in which he admits to being 'startled' to find 'how accurately' his mood while making *Nostalgia* was transferred to the screen:

> a profound and increasingly wearing sense of bereavement, away from home and loved ones, filling every moment of existence. To this inexorable, insidious awareness of your own dependence on your past, like an illness that grows ever harder to bear, I gave the name 'Nostalgia'.

And so the sense of nostalgia as a physical, almost medical condition returns.

> Ultimately I wanted *Nostalgia* to be free of anything irrelevant or incidental that would stand in the way of my principal objective: the portrayal of someone in a state of profound alienation from the world and himself, unable to find a balance between reality and the harmony for which he longs, in a state of *nostalgia* provoked not only by his remoteness from his country but also by a global yearning for the wholeness of existence.[6]

The final image of the film is a slow pull back from a remembered childhood scene until the whole is held within a massive ruined church, open to the sky. *Nostalghia* (the Russian title) appeared before the collapse of the Soviet empire in 1989–91 when, as with so many who have fled their countries in our time, émigré Russians would yearn in vain for the possibility of return.

Clearly it is well worth considering the various aesthetic equivalents for the representation of nostalgia beyond writing, including those literary genres that are not strictly narrative, such as drama, poetry, and song (I referred to poetry and oral performance in Chapter 3), but also music, film, and architecture. The most striking and richly ambiguous examples are the filmic or pictorial: Naipaul's use of De Chirico was referred to in Chapter 2, but more could be made, for example, of the way that melancholy artist's own nostalgia towards classical Greece and Rome, superimposed upon personal memories of Turin, expressed a complex form of nostalgia that is used by the writer as a means of communicating his own divided identification with, and resistance to, the Western influences upon his sense of himself. It is in W. G. Sebald's work that the possibilities of the visual, specifically of the photographic, in relation to memory, melancholy, and nostalgia are most obviously present.

As I have suggested (in Chapter 5), Sebald's narrators typically wander through a thicket of images—photos, drawings, newspaper clippings, maps—that simultaneously evoke the material survivals of the past, and the ephemerality of those survivals. These images, and their often apparently random, captionless placing in his texts, highlight the importance of the visual in all memory work; but it is an importance all the more telling in that it was for many the visual record of the Holocaust that reverberated, conjuring up a sense of horror, shame, and guilt. Sebald's art is an art of indirection and allusion, and so on the rare occasion when he uses an explicit image—a newspaper photograph of corpses in the wood at Bergen Belsen in *The Rings of Saturn*, for example—the resultant shock for the reader is all the more powerful. The function of photographs in his work is highly but complexly evocative: veering from their role in suggesting an actuality that demands witnessing to, more often, that of elegiac remembrance. His art is like that of the émigré German Jewish artist, Max Ferber, who appears in the final story of *The Emigrants*, and whose art is an art of traces, tending towards dust or nothingness, and yet which survives through the act of creation, the telling, the writing, the imagery.

As Sylviane Agacinski suggests, the significance of images in the present can hardly be underestimated, although their impact is ambiguous, serving memory less than supplanting it. As vestiges, remains, and traces, they seem more real than memory, than nostalgia, which is as we have seen vague and elusive. But images are after all a method of representation that we can see and think about, aware of the extent to which they conceal as much as they reveal. In our time of the increased compression of time by the media, images and words can work together to resist the simple consumption of what is past, or passing, and to come.[7]

I would like to think that those of us committed to the postcolonial project, through 'thick' or 'thin' relationships, share a sense of the importance of remembering the radical evils marking the long histories of empire and colonisation, as part of our contingent sense of who we are in the present. One way of creating or sustaining such a community of memory is through embodying certain quite specific representations of the past—representations that acknowledge an ethical dimension to the struggle to understand the meanings of identity, identification, and reflective recall prompted by nostalgia. Such representations may not be aesthetic or literary; although the mix of experiential intensity and reflective detachment characteristic of artistic forms carries the potential to affect debates about who we are and about how nostalgia may or may not contribute to that fragile, contingent sense of ourselves in a way that is more than merely a matter of theory.

Notes

Notes to Chapter 1

1. Jean-Jacques Rousseau, *Confessions*, 1782–89, transl. Angela Scholar, ed. Patrick Coleman, Oxford: Oxford University Press, 2000, Book Six, p.221.
2. A. E. Housman, 'A Shropshire Lad', *The Collected Poems of A. E. Housman*, Ware, Herts: Wordsworth Editions, 2005, p.55.
3. Marcel Proust, *By Way of Sainte-Beuve,* 1908, transl. Sylvia Townsend Warner, London: The Hogarth Press, 1984, p.63.
4. Lenrie Peters, 'Home Coming', 1981, reptd in *The Heinemann Book of African Poetry in English*, selected by Adewale Maja-Pearce, Oxford and Portsmouth, NH: Heinemann Educational, 1990, p.32.
5. E. J. Hobsbawm, *The Age of Empire: 1875–1914*, London: Abacus, 1989, p.3.
6. As Fred Davis observes in a useful survey of *Yearning for Yesterday: A Sociology of Nostalgia,* London and New York: Macmillan: The Free Press, 1979, p.101.
7. See Graham Huggan, *The Postcolonial Exotic: Marketing the Margins*, London and New York: Routledge, 2003, especially the Conclusion.
8. Dennis Walder, *Post-colonial Literatures in English: History, Language, Theory*, Oxford: Basil Blackwell, 1998, pp.207–08.
9. See Robert J. C. Young, *Postcolonialism: A Very Short Introduction*, Oxford: Oxford University Press, for a useful summary of the standard position.
10. *Heart of Darkness*, 1899, ed. Owen Knowles, London: Penguin Classics, 2007, p.5
11. See Ashis Nandy, *The Intimate Enemy: Loss and Recovery of Self under Colonialism*, New Delhi: Oxford University Press, 1983; Homi Bhabha, *The Location of Culture*, London and New York: Routledge, 1994.
12. For an analysis of the current cultural obsession with memory, see Andreas Huyssen, *Twilight Memories: Marking Time in a Culture of Amnesia*, London and New York: Routledge, 1995; and Andreas Huyssen, *Present Pasts: Urban Palimpsests and the Politics of Memory*, Stanford: Stanford University Press, 2003. A succinct survey of the concept may be found in Anne Whitehead, *Memory*, London and New York: Routledge, 2009. See also Michael Rossington and Anne Whitehead, eds, *Theories of Memory: A Reader,* Edinburgh: Edinburgh University Press, 2007.
13. Fred Davis, op. cit., is a notable exception. See also Linda Hutcheon, 'Irony, Nostalgia, and the Postmodern', http://www.library.utoronto.ca/utel/criticism/hutchinp/html accessed 22 June 2004.

14. Gerald Clarke, 'The Meaning of Nostalgia', *Time*, 3 May 1971: http://www.time.com/time/o,8816,876989,00.html accessed 12 Feb. 2009.
15. Andrew Marr, *The Making of Modern Britain: From Queen Victoria to V.E. Day*, London: Macmillan, 2009.
16. See http://www.bestofbritishmag.co.uk/ accessed 12 Feb. 2009.
17. Tony Judt, *Postwar: A History of Europe Since 1945*, London: William Heinemann, 2005, p.774.
18. See Dominick LaCapra, *History and Memory After Auschwitz*, Ithaca: Cornell University Press, 1998; *Writing History, Writing Trauma*, Baltimore: Johns Hopkins University Press, 2001.
19. Jay Naidoo, *Tracking Down Historical Myths*, Johannesburg: Ad Donker, 1989, p.69.
20. See Benita Parry on Spivak and Bhabha in 'Problems in Current Theories of Colonial Discourse', 1987, reptd in Bill Ashcroft, Gareth Griffiths, and Helen Tiffin, eds, *The Post-Colonial Studies Reader*, 2nd edn., London and New York: Routledge, 2006, pp.44–50. This Reader also contains the relevant extracts from Spivak and Bhabha's well-known work.
21. Peter Hulme, 'Beyond the Straits', *Postcolonial Studies and Beyond*, eds Ania Loomba et al., Durham and London: Duke University Press, 2005, p.42.
22. See Dipesh Chakrabarty, *Provincializing Europe: Postcolonial Thought and Historical Difference*, new edn., Princeton: Princeton University Press, 2007.
23. See Carolyn Hamilton, Verne Harris, and Graeme Reid, *Refiguring the Archive*, Cape Town, Dordrecht and Norwell, MA: David Philip/Kluwer Academic, 2002, passim.
24. Richard Kearney, *On Stories*, London and New York: Routledge, 2002, p.5.
25. Antonio Damasio, *The Feeling of What Happens: Body, Emotion and the Making of Consciousness*, London: William Heinemann, 1999, p.172. See also Evelyne Ender, *Architexts of Memory: Literature, Science, and Autobiography*, Ann Arbor: University of Michigan Press, 2005, pp.106–07.
26. For a useful discussion of the relation of narrative to memory, see: Peter Middleton and Tim Woods, *Literatures of Memory: History, Time and Space in Postwar Writing*, Manchester and New York: Manchester University Press, 2000, especially pp.54–80.
27. Adam Muller, 'Notes Towards a Theory of Nostalgia: Childhood and the Evocation of the Past in Two European "Heritage" Films', *New Literary History*, 37 (2007), p.739. Muller goes on to develop a position derived from Svetlana Boym's account of nostalgia (see below).
28. 'You Can't Go Home Again' (1974), in Paul Barker, ed., *Arts in Society*, London: Fontana/Collins, 1977, p.21.
29. Raymond Williams, *The Country and the City*, London: Paladin, 1975, p.21.
30. Svetlana Boym, *The Future of Nostalgia*, New York: Basic Books, 2001, p.355. Hutcheon, op. cit., argues along the same lines, while suggesting that it is the postmodern that is aware of the dangers of nostalgia (p.8).
31. Andreea Deciu Ritivoi, *Yesterday's Self: Nostalgia and the Immigrant Identity*, Lanham, MD, and Oxford: Rowman and Littlefield, 2002.
32. Op. cit., p.3.
33. See translation by Carolyn Kiser Anspach, 'Medical Dissertation on Nostalgia by Johannes Hofer, 1688', *Bulletin of the Institute of the History of Medicine*, 2 (1934), pp.376–91.

34. Jean Starobinski, 'The Idea of Nostalgia', transl. William S. Kemp, *Diogenes*, 54 (1966), p.96.
35. See Simon Bunke, *Heimweh: Studien zur Kultur- und Literaturgeschichte*, Freiburg im Breisgau, 2009, pp.127–30. Bunke provides a comprehensive account of the shift from medical to more broadly literary and cultural discourse in the understanding of nostalgia.
36. Antonio Melechi, '*Temps Perdu*', *Fugitive Minds: On Madness, Sleep and other Twilight Afflictions*, London: Arrow Books, 2003, pp.112–16.
37. Op. cit., p.7.
38. Op. cit., Introduction, pp.xvi–xvii; see also Susan Stewart, *On Longing: Narratives of the Miniature, the Gigantic, the Souvenir, the Collection*, Durham, NC: Duke University Press, 1996, pp.23–24.
39. Milan Kundera, *Ignorance*, 2002, transl. Linda Asher, London: Faber and Faber, 2003, p.5.
40. Malcolm Chase and Christopher Shaw, 'The Dimensions of Nostalgia', *The Imagined Past: History and Nostalgia*, Manchester and New York: Manchester University Press, 1989, pp.2–4.
41. See, for example, Friedrich Nietzsche, 'On the Advantage and Disadvantage of History for Life', 1874, transl. Peter Preuss, Indianapolis: Hackett Publishing, 1988.
42. T. S. Eliot, '*Ulysses*, Order and Myth', 1923, *Selected Prose*, ed. Frank Kermode, London: Faber & Faber, 1975, p.177.
43. 'Theses on the Philosophy of History', 1940, reptd in *Literature in the Modern World*, ed. Dennis Walder, Oxford: Oxford University Press, 2003, p.436.
44. Ibid., p.435.
45. Boym, op. cit., pp.xviii, 28, 41, 78.
46. A re-reading that Punter seems to feel pessimistic about: David Punter, *Postcolonial Imaginings: Fictions of a New World Order*, Edinburgh: Edinburgh University Press, 2000, pp.75–78. See also Arundhati Roy, *The God of Small Things*, London: Flamingo, 1997; Michael Hardt and Antonio Negri, *Empire*, Cambridge, Mass.: Harvard University Press, 2000, pp. 43ff.
47. Salman Rushdie, 'Imaginary Homelands', 1982, *Imaginary Homelands*, London: Granta Books, 1991, pp.9–11.
48. Neil Lazarus, 'The Politics of Postcolonial Modernism', *The European Legacy: Special Issue: Europe and Post Colonial Narratives*, ed. Rajeev Patke, 7, 6 (Dec. 2002), p.772. Lazarus is (rightly) objecting to the repeated use of a limited few 'canonical' texts in postcolonial criticism and theory.
49. Jonathan Freedland, 'Sixty Years On, D-Day Veterans Pass Torch into the Hands of History', *Guardian*, 7 June 2004, p.1.
50. Anne Frank, *Diary of a Young Girl, The Definitive Edition*, transl. Susan Massotty, eds, Otto H. Frank and Mirjam Pressler, London: Viking, 2001, pp.314–15.
51. Stuart Hall, 'Cultural Identity and Diaspora', in *Identity: Community, Culture, Difference*, ed. Jonathan Rutherford, London: Lawrence & Wishart, 1990, p.222.
52. Stuart Hall, 'When was "The Post-colonial"? Thinking at the Limit', in *The Post-Colonial Question*, eds Iain Chambers and Lidia Curti, London and New York: Routledge, 1996, pp.242–46.
53. Derek Walcott, 'The Muse of History', 1974, in *What the Twilight Says: Essays*, London: Faber and Faber, 1998, p.37.

54. Trinh T. Minh-ha, *Woman, Native, Other: Writing Postcoloniality and Feminism*, Bloomington: Indiana University Press, 1989, p.28. Grace Nichols, *I is a long memoried woman*, London: Karnak House, 1983.
55. Hall, '"When was the Post-colonial?"', p.247.
56. Ania Loomba, *Colonialism/Postcolonialism*, 2nd edn., London and New York: Routledge, 2005.
57. Edward Said, *Out of Place: A Memoir*, London: Granta Books, 1999, pp.216–17.
58. Op. cit., p.37; see also Bart Moore-Gilbert, *Postcolonial Life-Writing: Culture, Politics and Self-Representation*, London and New York: Routledge, 2009, pp.115–21, in which the writing of the memoir is seen as a 'willed act of resistance' to the denial of Said's identity as a Palestinian.
59. Rey Chow, *Writing Diaspora: Tactics of Intervention in Contemporary Cultural Studies*, Bloomington: Indiana University Press, 1993, p.13.
60. Breyten Breytenbach, 'The Exile as African', in *Altogether Elsewhere: Writers on Exile*, ed. Marc Robinson, Boston and London: Faber and Faber, 1994, p.181.
61. Kimberly K. Smith, 'Mere Nostalgia: Notes on a Progressive Paratheory', *Rhetoric & Public Affairs*, 3, 4 (2000), pp.518–19.
62. Elleke Boehmer, *Colonial and Postcolonial Literature*, 2nd edn., Oxford: Oxford University Press, 2005, pp.112–17.
63. Eric Hobsbawm, *Globalisation, Democracy and Terrorism*, London: Abacus, 2008, p.78.
64. Sarah Nuttall and Carli Coetzee, eds, *Negotiating the Past: The Making of Memory in South Africa*, Cape Town: Oxford University Press, 1998, Introduction, p.5.
65. Lewis Nkosi, 'The Republic of Letters after the Mandela Republic', 2001, in *Still Beating the Drum: Critical Perspectives on Lewis Nkosi*, eds Lindy Stiebel and Liz Gunner, Amsterdam-New York: Rodopi, 2005, pp.320–21.
66. See Dennis Walder, *Athol Fugard*, Tavistock, Devon: Northcote House, Writers and Their Work Series, 2003, chapter 5.
67. Jacob Dlamini, *Native Nostalgia*, Auckland Park, South Africa: Jacana, 2009, p.156.
68. Deborah Hoffman, interviewed by Fergal Keane, Tricycle Theatre Cinema, London, 24 May 2001.
69. Avishai Margalit, *The Ethics of Memory*, Cambridge, MA: Harvard University Press, 2002, pp.69, 74, 78, 83.
70. John J. Su, *Ethics and Nostalgia in the Contemporary Novel*, Cambridge: Cambridge University Press, 2005, p.57.
71. J. M. Coetzee, *White Writing: On the Culture of Letters in South Africa*, New Haven and London: Yale University Press, 1998, pp.1–11. Coetzee's 'memoirs' include: *Boyhood: Scenes from Provincial Life*, London: Secker & Warburg, 1997; *Youth*, London: Secker & Warburg, 2002; and *Summertime: Scenes from Provincial Life*, London: Harvill Secker, 2009.

Notes to Chapter 2

1. Interview with Charles Michener, *Newsweek*, 16 Nov. 1981, p.108.
2. V. S. Naipaul, *A Writer's People; Ways of Looking and Feeling*, London: Picador, 2007, p.2

3. Salman Rushdie, '*The Enigma of Arrival* by V. S. Naipaul', *Guardian*, 13 March 1987, www.guradian.co.uk/books/1987/mar/13/fiction.vsnaipaul accessed 10 July 2009.
4. Stuart Hall, 'Introduction: Who Needs Identity?', in Stuart Hall and Paul du Gay, eds, *Questions of Cultural Identity*, London and New Delhi: Sage, 1996, p.1. Subsequent in-text references are to this edition.
5. See, for example, Selwyn R. Cudjoe, *V. S. Naipaul: A Materialist Reading*, Amherst: University of Massachusetts Press, pp.209–23, and Rob Nixon, *London Calling: V. S. Naipaul: Postcolonial Mandarin*, Oxford: Oxford University Press, 1992, pp.160–63. The most influential voice among those attacking Naipaul has been Edward Said's in, for example, *Culture and Imperialism*, London: Vintage, 1994, pp.20, 320–21; more sympathetic is Helen Hayward's *The Enigma of V. S. Naipaul*, Houndmills, Basingstoke: Palgrave Macmillan, 2002. John J. Su, *Ethics and Nostalgia in the Contemporary Novel*, Cambridge: Cambridge University Press, 2005, pp.66–80, suggests that, *contra* Said, Naipaul's 'strategic' nostalgia permits him to express an 'ethical' position on empire and its aftermath.
6. V. S. Naipaul, 'Images', in Robert D. Hamner, ed., *Critical Perspectives on V. S. Naipaul*, London: Heinemann, 1979, pp.26–27.
7. See Patrick French, *The World Is What It Is: The Authorized Biography of V. S. Naipaul*, London: Picador, 2009.
8. 'East Indian', in V. S. Naipaul, *The Overcrowded Barracoon*, 1965, Harmondsworth, Middlesex: Penguin, 1976, p.36.
9. R. K. Narayan, *The English Teacher*, Madras: Indian Thought Publications, 1984, chapter 8, p.220.
10. Ibid., p.221.
11. Gauri Viswanathan, *Masks of Conquest: Literary Study and British Rule in India*, New York: Columbia University Press, 1989.
12. Jacques Derrida, *Of Grammatology*, 1967, trans. Gayatri Chakravorty Spivak, Baltimore: Johns Hopkins University Press, 1977, p.19.
13. V. S. Naipaul, *Reading & Writing: A Personal Account*, New York: New York Review of Books, 2000, p.55.
14. Stuart Murray, 'Naipaul Among the Critics', *Moving Worlds*, 2, 1 (2002), p.58.
15. V.S. Naipaul, *The Enigma of Arrival: A Novel in Five Sections*, London: Penguin Books, 1987, p.135. Subsequent in-text references are to this edition.
16. Andreea Deciu Ritivoi, *Yesterday's Self: Nostalgia and the Immigrant Identity*, Lanham, MD: Rowman & Littlefield, 2002, pp.39, 45, 68. Ritivoi analyses a range of 'immigrants', both fictional (Odysseus, Crusoe) and non-fictional (Eva Hoffman).
17. For details, see French, op. cit., pp.426–30.
18. See Raymond Williams, *The Country and the City*, London: Paladin, 1975, passim.
19. Robert Winder, *Bloody Foreigners: The Story of Immigration to Britain*, London: Abacus, 2005, p.334.
20. Brathwaite gave himself the new forename Kamau to recreate the forgotten link with his African ancestors. 'Caribbean Voices' was a BBC show broadcast to the Caribbean from London from 1946 under the direction of Henry Swanzy: see French, op. cit., pp.84ff.
21. See French, op. cit., pp.427–28.

22. See, for example, Adewale Maja-Pearce, 'The Naipauls on Africa: An African View', *Journal of Commonwealth Literature*, 20, 1 (1985), pp.111–15, and my response, 'V. S. Naipaul and the Postcolonial Order', in Jonathan White, ed., *Recasting the World: Writing after Colonialism* (Baltimore and London: Johns Hopkins University Press, 1993), pp.111–14.
23. Nayantarah Sahgal, 'The Schizophrenic Imagination', reptd in Anna Rutherford, ed., *From Commonwealth to Post-Colonial*, Coventry: Dangaroo Press, 1992, p.36.
24. V. S. Naipaul, *A Writer's People: Ways of Looking and Feeling*, London: Picador, 2007, p.2.
25. Lucienne Loh writes of the recurring image of a condensed milk tin label depicting 'English cows', in 'Rural Routes/Roots: India, Trinidad and England in V. S. Naipaul's *The Enigma of Arrival*', *Journal of Postcolonial Writing*, 45, 2 (June 2009), pp.157,159.
26. Salman Rushdie, 'A Sad Pastoral', *Guardian*, 13 March 1987, http://books.guardian.co.uk/review/generalfiction/0,6121,567657,00.html accessed 10 June 2005.
27. James Thrall Soby, *Giorgio de Chirico*, rept edn., New York: Museum of Modern Art, 1966, pp.45–46. Soby argues that de Chirico himself gave the titles to his early works, while agreeing that Apollinaire was the painter's 'champion'.
28. Robert Hughes, 'Giorgio de Chirico', *Nothing if not Critical: Selected Essays on Art and Artists*, 1982, London: The Harvill Press, 2001, p.163.
29. See French, op. cit., p.453.
30. Rushdie, 'A sad pastoral'.
31. See for example, Florence Labaune-Demeule, 'De Chirico Revisited: The Enigma of Creation in V. S. Naipaul's *The Enigma of Arrival*', *Commonwealth*, 22, 2 (2000), pp.107–18.
32. V. S. Naipaul, *Reading & Writing*, op. cit, p.17.
33. V. S. Naipaul, 'Prologue to an Autobiography', *Finding the Centre*, Harmondsworth, Middlesex: Penguin Books, 1985, pp.35–36.
34. See L. Loh, op. cit., pp.151–61, for a useful account of 'connective triangulated threads between rural India, rural Trinidad and rural England' in the book.
35. V. S. Naipaul, *Reading & Writing*, p. 37.
36. Ibid., p.35.
37. V. S. Naipaul, *An Area of Darkness*, Harmondsworth, Middlesex: Penguin, 1968, p.30.
38. V. S. Naipaul, *India: A Wounded Civilization*, Harmondsworth, Middlesex: Penguin, 1979, p.10.
39. V. S. Naipaul, *India: A Million Mutinies Now*, London: Minerva, 1990, p.517.
40. Ibid., pp.7–8.
41. *An Area of Darkness*, p.266.
42. Eric R. Kandel, *In Search of Memory*, London and New York: W.W. Norton & Co., 2006, p.281.
43. Saint Augustine, *Confessions*, transl. Henry Chadwick, Oxford: Oxford World Classics, 1998, pp.184–88; Oliver Sacks, 'A Matter of Identity', *The Man Who Mistook His Wife For A Hat*, London: Picador, 1986, pp.103–10.
44. Thomas Docherty, 'Now, here, this', *Literature and the Contemporary: Fictions and Theories of the Present*, eds, Roger Luckhurst and Peter Marks, London: Longman, 1999, pp.50–53.

45. V. S. Naipaul, 'Jasmine', *The Overcrowded Barracoon*, p.24.
46. Frank Kermode, 'Memory', *Pieces of My Mind: Writings 1958–2002,* London: Allen Lane, 2003, p.296.
47. Jean-Jacques Rousseau, *Confessions*,1782–89, transl. Angela Scholar, Oxford: Oxford University Press World Classics, 2000, p.5.
48. Qtd in Charles Nicholl, *Somebody Else: Arthur Rimbaud in Africa 1880–91*, London: Vintage, 1998, p.12.
49. Primo Levi, *The Drowned and the Saved*, transl. R. Rosenthal, London: Abacus, 1985, p.12.
50. V. S. Naipaul, *The Middle Passage*, 1962, Harmondsworth, Middlesex: Penguin, 1985, p.29.
51. V. S. Naipaul, *A Way in the World: A Sequence*, London: Minerva, 1995, p.73.

Notes to Chapter 3

1. [Diä!kwain/David Hoesar],'Bushman Notebook', [William Bleek/Lucy Lloyd] [unpublished], L.V. 15, p.5104.
2. Claude Levi-Strauss, *Tristes Tropiques*, 1955, transl. John and Doreen Weightman, New York: Penguin Books, 1992, p.414.
3. See Alan Barnard, *Hunters and Herders of Southern Africa: A Comparative Ethnography of the Khoisan Peoples*, Cambridge: Cambridge University Press, 1992, pp.7–12; Shane Moran, *Representing Bushmen: South Africa and the Origin of Language*, Rochester, NY: University of Rochester Press, 2009, pp.3–6.
4. Edwin Wilmsen, 'To See Ourselves as We Need to See Us: Ethnography's Primitive Turn in the Early Cold War Years', with commentaries and responses, ed. Joost Fontein, *Critical African Studies*, Issue 1 (June 2009) p.4; pp.1–76: http://www.criticalafricanstudies.ed.ac.uk/index.php/cas/issue/view/3 accessed 1 Nov. 2009.
5. Peter Ackroyd, *T. S. Eliot*, London: Hamish Hamilton, 1984, p.88.
6. *Global Diasporas: An Introduction*, London: UCL Press, 1997, pp.174–75.
7. Benedict Anderson, *Imagined Communities*, rev. edn London: Verso, 1991, pp.204–05.
8. See C. J. Wickham, *Constructing Heimat in Postwar Germany*, Lewiston, NY: The Edwin Mellen Press, 1999.
9. Terence Ranger, 'The Invention of Tradition in Colonial Africa', in E. J. Hobsbawm and T. Ranger, eds, *The Invention of Tradition*, 1983, Cambridge: Cambridge University Press, 1992, p.211.
10. Rosemary Marangoly George, *The Politics of Home: Postcolonial Relocations and Twentieth-Century Fiction*, Berkeley and Los Angeles: University of California Press, 1999.
11. See Alison Blunt and Robyn Dowling, *Home*, London: Routledge, 2006, pp.140–95.
12. See E. Boa and R. Palfreyman, *Heimat: A German Dream: Regional Loyalties and National Identity in German Culture 1890–1990*, Oxford: Oxford University Press, 2000, p.5.
13. Laurens van der Post, *The Lost World of the Kalahari*, 1958, London: Vintage, 2004, p.11.

14. See Reinhart Kössler, 'Public Memory, Reconciliation and the Aftermath of War', ed. Henning Melber, *Re-examining Liberation in Namibia: Political Culture Since Independence*, Stockholm: Nordiska Afrikainstitutet, 2003, pp.99–112.
15. van der Post, op. cit., p.59.
16. Athol Fugard, *Notebooks: 1960–1977*, ed. Mary Benson, London: Faber and Faber, 1983, p.22.
17. William James, *The Varieties of Religious Experience*, 1902, London/New York: Collier Macmillan, 1961, p.43.
18. Van der Post, op. cit., pp.30–31.
19. Qtd in J.D.F. Jones, *Storyteller: The Many Lives of Laurens van der Post*, London: Murray, 2001, p.227. As Jones points out, there were certainly at one time many Bushmen near van der Post's hometown of Philippolis, just north of the Orange River (p.212).
20. Laurens van der Post, 'A Region of Shadow', *The Listener*, 5 August 1971, pp.168–70.
21. For a further analysis of van der Post from a sympathetic, informed perspective, see Edwin Wilmsen's *Land Filled with Flies: A Political Economy of the Kalahari*, Chicago: Chicago University Press, 1989; and 'Primitive Politics in Sanctified Landscapes: The Ethnographic Fictions of Laurens van der Post', *Journal of Southern African Studies*, 21 (1995), pp.201–23.
22. Michael Cope, *Intricacy: A Meditation on Memory*, Cape Town: Double Storey Books, 2005, pp.138–39.
23. Qtd in Lotte Hughes, *The No-Nonsense Guide to Indigenous Peoples*, London: Verso, 2003, p.39.
24. Qtd in Andrew Bank, *Bushmen in a Victorian World: The Remarkable Story of the Bleek–Lloyd Collection of Bushman Folklore*, Cape Town: Double Storey, 2006, pp.39–40.
25. Olive Schreiner, *The Story of an African Farm*, 1883, ed. J. Bristow, Oxford: World's Classics, 1992, chap. 2, pp.10,16.
26. Qtd Leon Rousseau, *The Dark Stream: The Story of Eugène Marais*, Johannesburg: Jonathan Ball, 1999, p.266.
27. Op. cit., p.5.
28. J. M. Coetzee, *White Writing: The Culture of Letters in South Africa*, New Haven and London: Yale University Press, 1989, p.177.
29. J. M. Coetzee, *In the Heart of the Country*, Harmondsworth, Middlesex: Penguin Books, 1977, pp.136–38.
30. For a good survey of Coetzee criticism, see Dominic Head, *The Cambridge Introduction to J. M. Coetzee*, Cambridge: Cambridge University Press, 2009.
31. Foreword, Sandy Gall, *The Bushmen of Southern Africa: Slaughter of the Innocent*, London: Pimlico, 2002, p.xvi.
32. *South Africa: Historical Introduction*, Harmondsworth, Middlesex: Penguin, 1975, p.11.
33. Tom Nairn, *The Break-up of Britain: Crises and Neo-Nationalism*, London: New Left Books, 1997, p.348.
34. As Linda Colley shows in *Britons: Forging the Nation 1707–1837*, London: Pimlico, 1992.
35. The Azanian People's Organisation, an off-shoot of the Pan African Congress: in the 1999 elections, AZAPO managed only a single seat; but it survives to this day (see www.azapo.org.za/) accessed 15 December 2009

36. Shula Marks and Stanley Trapido, *The Politics of Race, Class and Nationalism in Twentieth Century South Africa*, New York: Longmans, 1987, p.1.
37. See Allister Sparks, *The Mind of South Africa*, London: Heinemann, 1990, pp.177–79.
38. Leonard Thompson, *A History of South Africa*, 3rd edn., New Haven and London: Yale University Press, 2001, pp.191–95.
39. See Marc Ferro, *The Use and Abuse of History, or How the Past is Taught to Children*, 1981, rev edn., transl. Norman Stone and Andrew Brown, London & New York: Routledge, 2000, pp.14–15.
40. See http://www.independent.co.uk/news/world/africa/apartheids-last-stand-757717.html; http://www.afrol.com/articles/11036 both accessed Dec. 2009.
41. Michael Chapman, ed., *The Paperbook of South African English Poetry*, Parklands, South Africa: Ad Donker, 1990, p.33.
42. Qtd Guy Butler, ed., *A Book of South African Verse*, London: Oxford University Press, 1959, p.2, note 1.
43. See Michael Chapman, *Southern African Literatures*, London and New York: Longman, 1996, p.98.
44. See Michael Chapman, *Paperbook of South African Poetry*, p.36.
45. Quoted by Annie Gagiano, '"By what authority?" Presentations of the Khoisan in South African English Poetry', http://singh.reshma.tripod.com/alternation/alternation6_1/11GAGI.htm accessed 27 Aug. 2008.
46. The best account is in Robert J. Gordon and Stuart Sholto Douglas, *The Bushman Myth,* 2nd edn., Boulder, CO, Oxford: Westview Press.
47. See A. Jones, Introduction, *The First Bushman's Path: Stories, Songs and Testimonies of the /Xam of the Northern Cape*, Pietermaritzburg: University of Natal Press, 2001, pp.15–27.
48. J. Cope and U. Krige, eds, *The Penguin Book of South African Verse*, Harmondsworth, Middlesex: Penguin Books, 1968, p.18.
49. See Robert J. Gordon, '"Captured on Film": Bushmen and the Claptrap of Performative Primitives', in Paul S. Landau and Deborah D. Kaspin, eds, *Images and Empires: Visuality in Colonial and Postcolonial Africa*, London, Berkeley: University of California Press, 2002, pp.212–32.
50. 'Dai-Kwain' [sic], 'The Broken String', in Jack Cope and Uys Krige, eds, *The Penguin Book of South African Verse*, p.248.
51. Stephen Watson, *Return of the Moon: Versions of the /Xam*, Cape Town: The Carrefour Press, 1991, pp.59–60.
52. See W.H.I Bleek and L. C. Lloyd, *Specimens of Bushman Folklore*, 1911, ed. L. C. Lloyd, intro. George McCall Theal, reptd London: Bibliobazaar, 2007, p.134. A facsimile reprint.
53. Stephen Watson, 'A Version of Melancholy', *Selected Essays 1980–1990*, Cape Town: The Carrefour Press, 1990, p.176.
54. Duncan Brown, *Voicing the Text: South African Oral Poetry and Performance*, Cape Town: Oxford University Press, 1998, pp.67–70.
55. Op. cit., pp.71–73.
56. Stephen Finn and Rosemary Gray, eds, *Broken Strings: The Politics of Poetry in South Africa*, Cape Town: Maskew Miller Longman,1992, pp.iii,v, 134–35.
57. Qtd in Martin Legassick, 'From Prisoners to Exhibits: Representations of "Bushmen" of the Northern Cape, 1880–1900', in Annie Coombs, ed. *Rethinking Settler Colonialism*, Manchester: Manchester University Press, 2006, p.66.

58. See Dorian Haarhof, *The Wild South-West: Frontier Myths and Metaphors in Literature Set in Namibia 1760–1988*, Johannesburg: Witwatersrand University Press, 1991, pp.172–73.
59. See George Steinmetz, *The Devil's Handwriting: Precoloniality and the German Colonial State in Qingdao, Samoa, and Southwest Africa*, Chicago and London: University of Chicago Press, 2007, pp.135ff. Steinmetz considers the link between German colonial policies and Nazism to be overplayed.
60. See Elena Bregin, 'Miscast; Bushmen in the Twentieth Century', *Current Writing*, 13, 1 (2001), pp.99–101 for a good account of the exhibition and the reactions to it.
61. N. Bennun, *The Broken String: The Last Words of an Extinct People*, London: Viking Penguin, 2004, p.1.
62. Zoë Wicomb, *Playing in the Light*, New York: The New Press, 2006, pp.183–84.
63. See Antjie Krog, 'It Takes a Lot of God to Survive Here', in Paul Weinberg, ed., *Once We Were Hunters*, Cape Town: David Philip, Amsterdam: Mets & Schilt, 2000, pp.55–72.
64. A. Krog, *the stars say 'tsau'*, Cape Town: Kwela Books, 2004, p.11; blurb, the words of Gus Ferguson.
65. Krog, op. cit., p.13.
66. An issue developed by Michael Wessels, 'Antjie Krog, Stephen Watson and the Metaphysics of Presence', *Current Writing*, 19 (2). 2007
67. Krog, op. cit., p.9.
68. Bank, op. cit., p.262.
69. Duncan Brown, *To Speak of this Land: Identity and Belonging in South Africa and Beyond*, Scottsville: University of KwaZulu-Natal Press, 2006, p.xiii. For Brown, Bushman rock art represents 'a script of belonging' (p.22).
70. See Dan Wylie, '"Now Strangers Walk in that Place": Antjie Krog, Modernity, and the Making of //Kabbo's Story', *Current Writing*, 19, 2 (2007), 49–71.
71. See Dennis Walder, *Athol Fugard*, Horndon, Tavistock: 2003, chapter 5.
72. Alan Barnard, 'Coat of Arms and the Body Politic: Khoisan Imagery and the South African National Identity', *Ethnos: Journal of Anthropology*, 69, 1 (March 2004), pp.5–22.
73. See http://www.info.gov.za/aboutgovt/symbols/coa/index.htm for Mbeki's speech and related information, including an image of the new National Coat of Arms, accessed 22 Feb. 2005.
74. Pippa Skotnes, 'The Legacy of Bleek and Lloyd', in Pippa Skotnes, ed., *The Archive of Wilhelm Bleek and Lucy Lloyd: Claim to the Country*, Athens, OH; Auckland Park, South Africa: Ohio University Press and Jacana Media, 2007, p.72. This massive and copiously illustrated book is itself another example of nostalgic (attempted) restitution.
75. Fred Bridgland, 'Bushmen Win the Right to Go Home', *The Times*, 14 Dec. 2006, p.43.
76. For an initial comparative discussion, see: Terence Ranger, '"Great Spaces Washed with Sun": The Matopos and Uluru Compared', in Kate Darian-Smith, Liz Gunner, Sarah Nuttall, eds, *Text, Theory, Space,* London and New York: Routledge, 1996, pp.157–71.
77. See Andy Smith, Candy Malherbe et al., *The Bushmen of Southern Africa*, Claremont, Cape and Athens, OH: David Philip and Ohio University Press, 2000, pp.91–99.

Notes to Chapter 4

1. Doris Lessing, *Under My Skin: Volume One of My Autobiography*, London: Flamingo, 1995, pp.185, 195.
2. In Paul Schlueter, ed., *A Small Personal Voice: Essays, Reviews, Interviews*, London: Flamingo, 1994, p.50.
3. See Ibid., pp.161–84; 207–16.
4. Doris Lessing, 'Desert Child', *New Statesman* 15 Nov. 1958, 700.
5. J. M. Coetzee, *White Writing: On the Culture of Letters in South Africa*, New Haven and London: Yale University Press, 1988, pp.4–6 and passim.
6. Doris Lessing, *African Laughter: Four Visits to Zimbabwe*, London: Flamingo, 1993, p.426.
7. *The Poetics of Space*, 1958, transl. M. Jolas, Boston: Beacon Press, 1969, pp.8–9.
8. Fredric Jameson, *Postmodernism, Or the Cultural Logic of Late Capitalism*, Durham, NC: Duke University Press, 1991, p.20.
9. See http://www.info.gov.za/speeches/2004/04111808451002.htm accessed 7 June 2008.
10. See Wole Soyinka, *Myth, Literature and the African World*, 1978, Cambridge: Cambridge University Press, 2000, Preface, and pp.126–34.
11. Chinua Achebe, 'Thoughts on the African Novel', 1973, reptd in *Hopes and Impediments: Selected Essays*, New York: Doubleday Anchor, 1989, pp.92–93, 99.
12. 'Preface for the 1964 Collection', *This Was the Old Chief's Country: Collected African Stories, Volume One*, London: Flamingo, 2003, pp.7–8.
13. Lorna Sage, *Doris Lessing*, London and New York: Methuen, 1983, p.77.
14. *African Laughter*, p.11.
15. See C. J. Driver, 'Profile 8: Doris Lessing', *The New Review*, 1, 8 (Nov. 1974): 17–23.
16. *Under My Skin*, p.383.
17. Ibid., pp. 218,384.
18. See Doris Lessing, 'The Small Personal Voice', 1957, reptd in Doris Lessing, *A Small Personal Voice*, ed. Paul Schlueter, London: Flamingo, 1994, pp.7–25; Margaret Drabble, 'Ahead of Her Time', *Guardian Saturday Review*, 6 Dec. 2008, p.19.
19. For a good brief account of Africa's earlier civilisations, see Roland Oliver and J. D. Fage, *A Short History of Africa*, many editions, Harmondsworth: Penguin, 1962 and subsequent.
20. *Mara and Dann*, London: Flamingo, 1999, p.166.
21. Ibid., pp.168–69.
22. 'Lessing's Work: Mara and Dann', BBC World Service (interview), http://www.bbc.co.uk/worldservice/arts/features/womenwriters/lessing_work.shtml accessed 7 June 2007.
23. Svetlana Boym, *The Future of Nostalgia*, New York: Basic Books, 2001, p.351.
24. Quoted on the flyleaf, *The Memoirs of a Survivor*, London: Picador, 1976.
25. Doris Lessing, *Under My Skin*, pp.12–13.
26. Doris Lessing, *Martha Quest*, 1952, London: Flamingo, 1993, p.35.
27. Ibid., pp.75; 272;189–90;163.
28. Doris Lessing, *A Proper Marriage*, 1954, London: Flamingo, pp.169–70.
29. Doris Lessing *The Golden Notebook*, 1962, London: Flamingo, 2002, p.414.

30. Doris Lessing, *Walking in the Shade*, p.308.
31. Ibid., p.309. For a good account of how the novel continues to exert an impact as a critique of gender relations, see Louise Yelin, *From the Margins of Empire: Christina Stead, Doris Lessing, Nadine Gordimer*, New York: Cornell University Press, pp.71–90.
32. Roberta Rubinstein, *Home Matters: Longing and Belonging, Nostalgia and Mourning in Women's Fiction*, New York: Palgrave, 2001, pp.20–21.
33. Doris Lessing, *The Golden Notebook*, London: Flamingo, 2002, pp.147–48.
34. Doris Lessing, *African Laughter: Four Visits to Zimbabwe*, London: Flamingo, 1993, pp.314–15; 318 (Lessing's ellipsis).
35. Doris Lessing, 'Desert Child', p.700.
36. *Under My Skin*, p.160.
37. Eve Bertelsen, 'Veldtanschauung: Doris Lessing's Savage Africa', *Modern Fiction Studies*, 37, 4 (Winter 1991), 657 (647–58).
38. Doris Lessing, *The Grass is Singing*, 1950, London: Flamingo, 2000, p.198.
39. Qtd in Eve Bertelsen, 'Interview with Doris Lessing', 9 Jan. 1984, Eve Bertelsen, ed., *Doris Lessing*, Johannesburg: McGraw-Hill Book Company, 1985, p.102 (93–118).
40. Andrew Foley defends Paton against this criticism in *The Imagination of Freedom*, Johannesburg: Wits University Press, 2009, pp.53–71.
41. Karen Blixen (Isak Dinesen), *Out of Africa*, London: Penguin Classics, 2001, p.92.
42. Ibid, p.319.
43. Ibid., p.284.
44. Ibid., p.319.
45. Ibid., pp.122, 141, 178.
46. Ibid., p.319.
47. Judith Thurman, *Isak Dinesen: The Life of a Storyteller*, New York: St Martin's Press, 1982, p.127.
48. Ruth Mayer, *Artificial Africas: Colonial Images in the Times of Globalization*, Hanover and London: University Press of New England, 2002, p.132. See also Fredric Jameson, *Postmodernism: or, the Cultural Logic of Late Capitalism*, Durham: Duke University Press, 1990, p.19.
49. Doris Lessing, 'The Old Chief Mshlanga', *This Was the Old Chief's Country: Collected African Stories, Volume One*, London: Flamingo, 2003, pp.13–14.
50. Ibid., p.17.
51. Doris Lessing, *Going Home*, London: Flamingo, 1992, p.8.
52. See Lessing's story 'Eldorado', *This Was the Old Chief's Country*, pp.299–355.
53. See Michael Thorpe, *Doris Lessing's Africa*, London: Evans Brothers Limited, 1978, pp.22–24, for a good account of this background.
54. 'The Old Chief Mshlanga', p.20.
55. Ian Holding, *Unfeeling*, London: Pocket Books, 2006, p.113, for example. And see Ranka Primorac on recent Zimbabwean fiction as an expression on the lack of 'spatio-temporal' rights in the country: *The Place of Tears: The Novel and Politics in Modern Zimbabwe*, London: Tauris Academic Studies, 2006.
56. Ibid., p.23.
57. Doris Lessing, 'The Tragedy of Zimbabwe', *Time Bites: Views and Reviews*, London: Harper, p.237.

58. Ibid., p.25.
59. Doris Lessing, Preface, 1971, *The Golden Notebook*, London: Flamingo, 2002, p.14.
60. 'Doris Lessing, 'The History of *The Golden Notebook*'s Troubled Reception', *Guardian Review*, 27 Jan. 2007, p.7.
61. Doris Lessing, *'The Sufis'*, *Time Bites: Views and Reviews*, London: Harper Perennial, 2005, p.266.
62. George Steiner, *Nostalgia for the Absolute*, 1974, Concord, Ontario: House of Anansi Press, 1997, p.48.
63. Qtd Gillian Stead Eilersen, *Bessie Head: Thunder Behind her Ears*, Claremont, South Africa: David Philip, 1995, p.189.
64. Bessie Head, *A Question of Power*, London: Heinemann Educational Books, 1974, p.206.

Notes to Chapter 5

1. 1941, qtd in *Hitler in Colour*, DVD dir David Batty, September 2005.
2. Frantz Fanon, *Black Skin, White Masks*, 1962 transl. Charles Lam Markmann, London and Sydney: Pluto Press, 1986, p.122.
3. One exception might have been Stephen Clingman, who however skirts postcolonial issues in his excellent account of Sebald's work as 'transnational', 'uncanny transfiction' in *The Grammar of Identity: Transnational Fiction and the Nature of the Boundary*, Oxford: Oxford University Press, 2009, pp.167–204.
4. Niall Ferguson, *Colossus: The Rise and Fall of the American Empire*, London: Penguin, 2005, pp.171–73; 286–89.
5. *Preface*, Frantz Fanon, *The Wretched of the Earth*, 1961, transl. Constance Farrington, Harmondsworth, Middlesex: Penguin, 1967, p.21.
6. See Larissa Förster, Dag Henrichsen, Michael Bollig, eds, *Namibia-Deutschland: Eine Geteilte Geschichte*, Wolfratshausen: Minerva, 2004.
7. For further discussion, see: Dennis Walder, 'Literature, Memory and Nation', *War, Culture and Memory*, eds Clive Emsley, Milton Keynes: The Open University, 2003, pp.69–102.
8. Eva Hoffman, *After Such Knowledge: Memory, History and the Legacy of the Holocaust*, New York: Public Affairs Press, 2004, pp.119–20.
9. Bill Ashcroft, 'The Rhizome of Post-colonial Discourse', *Literature and the Contemporary*, eds Roger Luckhurst and Peter Marks, Harlow, Essex: Pearson Education, 1999, p.116.
10. Hannah Arendt, *The Origins of Totalitarianism*, new edn., New York: Harvest/Harcourt, Inc., 1976, p.185.
11. See Robert Eaglestone, *The Holocaust and the Postmodern*, Oxford: Oxford University Press, 2008, pp.343–44.
12. Wibke Bruhns, *My Father's Country: The Story of a German Family*, 2004, transl. Shaun Whiteside, London: Arrow Books, 2009, pp.50–51, 267.
13. Elizabeth Harvey, 'Management and Manipulation: Nazi Settlement Planners and Ethnic German Settlers in Occupied Poland', in *Settler Colonialism in the Twentieth Century*, eds Caroline Elkins and Susan Pedersen, London: Routledge, 2005, pp.95–112.
14. *'Exterminate all the Brutes': One Man's Odyssey into the Heart of Darkness*, London/New York: The New Press, 1992, p.10.

15. Wibke Bruhns, *My Father's Journey*, p.51.
16. See Michael Hardt and Antonio Negri, *Empire*, Cambridge, MA: Harvard University Press, 2000. Their views have been subject to considerable debate.
17. See Matthew Jefferies, *Contesting the German Empire 1871–1918*, Oxford: Blackwell, 2008, pp.172–78.
18. See Ernestine Schlant, *The Language of Silence: West German Literature and the Holocaust*, London: Routledge, 1999, pp.8–9.
19. See Michael Hamburger, *The Truth of Poetry*, Harmondsworth, Middlesex: Penguin, 1969, pp.320–25.
20. George Steiner, 'The Hollow Miracle', *Language and Silence: Essays 1958–1966*, 1959, Harmondsworth, Middlesex: Peregrine Books, 1979, pp.150–51.
21. W. G. Sebald, 'Between History and Natural History', 1982, in *Campo Santo*, London: Hamish Hamilton, 2005, p.95.
22. See Tony Judt, *Postwar: A History of Europe Since 1945*, London: William Heinemann, 2005, p.274.
23. See Alan Watson, *The Germans: Who Are They Now?* London: Mandarin, 1994, p.134.
24. Qtd Arthur Lubow, 'Crossing Boundaries' (2002), in *The Emergence of Memory: Conversations with W. G. Sebald*, ed. Lynne Sharon Schwartz, New York: Seven Stories Press, 2007, p.162.
25. Qtd Maya Jaggi, 'The Last Word' (interview), *Guardian G2*, 21 Dec. 2001, p.4.
26. Qtd Jaggi, 'The Last Word', *Guardian G2*, p.4.
27. See Lise Patt, ed., *Searching for Sebald: Photography after W. G. Sebald*, Los Angeles: Institute of Cultural Inquiry, 2007, for a series of essays on the visual dimension of his work.
28. All quotations in what follows from: W. G. Sebald, *The Emigrants*, 1993, transl. Michael Hulse, London: Vintage, 2002.
29. See John Zilcosky, 'Sebald's Uncanny Travels', in *W. G. Sebald—A Critical Companion*, eds J. J. Long and Anne Whitehead, Seattle: University of Washington Press, 2004, p.113.
30. Zilcosky, p.113.
31. W. G. Sebald, *Vertigo*, 1990, transl. Michael Hulse, London: Vintage, 2002, p.185.
32. Interview, 7 October 2001, qtd Christopher Bigsby, *Remembering and Imagining the Holocaust: The Chain of Memory* (Cambridge: Cambridge University Press, 2006), p.60.
33. Qtd in Jaggi, 'The last word', p.4.
34. All quotations following from W. G. Sebald, *The Rings of Saturn*, 1995, transl. Michael Hulse, London: The Harvill Press, 1999.
35. Adam Hochschild, *King Leopold's Ghost: A Story of Greed, Terror and Heroism in Colonial Africa*, updated edn., London: Pan Books, 2006, p.294.
36. Jennifer Wenzel, 'Remembering the Past's Future: Anti-imperialist Nostalgia and Some Versions of the Third World', *Cultural Critique*, 62 (Winter 2006), p.7.
37. 'Author's Note', 1917, in Joseph Conrad, *Heart of Darkness and Other Tales*, ed. Cedric Watts, Oxford: World's Classics, 2008, p.189.
38. Ian Watt, *Conrad in the Nineteenth Century*, London: Chatto & Windus, 1980, p.138.
39. André Aciman, 'Out of Novemberland', *The New York Review of Books*, 45, 19 (3 Dec. 1998), 6–7.

40. Quotations are taken from W. G. Sebald, *Austerlitz*, transl. Anthea Bell, London: Hamish Hamilton, 2001, p.9.
41. W. G. Sebald, 'Between History and Natural History', *Campo Santo*, p.77.
42. Qtd Maya Jaggi, 'Recovered Memories', *The Guardian*, 22 Sept. 2001: http://www.guardian.co.uk/books/2001/sep/22/artsandhumanities/ accessed 31 July 2009, p.8.
43. Tzvetan Todorov, *Hope and Memory: Reflections on the Twentieth Century*, transl. David Bellos, London: Atlantic Books, 2005, pp.117–18; 127.
44. Qtd Christopher Bigsby, ed., *Writers in Conversation*, Norwich: Pen and Inc Press, vol. II, p.144
45. 'Reading Room: Erosion and Sedimentation in Sebald's Suffolk', in *W. G. Sebald–A Critical Companion*, eds J. J. Long and Anne Whitehead, Seattle: University of Washington Press, 2004, pp.76, 86.
46. Qtd Jaggi, 'Recovered Memories, 2001, pp.3, 8. Sebald also changed the name Aurach to Ferber for the artist in the English version of *The Rings of Saturn*, since he was to some extent modelled on Frank Auerbach, who objected. See also Clingman, *The Grammar of Identity*, pp.193–95.
47. Qtd Jaggi, 'The Last Word', p.5.

Notes to Chapter 6

1. Christopher Okigbo, 'Elegy for Slit-Drum', 1964, in *The Heinemann Book of African Poetry in English*, selected by Adewale Maja-Pearce, 1990, London: Heinemann, p.28.
2. Jean Starobinski, 'The Idea of Nostalgia', transl. William S. Kemp, *Diogenes*, 54, 1966, p.103.
3. Ngugi wa Thiong'o, *Decolonising the Mind: The Politics of Language in African Literature*, 1986, Oxford, Nairobi, Portsmouth, NH: James Currey/Heinemann, 2006, p.85.
4. 'Out of Nigeria', *South Bank Show*, UK ITV1, 10 May 2009.
5. Wole Soyinka, *The Climate of Fear: The Reith Lectures 2004*, London: Profile Books, 2004, p.79.
6. Martin Meredith, *The State of Africa: A History of Fifty Years of Independence*, London: The Free Press, 2006, p.580.
7. Achille Mbembe, *On the Postcolony*, Berkeley and Los Angeles, and London: University of California Press, 2001, p.12.
8. Frantz Fanon, *The Wretched of the Earth*, 1961, transl. Constance Farrington, Harmondsworth, Middlesex: Penguin, 1967, p.200.
9. Frederick Cooper, *Colonialism in Question: Theory, Knowledge, History*, Berkeley, CA: University of California Press, 2005, pp.88–89.
10. See Ato Quayson, 'Realism, Criticism and the Disguises of Both: A Reading of Chinua Achebe's *Things Fall Apart*', *Research in African Literatures*, 25, 4 (Winter 1994), pp.117–36.
11. Tim Woods, *African Pasts: Memory and History in African Literatures*, Manchester and New York: Manchester University Press, 2007, p.3.
12. See Meredith, *State of Africa*, p.677.
13. André Brink, 'Stories of History: Reimagining the Past in Post-apartheid Narrative', in Sarah Nuttall and Carli Coetzee, eds, *Negotiating the Past: The*

Making of Memory in South Africa, Cape Town: Oxford University Press, 1998, pp.30–33.
14. Aimé Césaire, *Cahier d'un retour au pays natal/Notebook of a Return to my Native Land*, 1939, Bilingual Edition, transl. Mireille Rosello with Annie Pritchard, Tarset, Northumberland: Bloodaxe Books, 1995, p.84.
15. See Elleke Boehmer, 'Stories of Women and Mothers: Gender and Nationalism in the Early Fiction of Flora Nwapa' and C. L. Innes, 'Mothers or Sisters? Identity, Discourse and Audience in the Writing of Ama Ata Aidoo and Mariama Bâ', in Susheila Nasta, ed. *Motherlands: Black Women's Writing from Africa, the Caribbean and South Asia*, London: The Women's Press, 1991, pp.3–23; 129–51; Gay Wilentz, *Binding Cultures: Black Women Writers in Africa and the Diaspora*, Bloomington: Indiana University Press, 1992; and Stephanie Newell, 'Feminism and Women's Writing', *West African Literatures: Ways of Reading*, Oxford: Oxford University Press, 2006, pp.136–58.
16. Quoted in Mineke Schipper, 'Mother Africa on a Pedestal: The Male Heritage in African Literature and Criticism', in Eldred Jones, Eustace Palmer, and Marjorie Jones, eds, *Women in African Literature Today*, London: James Currey, 1987, p.47.
17. Lily Mabura goes so far as to see Adichie's texts as derivative of European Gothic: Lily G. N. Mabura, 'Breaking Gods: An African Postcolonial Gothic Reading of Chimamanda Ngozi Adichie's *Purple Hibiscus* and *Half of a Yellow Sun*', *Research in African Literatures*, 39, 1 (Winter 2008), 203–22.
18. Salman Rushdie, 'Imaginary Homelands', 1982, *Imaginary Homelands: Essays and Criticism 1981–1991*, London: Granta Books, 1991, p.10.
19. 'Reinventing Home: Michael Ondaatje & Chimamanda Ngozi Adichie', *Pen America 7: World Voices*, 2005, http://www.pen.org/viewmedia.php/prmMID/1420/prmID/1644 accessed 20 Aug. 2009.
20. Chinua Achebe, *Home and Exile*, New York: Oxford University Press, 2000, pp.1–14.
21. Achebe, *Home and Exile*, p.39.
22. Chinua Achebe, 'The Novelist as Teacher', 1965, reptd in *Hopes and Impediments: Selected Essays*, London and New York: Doubleday Anchor, 1989, p.44.
23. Chinua Achebe, 'The Role of the Writer in a New Nation', 1964, reptd in *African Writers on African Writing*, ed. G. D. Killam, London: Heinemann Educational, 1973, p.9.
24. Chinua Achebe, 'Named for Victoria, Queen of England', 1973, reptd in *Hopes and Impediments: Selected Essays*, p.38.
25. Qtd Clare Garner, 'Profile of Chimamanda Ngozie Adichie', in 'About the Author', Chimamanda Ngozie Adichie, *Purple Hibiscus*, 2004, London: Harper Perennial, 2008, p.3. Quotations in what follows will be from this edition of the novel.
26. Elleke Boehmer, 'Achebe and his Influence in Some Contemporary African Writing', *Interventions*, 11, 2 (2009), p. 148.
27. Chinua Achebe, *Things Fall Apart*, 1958, London: Everyman's Library, 1992, pp.30, 152.
28. F. Abiola Irele, 'The Crisis of Cultural Memory in Chinua Achebe's *Things Fall Apart*', 2001, reptd in F. Abiola Irele, ed., *Things Fall Apart*, London and New York: Norton, 2008, p.459.

29. Sam Durrant, 'Storytellers, Novelists and Postcolonial Melancholia: Displaced Aesthetics in *Things Fall Apart*', in Sam Durrant and Catherine M. Lord, eds, *Essays in Migratory Aesthetics*, Amsterdam-New York: Rodopi, 2007, p.149.
30. Chimamanda Ngozie Adichie, 'Tiny Wonders', 2003, reptd in 'About the Book', in *Purple Hibiscus*, 2008, pp.7–8.
31. 'Reinventing Home', 2005.
32. See, e.g., Ato Quayson, 'Realism, Criticism, and the Disguises of Both, pp.117–36.
33. Brenda Cooper, *A New Generation of African Writers*, Pietermaritzburg: University of KwaZulu-Natal Press, 2008, p.120.
34. See Ibid., pp.116–17.
35. Helen Dunmore, 'Half of a Yellow Sun by Chimamanda Ngozi Adichie', *The Times*, 26 Aug. 2006: http://entertainment.timesonline.co.uk/tol/arts_and_entertainment/books/fiction/article61863 accessed 15 Sept. 2009.
36. Chinua Achebe, *The Trouble with Nigeria*, London: Heinemann Educational Books, 1984, pp.46–47. There is of course a scholarly literature about the Igbo: see for example Elizabeth Isichei, *A History of the Igbo People*, New York: St Martin's Press, 1976.
37. See C. L. Innes, *Chinua Achebe*, Cambridge: Cambridge University Press, 1990, p.109.
38. Chimamanda Ngozi Adichie, 'The Stories of Africa: Q & A with Chimamanda Ngozi Adichie', *Half of a Yellow Sun*, 2006, London: Harper Perennial, 2007, p.2. All subsequent references are to this edition.
39. Chimamanda Adichie, 'Author's Note', *Half of a Yellow Sun*, 2006, London: Fourth Estate, p.435.
40. See Craig McLuckie, *Nigerian Civil War Literature*, New York: Edwin Mellen Press, 1990.
41. John Marx, 'Failed-State Fiction', *Contemporary Literature*, XLIX, 4 (2008), pp.597–633.
42. See Alcinda Honwana, *Child Soldiers in Africa*, Philadelphia: University of Pennsylvania Press, 2007.
43. See Boehmer, op. cit., pp.148–49, for an account of this novel's interest in 'twoness' and twins.
44. Christopher Anyokwu, '"May We Always Remember": Memory and Nationhood in Chimamanda Ngozi Adichie's *Half of a Yellow Sun*', *NTU Studies in Language and Literature*, 20 (Dec. 2008), p.179.
45. This argument is taken up by Brenda Cooper, citing Mamdani, 'Darfur: The Politics of Naming', *The Mail & Guardian*, 16–22 March 2007, in *A New Generation of African Writers*, , Scottsville South Africa: University of KwaZulu-Natal Press, 2008, pp.139–42.
46. Nicola King, *Memory, Narrative, Identity: Remembering the Self*, Edinburgh: Edinburgh University Press, 2000, p.124.
47. Conversation with John Mullan, *Guardian Review Book Club: Chimamanda Ngozie Adichie*, King's Place, London, 13 Oct. 2009.
48. Ibid.
49. Chimamanda Ngozi Adichie, *Half of a Yellow Sun*, 2006, London: Harper Perennial, 2007, pp.423–24. Subsequent quotations are taken from this edition.

186 *Notes*

50. Rob Nixon, 'A Biafran Story', *New York Times*, 1 Oct. 2006, http://www.nytimes.com/2006/10/01/books/review/Nixon.t.html accessed 20 Sept. 2009.
51. Chimamanda Ngozi Adichie, *The Thing Around Your Neck*, London: Fourth Estate, 2009, pp.65,73,125.

Notes to Chapter 7

1. Michel de Montaigne, *Essais*, livre 3, chap 2, 'Du repentir', reptd www.bribes.org/trismegiste/es3ch02.htm accessed 30 Dec. 2009.
2. '"The Next Five Minutes": Literature and History', BBC Open University TV A319/15, 1991.
3. J. G. Ballard, 'A City of Excess' (review), *Daily Telegraph Weekend*, 2 Feb. 1991, p.XV.
4. J. G. Ballard, 'Look Back at Empire', *Saturday Guardian Review*, 4 March 2006, p.14.
5. Guy Debord, *The Society of the Spectacle*, 1967, transl. Donald Nicholson-Smith, New York: Zone Books, 2008.
6. Andrzej Gasiorek, *J. G. Ballard*, Manchester and New York: Manchester University Press, 2005, pp.206–07.
7. Robert Hewison, *The Heritage Industry: Britain in a Climate of Decline*, London: Methuen, 1988, p.135.
8. Angela Carter, quoted inside cover, J. G. Ballard, *Empire of the Sun*, 1984, London: Grafton Books, 1985.
9. Dipesh Chakrabarty, *Provincializing Europe: Postcolonial Thought and Historical Difference*, Princeton: Princeton University Press, 2007.
10. J. G. Ballard, *Miracles of Life: From Shanghai to Shepperton*, London: Fourth Estate, 2008, p.248. Subsequent references are to this edition.
11. J. G. Ballard, 'Airports', *The Observer*, 14 Sept. 1997, http://www.jgballard.com/airports.htm accessed 10 Oct. 2009.
12. J. G. Ballard, *Empire of the Sun*, 1984, London, New York: Harper Perennial, 2006, p.267. Quotations in what follows are from this edition.
13. Richard Jones, 'Lands of Terror', *The Listener*, 20 Sept. 1984, p.27.
14. J. M. Roberts, *Pelican History of the World*, Harmondsworth, Middlesex: Penguin, 1988, p.847.
15. Anne Whitehead, *Memory*, London & New York: Routledge, 2009, pp.148–49.
16. See Alan Munton, *English Fiction of the Second World War*, London: Faber and Faber, 1989; Alison Lee, *Realism and Power: Postmodern British Fiction*, London and New York: 1990.
17. Roger Lewis, 'Lost Boy', *New Statesman*, 21 Sept. 1984, p.29. See also, e.g., Claire Tomalin, 'The Artist as a Young Prisoner', *Sunday Times*, 9 Sept. 1984, p.43, referring to an 'adventure' story; Philip Howard, 'Sharp Eyes Behind the Barbed Wire', *The Times*, 20 Sept. 1984, p.11, comparing it to *Lord of the Flies*; and Julian Symons, 'Unlucky Jim', *London Review of Books*, 10 Oct. 1991, p.16, still calling it an 'adventure story'.
18. *The Listener*, 11 October 1984.
19. Martin Amis, 'Ballard's Worlds', *The Observer*, 2 Sept. 1984, reptd in http://www.jgballard.ca/interviews/observer_amis_1984.html accessed 10 Jan. 2010.

20. One critic sees in Ballard's work a visionary recognition of 'the realm of the eternal': Gregory Stephenson, *Out of the Night and Into the Dream: A Thematic Study of the Fiction of J. G. Ballard*, New York: Greenwood Press, 1991, p.161. This misses the historical, realistic level of his imagination as evinced in *Empire of the Sun*.

Notes to Chapter 8

1. Louis MacNeice, *Selected Poems*, ed. Michael Longley, London: Faber and Faber, 1988, p.v.
2. Judith Wright, Introduction, *Preoccupations in Australian Poetry*, Melbourne: Oxford University Press, 1965, p.xviii.
3. Doris Lessing, *The Golden Notebook*, 1962, London: Flamingo, 2002, p.78.
4. Ibid., p.77.
5. Fredric Jameson, *Signatures of the Visible*, 1992, London and New York: Routledge, 2007, pp.116–17, 124–25, 303–07; see also his 'Postmodernism and Consumer Society', *The Cultural Turn: Selected Writings on the Postmodern, 1983–1998*, London and New York: Verso, 1998, pp.7–10.
6. Andrey Tarkovsky, *Sculpting in Time; Reflections on the Cinema*, 1986, transl. Kitty Hunter-Blair, Austin: University of Texas Press, 1987, pp.204–06.
7. See Sylviane Agacinski, *Time Passing: Modernity and Nostalgia*, transl. Jody Gladding, New York: Columbia University Press, 2003, pp.102–03, 170–71.

Bibliography

Achebe, Chinua ([1958] 1992) *Things Fall Apart*, London: Everyman's Library.
———. ([1964] 1973) 'The Role of the Writer in a New Nation', in *African Writers on African Writing*, ed. G. D. Killam, London: Heinemann Educational: 7–13.
———. ([1965] 1989) 'The Novelist as Teacher', in *Hopes and Impediments: Selected Essays*, London and New York: Doubleday Anchor: 40–46.
———. ([1973] 1989) 'Thoughts on the African Novel', in *Hopes and Impediments: Selected Essays*, New York: Doubleday Anchor: 92–99.
———. ([1973] 1989) 'Named for Victoria, Queen of England', in *Hopes and Impediments: Selected Essays*, London and New York: Doubleday Anchor: 30–39.
———. (1973) *Christmas in Biafra and Other Poems*, New York: Doubleday.
———. (1984) *The Trouble with Nigeria,* London: Heinemann Educational Books.
———. (2000) *Home and Exile*, New York: Oxford University Press.
Aciman, André (1998) 'Out of Novemberland', *The New York Review of Books*, 45 (19), 3 December: 6–7.
Ackroyd, Peter (1984) *T. S. Eliot*, London: Hamish Hamilton.
Adichie, Chimamanda Ngozi ([2003] 2008) 'Tiny Wonders', in 'About the Book', *Purple Hibiscus*: 7–12.
———. ([2004] 2008) *Purple Hibiscus*, London: Harper Perennial.
———. (2005) Interview, 'Reinventing Home: Michael Ondaatje & Chimamanda Ngozi Adichie', *Pen America 7: World Voices* http://www.pen.org/viewmedia.php/prmMID/1420/prmID/1644 accessed 20 August 2009.
———. ([2006]2007) *Half of a Yellow Sun*, London: Harper Perennial.
———. (2007) 'The Stories of Africa: Q & A with Chimamanda Ngozi Adichie', *Half of a Yellow Sun*, London: Harper Perennial.
———. (2009) 'Out of Nigeria', *South Bank Show*, director and interviewer Melvyn Bragg, UK ITV1, 10 May.
———. (2009) Conversation with John Mullan, *Guardian Review Book Club: Chimamanda Ngozie Adichie*, King's Place, London, 13 October.
———. (2009) *The Thing Around Your Neck*, London: Fourth Estate
Agacinski, Sylviane (2003) *Time Passing: Modernity and Nostalgia*, transl. Jody Gladding, New York: Columbia University Press.
Anderson, Benedict (1991) *Imagined Communities*, rev edn London: Verso.
Anyokwu, Christopher (2008) '"May We Always Remember": Memory and Nationhood in Chimamanda Nogozi Adichie's *Half of a Yellow Sun*', *NTU Studies in Language and Literature*, 20 (December): 179–96.
Arendt, Hannah ([1950] 1976) *The Origins of Totalitarianism*, new edn. New York: Harvest/Harcourt, Inc.

Bibliography

Ashcroft, Bill (1999) 'The Rhizome of Post-colonial Discourse', in *Literature and the Contemporary*, eds Roger Luckhurst and Peter Marks, Harlow, Essex: Pearson Education: 111–25.
Ashcroft, Bill, Gareth Griffiths, and Helen Tiffin, eds (1995) *The Post-Colonial Studies Reader*, 2nd edn. Oxford and New York: Routledge.
Augustine, St ([397–400] 1998) *Confessions*, transl. Henry Chadwick, Oxford: Oxford World Classics.
Bachelard, Gaston ([1958] 1969) *The Poetics of Space*, transl. M. Jolas, Boston: Beacon Press.
Bal, Mieke and others, eds (1999) *Acts of Memory: Cultural Recall in the Present*, Hanover, NH, and London: University Press of New England.
Ballard, J. G. ([1984] 2006) *Empire of the Sun*, London, New York: Harper Perennial.
———. (1991) '"The Next Five Minutes": Literature and History', BBC Open University TV A319/15, including documentary extracts.
———. (1991) 'A City of Excess' (review), *Daily Telegraph Weekend*, 2 February: XV
———. (1997) 'Airports', *The Observer*, 14 September http://www.jgballard.com/airports.htm accessed 10 October 2009.
———. (2006) 'Look Back at Empire', *Saturday Guardian Review*, 4 March: 14.
———. (2008) *Miracles of Life: From Shanghai to Shepperton*, London: Fourth Estate.
Bank, Andrew (2006) *Bushmen in a Victorian World: The Remarkable Story of the Bleek-Lloyd Collection of Bushman Folklore*, Cape Town: Double Storey.
Barnard, Alan (1992) *Hunters and Herders of Southern Africa: A Comparative Ethnography of the Khoisan Peoples*, Cambridge: Cambridge University Press.
———. (2004) 'Coat of Arms and the Body Politic: Khoisan Imagery and the South African National Identity, *Ethnos: Journal of Anthropology*, 69 (1): 5–22.
Baronian, Marie-Aude and others, (2007) *Diaspora and Memory*, Amsterdam-New York: Rodopi.
Batty, David, director ([1941] 2005) *Hitler in Colour*, BBC TV documentary, DVD.
Beck, John (2004) 'Reading Room: Erosion and Sedimentation in Sebald's Suffolk', in *W. G. Sebald–A Critical Companion*, eds J.J. Long and Anne Whitehead, Seattle: University of Washington Press: 75–88.
Benjamin, Walter ([1940] 2003) 'Theses on the Philosophy of History', in *Literature in the Modern World*, ed. Dennis Walder, Oxford: Oxford University Press: 434–36.
Bennun, Neil (2004) *The Broken String: The Last Words of an Extinct People*, London: Viking Penguin.
Bertelsen, Eve (1991) 'Veldtanschauung: Doris Lessing's Savage Africa', *Modern Fiction Studies*, 37, 4: 647–58.
Bhabha, Homi (1994) *The Location of Culture*, London and New York: Routledge.
Bigsby, Christopher (2006) *Remembering and Imagining the Holocaust: The Chain of Memory*, Cambridge: Cambridge University Press.
Bleek W.H.I and L. C. Lloyd ([1911] 2007) *Specimens of Bushman Folklore*, ed. L. C. Lloyd, intro. George McCall Theal, facsimile reprint, London: Bibliobazaar.
Blixen, Karen [Isak Dinesen] (2001) *Out of Africa*, London: Penguin.
Blunt, Alison and Robyn Dowling (2006) *Home*, London: Routledge.
Boa, E. and R. Palfreyman (2000) *Heimat: A German Dream: Regional Loyalties and National Identity in German Culture 1890–1990*, Oxford, Oxford University Press.
Boehmer, Elleke (1991)'Stories of Women and Mothers: Gender and Nationalism in the Early Fiction of Flora Nwapa' in Nasta *Motherlands*: 3–23.
———. (2005) *Colonial and Postcolonial Literature*, 2nd edn, Oxford: Oxford University Press.
———. (2009) 'Achebe and his Influence in Some Contemporary African Writing', *Interventions*, 11 (2): 141–53.

Boym, Svetlana (2001) *The Future of Nostalgia*, New York: Basic Books.
Bregin, Elena (2001) 'Miscast: Bushmen in the Twentieth Century', *Current Writing*, 13 (1): 99–101.
Breytenbach, Breyten (1994) 'The Exile as African', in *Altogether Elsewhere: Writers on Exile*, ed. Marc Robinson, Boston and London: Faber and Faber: 179–82.
Bridgland, Fred (2006) 'Bushmen Win the Right to Go Home', *The Times*, 14 December: 43.
Brink, André (1998) 'Stories of History: Reimagining the Past in Post-apartheid Narrative', in *Negotiating the Past: The Making of Memory in South Africa*, Sarah Nuttall and Carli Coetzee, eds, Cape Town: Oxford University Press: 30–33.
———. ([2002] 2003) *The Other Side of Silence*, London: Vintage.
Brown, Duncan (1998) *Voicing the Text: South African Oral Poetry and Performance*, Cape Town: Oxford University Press.
———. (2006) *To Speak of this Land: Identity and Belonging in South Africa and Beyond*, Scottsville: University of KwaZulu-Natal Press.
Bruhns, Wibke ([2004] 2009) *My Father's Country: The Story of a German Family*, transl. Shaun Whiteside, London: Arrow Books.
Bunke, Simon (2009) *Heimweh: Studien zur Kultur- und Literaturgeschichte*, Freiburg im Breisgau.
Butler, Guy, ed. (1959) *A Book of South African Verse*, London: Oxford University Press.
Celan, Paul ([1972] 1996) *Selected Poems*, transl. and intro. Michael Hamburger, London: Penguin.
Césaire, Aimé ([1939] 1995) *Cahier d'un retour au pays natal/Notebook of a Return to my Native Land*, Bilingual Edition, transl. Mireille Rosello with Annie Pritchard, Tarset, Northumberland: Bloodaxe Books.
Chakrabarty, Dipesh (2007) *Provincializing Europe: Postcolonial Thought and Historical Difference*, new edn, Princeton: Princeton University Press.
Chapman, Michael, ed. (1990) *The Paperbook of South African English Poetry*, Parklands, South Africa: Ad Donker.
———. (1996) *Southern African Literatures*, London and New York: Longman.
Chase, Malcolm and Christopher Shaw (1989) 'The Dimensions of Nostalgia', in *The Imagined Past: History and Nostalgia*, eds Shaw and Chase, Manchester and New York: Manchester University Press: 1–94.
Chow, Rey (1993) *Writing Diaspora: Tactics of Intervention in Contemporary Cultural Studies*, Bloomington: Indiana University Press.
Clarke, Gerald (1971) 'The Meaning of Nostalgia', *Time*, 3 May http://www.time.magazine/article/0,8816,876989,00.html accessed 2 December 2009.
Clingman, Stephen (2009) *The Grammar of Identity: Transnational Fiction and the Nature of the Boundary*, Oxford: Oxford University Press.
Coetzee, J. M. (1977) *In the Heart of the Country*, Harmondsworth, Middlesex: Penguin.
———. (1988) *White Writing: On the Culture of Letters in South Africa*, New Haven and London: Yale University Press.
———. (1997) *Boyhood: Scenes from Provincial Life*, London: Secker & Warburg.
———. (2002) *Youth*, London: Secker & Warburg.
———. (2009) *Summertime: Scenes from Provincial Life*, London: Harvill Secker.
Cohen, Robin (1997) *Global Diasporas: An Introduction*, London: UCL Press.
Colley, Linda (1992) *Britons: Forging the Nation 1707–1837*, London: Pimlico.
Conrad, Joseph ([1899] 2007) *Heart of Darkness*, ed. Owen Knowles, London: Penguin Classics.
———. ([1917] 2008) 'Author's Note', in *Heart of Darkness and Other Tales*, ed. Cedric Watts, Oxford: World Classics: 188–89.
Coombes, Annie (2003), *History After Apartheid: Visual Culture and Public Memory in a Democratic South Africa*, Durham & London: Duke University Press.

Cooper, Brenda (2008) *A New Generation of African Writers*, Scottsville: University of KwaZulu-Natal Press.
Cooper, Frederick (2005) *Colonialism in Question: Theory, Knowledge, History*, Berkeley, CA: University of California Press.
Cope Jack and Uys Krige, eds (1968) *The Penguin Book of South African Verse*, Harmondsworth, Middlesex: Penguin Books.
Cope, Michael (2005) *Intricacy: A Meditation on Memory*, Cape Town: Double Storey Books.
D'Aguiar, Fred ([1994] 1995) *The Longest Memory*, London: Vintage.
———. (1997) *Feeding the ghosts*, London: Chatto & Windus.
Damasio, Antonio (1999) *The Feeling of What Happens: Body, Emotion and the Making of Consciousness*, London: William Heinemann.
Dangarembga, Tsitsi ([1988] 2004) *Nervous Conditions*, new intro. Kwame Anthony Appiah, Emeryville, California: Seal Press.
Davis, Fred (1979) *Yearning for Yesterday: A Sociology of Nostalgia*, London and New York: Macmillan: The Free Press.
Debord, Guy ([1967] 2008) *The Society of the Spectacle*, transl. Donald Nicholson-Smith, New York: Zone Books.
Derrida, Jacques ([1967] 1977] *Of Grammatology*, trans. Gayatri Chakravorty Spivak, Baltimore: Johns Hopkins University Press.
[Diä!kwain/David Hoesar] [1875] 'Bushman Notebook' [William Bleek/Lucy Lloyd] [unpublished MS] 28 July L.V.
Dlamini, Jacob (2009) *Native Nostalgia*, Auckland Park, South Africa: Jacana.
Docherty, Thomas (1999) 'Now, Here, This', in *Literature and the Contemporary: Fictions and Theories of the Present*, eds Roger Luckhurst and Peter Marks, London: Longman: 50–62.
Draaisma, Douwe (2004) *Why Life Speeds Up As You Get Older: How Memory Shapes Our Past*, transl. Arnold Pomerans, Cambridge: Cambridge University Press.
Drabble, Margaret (2008) 'Ahead of Her Time', *Guardian Saturday Review*, 6 December: 19.
Driver, C. J. (1974) 'Profile 8: Doris Lessing', *The New Review*, 1 (8): 17–23.
———. (1969) *Elegy for a Revolutionary*, London: Faber and Faber.
Dunmore, Helen (2006) 'Half of a Yellow Sun by Chimamanda Ngozi Adichie', *The Times*, 26 August: http://entertainment.timesonline.co.uk/tol/arts_and_entertainment/books/fiction/article61863 accessed 15 September 2009.
Durrant, Sam (2007) 'Storytellers, Novelists and Postcolonial Melancholia: Displaced Aesthetics in *Things Fall Apart*', in *Essays in Migratory Aesthetics*, eds Sam Durrant and Catherine M. Lord, Amsterdam-New York: Rodopi: 145–60.
Eaglestone, Robert (2008) *The Holocaust and the Postmodern*, Oxford: Oxford University Press.
Edwards, Justin D. (2008), 'Memory', in *Postcolonial Literature*, London: Palgrave Macmillan: 129–38.
Eilersen, Gillian Stead (1995) *Bessie Head: Thunder Behind her Ears*, Claremont, South Africa: David Philip.
Eliot, T. S. ([1923] 1975) '*Ulysses*, Order, and Myth', in *Selected Prose*, ed. Frank Kermode, London: Faber & Faber: 175–78.
———. (1968) *Collected Poems 1909–1962*, London: Faber and Faber Ltd.
Ender, Evelyne (2005) *Architexts of Memory: Literature, Science, and Autobiography*, Ann Arbor: University of Michigan Press.
Fanon, Frantz ([1961] 1967) *The Wretched of the Earth*, transl. Constance Farrington, Harmondsworth, Middlesex: Penguin.
———. ([1952] 1986) *Black Skin, White Masks*, transl. Charles Lam Markmann, foreword Homi Bhabha, London and Sydney: Pluto Press.

Felman, Shoshana and Dor Laub (1992) *Testimony: Crises of Witnessing in Literature, Psychoanalysis, and History*, New York and London: Routledge.
Ferguson, Niall (2005) *Colossus: The Rise and Fall of the American Empire*, London: Penguin.
Ferro, Marc ([1981] 2000) *The Use and Abuse of History, or How the Past is Taught to Children*, rev. edn, transl. Norman Stone and Andrew Brown, London & New York: Routledge.
Finn, Stephen and Rosemary Gray, eds (1992) *Broken Strings: The Politics of Poetry in South Africa*, Cape Town: Maskew Miller Longman.
Förster, Larissa and others, eds (2004) *Namibia-Deutschland: Eine Geteilte Geschichte*, Wolfratshausen: Minerva.
Foley, Andrew (2009) *The Imagination of Freedom*, Johannesburg: Wits University Press.
Frank, Anne ([1947, 1998] 2001) *Diary of a Young Girl, The Definitive Edition*, eds Otto H. Frank and Mirjam Pressler, transl. Susan Massotty, London: Viking.
Freedland, Jonathan (2004) 'Sixty Years On, D-Day Veterans Pass Torch into the Hands of History', *Guardian*, 7 June: 1.
French, Patrick (2009) *The World Is What It Is: The Authorized Biography of V. S. Naipaul*, London: Picador.
Fugard, Athol (1983) *Notebooks: 1960–1977*, ed. Mary Benson, London: Faber and Faber.
Gagiano, Annie (1999) '"By What Authority?", Presentations of the Khoisan in South African English Poetry', A*lternation* 6 (1) http://singh.reshma.tripod.com/alternation/alternation6_1/11GAGI.htm accessed 27 August 2008.
Gall, Sandy (2002) *The Bushmen of Southern Africa: Slaughter of the Innocent*, London: Pimlico.
Garner, Clare (2008) 'Profile of Chimamanda Ngozie Adichie', in 'About the Author', Chimamanda Ngozie Adichie, *Purple Hibiscus*, 2004, London: Harper Perennial: 2–5.
Gasiorek, Andrzej (2005) *J. G. Ballard*, Manchester and New York: Manchester University Press.
George, Rosemary Marangoly (1999) *The Politics of Home: Postcolonial Relocations and Twentieth-Century Fiction*, Berkeley and Los Angeles: University of California Press.
Gilroy, Paul (1993) *The Black Atlantic: Modernity and Double Consciousness*, Cambridge, MA: Harvard University Press.
Godwin, Peter (2007) *When a Crocodile Eats the Sun*, London: Picador.
Gordimer, Nadine ([1953] 1983) *The Lying Days*, London: Virago.
Gordon, Robert J. (2002) '"Captured on Film": Bushmen and the Claptrap of Performative Primitives', in *Images and Empires: Visuality in Colonial and Postcolonial Africa*, eds Paul S. Landau and Deborah D. Kaspin, London, Berkeley: University of California Press: 212–32.
Gordon, Robert J. and Stuart Sholto Douglas (2000) *The Bushman Myth: The Making of a Namibian Underclass*, 2nd edn Boulder, CO, Oxford: Westview Press.
Grass, Günter (2007) *Peeling the Onion*, transl. Michael Henry Heim, London: Harville Secker.
Haarhof, Dorian (1991) *The Wild South-West: Frontier Myths and Metaphors in Literature Set in Namibia 1760–1988*, Johannesburg: Witwatersrand University Press.
Hall, Stuart (1990) 'Cultural Identity and Diaspora', in *Identity: Community, Culture, Difference*, ed. Jonathan Rutherford, London: Lawrence & Wishart: 222–37.
———. (1996) 'Introduction: Who Needs Identity?', in Stuart Hall and Paul du Gay, eds. *Questions of Cultural Identity*, London and New Delhi: Sage: 1–17.
———. (1996) 'When Was "The Post-colonial"? Thinking at the Limit', in *The Post-Colonial Question*, eds Iain Chambers and Lidia Curti, London and New York: Routledge: 242–60.

Hamburger, Michael (1969) *The Truth of Poetry*, Harmondsworth, Middlesex: Penguin.
Hamilton, Carolyn and others, eds (2002) *Refiguring the Archive*, Cape Town, Dordrecht and Norwell, MA: David Philip/Kluwer Academic.
Haneke, Michael, director and scriptwriter (2009), *Das Weisse Band/The White Ribbon*, film, distr. Artificial Eye, DVD.
Hardt, Michael and Antonio Negri (2000) *Empire* Cambridge, MA: Harvard University Press.
Harrison, Nicholas, (2003) *Postcolonial Criticism: History, Theory and the Work of Fiction*, Cambridge: Polity Press.
Harvey, Elizabeth (2005) 'Management and Manipulation: Nazi Settlement Planners and Ethnic German Settlers in Occupied Poland', in *Settler Colonialism in the Twentieth Century*, eds Caroline Elkins and Susan Pedersen, London: Routledge: 95–112.
Hayward, Helen (2002) *The Enigma of V. S. Naipaul*, Houndmills, Basingstoke: Palgrave Macmillan.
Head, Bessie (1974) *A Question of Power*, London: Heinemann Educational Books.
Head, Dominic (2009) *The Cambridge Introduction to J. M. Coetzee*, Cambridge: Cambridge University Press.
Hobsbawm, E. J. (1989) *The Age of Empire: 1875–1914*, London: Abacus.
——— . (2008) *Globalisation, Democracy and Terrorism*, London: Abacus.
[Hofer, Johannes] ([1688] 1934) transl. Carolyn Kiser Anspach, 'Medical Dissertation on Nostalgia by Johannes Hofer, 1688', *Bulletin of the Institute of the History of Medicine*, 2 (1934): 376–91.
Hoffman, Eva (2004) *After Such Knowledge: Memory, History and the Legacy of the Holocaust*, New York: Public Affairs Press.
Hewison, Robert (1988) *The Heritage Industry: Britain in a Climate of Decline*, London: Methuen.
Hochschild, Adam (2006) *King Leopold's Ghost: A Story of Greed, Terror and Heroism in Colonial Africa*, London: Pan Books.
Holding, Ian (2006) *Unfeeling*, London: Pocket Books.
Honwana, Alcinda (2007) *Child Soldiers in Africa*, Philadelphia: University of Pennsylvania Press.
Hughes, Lotte (2003) *The No-Nonsense Guide to Indigenous Peoples*, London: Verso.
Hughes, Robert ([1982] 2001) 'Giorgio de Chirico', in *Nothing if not Critical: Selected Essays on Art and Artists*, London: The Harvill Press: 160–64.
Hulme, Peter (2005) 'Beyond the Straits: Postcolonial Allegories of the Globe', in *Postcolonial Studies and Beyond*, eds Ania Loomba and others, Durham and London: Duke University Press: 41–61.
Hutcheon, Linda (1998) 'Irony, Nostalgia, and the Postmodern', http://www.library.utoronto.ca/utel/criticism/hutchinp/html accessed 22 June 2004.
Huyssen, Andreas (1995) *Twilight Memories: Marking Time in a Culture of Amnesia*, London and New York: Routledge.
——— . (2003) *Present Pasts: Urban Palimpsests and the Politics of Memory*, Stanford: Stanford University Press.
Innes, C. L. (1990) *Chinua Achebe*, Cambridge: Cambridge University Press.
——— . (1991) 'Mothers or Sisters? Identity, Discourse and Audience in the Writing of Ama Ata Aidoo and Mariama Bâ', in *Motherlands: Black Women's Writing from Africa, the Caribbean and South Asia*, ed. Susheila Nasta, London: The Women's Press: 129–51.
Irele, F. Abiola ([2001] 2008) 'The Crisis of Cultural Memory in Chinua Achebe's *Things Fall Apart*', in *Things Fall Apart*, ed. F. Abiola Irele, London and New York: Norton: 453–91.
Isichei, Elizabeth (1976) *A History of the Igbo People*, New York: St Martin's Press.

James, William ([1902] 1961) *The Varieties of Religious Experience*, London/New York: Collier Macmillan.
Jameson, Fredric (1991) *Postmodernism, Or the Cultural Logic of Late Capitalism*, Durham, NC: Duke University Press.
———. ([1992] 2007) *Signatures of the Visible*, London and New York: Routledge.
———. (1998) 'Postmodernism and Consumer Society', *The Cultural Turn: Selected Writings on the Postmodern, 1983-1998*, London and New York: Verso: 7–10.
Jones, Alan (2001) *The First Bushman's Path: Stories, Songs and Testimonies of the /Xam of the Northern Cape*, Pietermaritzburg: University of Natal Press.
Jones, J.D.F. (2001) *Storyteller: The Many Lives of Laurens van der Post*, London: Murray.
Jones, Richard (1984) 'Lands of Terror', *The Listener*, 20 September: 27.
Jefferies, Matthew (2008) *Contesting the German Empire 1871-1918*, Oxford: Blackwell.
Judt, Tony (2005) *Postwar: A History of Europe Since 1945*, London: William Heinemann.
———. (2008) 'À la recherché du temps perdu: *France and Its Pasts*', in *Reappraisals: Reflections on the Forgotten Twentieth Century*, New York: Penguin: 196–218.
Kandel, Eric R. (2006) *In Search of Memory: The Emergence of a New Science of Mind*, London and New York: W.W. Norton & Co.
Kearney, Richard (2002), *On Stories*, London and New York: Routledge.
Kermode, Frank (2003) 'Memory', in *Pieces of My Mind: Writings 1958-2002,* London: Allen Lane: 289–306.
King, Nicola (2000) *Memory, Narrative, Identity: Remembering the Self*, Edinburgh: Edinburgh University Press.
Kössler, Reinhart (2003) 'Public Memory, Reconciliation and the Aftermath of War', in *Re-examining Liberation in Namibia: Political Culture Since Independence*, ed. Henning Melber, Stockholm: Nordiska Afrikainstitutet: 99–112.
Krog, Antjie (1998) *Country of My Skull*, London: Jonathan Cape.
———. (2000) 'It Takes a Lot of God to Survive Here', in *Once We Were Hunters*, ed. Paul Weinberg, Cape Town: David Philip, Amsterdam: Mets & Schilt: 55–72.
———. (2004) *the stars say 'tsau'* [sic], Cape Town: Kwela Books.
Kuhn, Annette (1995) *Family Secrets: Acts of Memory and Imagination*, new edn London and New York: Verso.
Kundera, Milan (2002), *Ignorance*, transl. Linda Asher, London: Faber and Faber.
Labaune-Demeule, Florence (2000) 'De Chirico Revisited: The Enigma of Creation in V. S. Naipaul's *The Enigma of Arrival*', *Commonwealth*, 22 (2): 107–18.
LaCapra, Dominick (1998) *History and Memory After Auschwitz*, Ithaca: Cornell University Press.
———. (2001) *Writing History, Writing Trauma*, Baltimore: Johns Hopkins University Press.
Langer, Lawrence L. (1995) *Admitting the Holocaust: Collected Essays*, New York: Oxford University Press.
Laye, Camera ([1953] 1994) *The Dark Child*, transl. James Kirkup and Ernest Jones, New York: Farrar, Straus and Giroux.
Lazarus, Neil (2002) 'The Politics of Postcolonial Modernism', *The European Legacy: Special Issue: Europe and Post Colonial Narratives*, ed. Rajeev Patke, 7 (6): 771–82.
Lee, Alison (1990) *Realism and Power: Postmodern British Fiction*, London and New York: Routledge.
Legassick, Martin (2006) 'From Prisoners to Exhibits: Representations of "Bushmen" of the Northern Cape, 1880–1900', in *Rethinking Settler Colonialism*, ed. Annie Coombs, Manchester: Manchester University Press.
Lessing, Doris ([1950] 2000) *The Grass is Singing,* London: Flamingo.

——. ([1951] 2003) 'The Old Chief Mshlanga', in *This Was the Old Chief's Country: Collected African Stories, Volume One*, London: Flamingo.
——. ([1952] 1993) *Martha Quest (Children of Violence*, vol. 1), 1952, London: Flamingo.
——. (1954) *A Proper Marriage (Children of Violence*, vol. 2), London: Flamingo.
——. ([1957] 1994) 'The Small Personal Voice', in *A Small Personal Voice: Essays, Reviews, Interviews*, ed. Paul Schlueter, London: Flamingo: 7–25.
——. (1958) 'Desert Child', *New Statesman*, 15 November: 700.
——. ([1962] 2002) *The Golden Notebook*, London: Flamingo.
——. ([1969] 1993) *The Four-Gated City (Children of Violence*, vol. 5), London: Flamingo.
——. (1976) *The Memoirs of a Survivor*, London: Picador .
——. ([1984] 1985) Interview with Eve Bertelsen, ed. *Doris Lessing*, Johannesburg: McGraw-Hill Book Company: 93–118.
——. (1992) *Going Home*, London: Flamingo.
——. (1993) *African Laughter: Four Visits to Zimbabwe*, London: Flamingo.
——. (1995) *Under My Skin: Volume One of My Autobiography, to 1949*, London: Flamingo.
——. ([1997] 1998) *Walking in the Shade: Volume Two of My Autobiography, 1949–1962*, London: Flamingo.
——. (1999) *Mara and Dann*, London: Flamingo.
——. (1999) Interview in 'Lessing's Work: Mara and Dann', BBC World Service http://www.bbc.co.uk/worldservice/arts/features/womenwriters/lessing_work.shtml accessed 7 June 2007.
——. ([2003] 2005) 'The Tragedy of Zimbabwe', *Time Bites: Views and Reviews*, London: Harper Perennial: 231–46.
——. (2005) '*The Sufis*', *Time Bites: Views and Reviews*, London: Harper Perennial: 254–68.
——. (2007) 'The History of *The Golden Notebook*'s Troubled Reception', *Guardian Review*, 27 January: 7.
Levi, Primo (1985) *The Drowned and the Saved*, transl. R. Rosenthal, London: Abacus.
Levi-Strauss, Claude ([1955] 1992) *Tristes Tropiques*, transl. John and Doreen Weightman, New York: Penguin Books.
Lewis, Roger (1984) 'Lost Boy', *New Statesman*, 21 September: 29.
Lindqvist, Sven (1992) *'Exterminate all the Brutes': One Man's Odyssey into the Heart of Darkness*, transl. Joan Tate, London/New York: The New Press.
Loh, Lucienne (2009) 'Rural Routes/Roots: India, Trinidad and England in V. S. Naipaul's *The Enigma of Arrival*', *Journal of Postcolonial Writing*, 45 (2):151–61.
Loomba, Ania (2005) *Colonialism/Postcolonialism*, 2nd edn London and New York: Routledge.
Lubow, Arthur ([2002] 2007) 'Crossing Boundaries', in *The Emergence of Memory: Conversations with W. G. Sebald*, ed. Lynne Sharon Schwartz, New York: Seven Stories Press: 159–72.
Mabura, Lily G. N. (2008) 'Breaking Gods: An African Postcolonial Gothic Reading of Chimamanda Ngozi Adichie's *Purple Hibiscus* and *Half of a Yellow Sun*', *Research in African Literatures*, 39 (1): 203–22.
MacNeice, Louis (1988) *Selected Poems*, ed. Michael Longley, London: Faber and Faber.
Maja-Pearce, Adewale (1985) 'The Naipauls on Africa: An African View', *Journal of Commonwealth Literature*, 20 (1): 111–15.
Margalit, Avishai (2002) *The Ethics of Memory*, Cambridge, MA: Harvard University Press.
Marks, Shula and Stanley Trapido (1987) *The Politics of Race, Class and Nationalism in Twentieth Century South Africa*, New York: Longmans.

Marx, John (2008) 'Failed-State Fiction', *Contemporary Literature*, XLIX, 4: 597–633.
Mayer, Ruth (2002) *Artificial Africas: Colonial Images in the Times of Globalization*, Hanover and London: University Press of New England.
Mbeki, Thabo (2000), 'Speech at the Launch of the Coat of Arms', Kwaggafontein, 27 April: http://www.info.gov.za/aboutgovt/symbols/coa/index.htm accessed 22 February 2005.
Mbembe, Achille (2001) *On the Postcolony*, Berkeley and Los Angeles, and London: University of California Press.
McLuckie, Craig (1990) *Nigerian Civil War Literature*, New York: Edwin Mellen Press.
Melechi, Antonio (2003) *'Temps Perdu'*, in *Fugitive Minds: On Madness, Sleep and other Twilight Afflictions*, London: Arrow Books: 112–16.
Meredith, Martin (2006) *The State of Africa: A History of Fifty Years of Independence*, London: The Free Press.
Middleton, Peter and Tim Woods, eds (2000) *Literatures of Memory: History, Time and Space in Postwar Writing*, Manchester and New York: Manchester University Press.
Minh-ha, Trinh T. (1989) *Woman, Native, Other: Writing Postcoloniality and Feminism*, Bloomington: Indiana University Press.
Montaigne, Michel de (1588) *Essais*, 'Du repentir', livre 3, chap 2: www.bribes.org/trismegiste/es3ch02.htm accessed 30 December 2009.
Moore-Gilbert, Bart (2009) *Postcolonial Life-Writing: Culture, Politics and Self-Representation*, London and New York: Routledge.
Moran, Shane (2009) *Representing Bushmen: South Africa and the Origin of Language*, Rochester, NY: University of Rochester Press.
Mudimbe, V. Y. ([1994] 2005) *The Idea of Africa*, Oxford: James Currey.
Muller, Adam (2007) 'Notes Towards a Theory of Nostalgia: Childhood and the Evocation of the Past in Two European "Heritage" Films', *New Literary History*, 37: 739–60.
Munton, Alan (1989) *English Fiction of the Second World War*, London: Faber and Faber.
Murray, Stuart (2002) 'Naipaul Among the Critics', *Moving Worlds*, 2 (1): 51–62.
Naipaul, V.S. ([1961] 1969) *A House for Mr. Biswas*, London: Penguin.
———. ([1962] 1985) *The Middle Passage*, Harmondsworth, Middlesex: Penguin.
———. ([1964] 1976) 'Jasmine', in *The Overcrowded Barracoon*, Harmondsworth, Middlesex: Penguin: 24–31.
———. ([1964] 1968) *An Area of Darkness*, Harmondsworth, Middlesex.
———. ([1965] 1976) 'East Indian', in *The Overcrowded Barracoon*, Harmondsworth, Middlesex: Penguin: 32–41.
———. ([1965] 1976) 'Images', in *Critical Perspectives on V. S. Naipaul*, ed. Robert D. Hamner, London: Heinemann: 26–29.
———. (1979) *India: A Wounded Civilization*, Harmondsworth, Middlesex: Penguin.
———. (1985) 'Prologue to an Autobiography', in *Finding the Centre*, Harmondsworth, Middlesex: Penguin Books.
———. (1987) *The Enigma of Arrival: A Novel in Five Sections*, London: Penguin Books.
———. (1990) *India: A Million Mutinies Now*, London: Minerva.
———. (1995) *A Way in the World: A Sequence*, London: Minerva.
———. (2000) *Reading & Writing: A Personal Account*, New York: New York Review of Books.
———. ([2001] 2002) *Half a Life*, London, Picador
———. (2007) *A Writer's People; Ways of Looking and Feeling*, London: Picador.
Nairn, Tom (1997) *The Break-up of Britain: Crises and Neo-Nationalism*, London: New Left Books.

Nalbantian, Suzanne (2003) *Memory in Literature: From Rousseau to Neuroscience*, Houndmills, Basingstoke and New York: Palgrave Macmillan.
Nandy, Ashis (1983) *The Intimate Enemy: Loss and Recovery of Self under Colonialism*, New Delhi: Oxford University Press.
———. (1995) 'History's Forgotten Doubles', *History and Theory*, 34 (2): 44–66.
Narayan, R. K. (1984) *The English Teacher*, Madras: Indian Thought Publications.
Newell, Stephanie (2006) 'Feminism and Women's Writing', *West African Literatures: Ways of Reading*, Oxford: Oxford University Press: 136–58.
Ngugi wa Thiong'o ([1986] 2006) *Decolonising the Mind: The Politics of Language in African Literature*, Oxford, Nairobi, Portsmouth, NH: James Currey/Heinemann.
Nicholl, Charles (1998) *Somebody Else: Arthur Rimbaud in Africa 1880–91*, London: Vintage.
Nietzsche, Friedrich ([1874] 1988) 'On the Advantage and Disadvantage of History for Life', transl. Peter Preuss, Indianapolis: Hackett Publishing.
Nixon, Rob (1992) *London Calling: V. S. Naipaul: Postcolonial Mandarin*, Oxford: Oxford University Press, 1992.
———. (2006) 'A Biafran Story', *New York Times*, 1 October http://www.nytimes.com/2006/10/01/books/review/Nixon.t.html accessed 20 September 2009.
Nkosi, Lewis ([2001] 2005) 'The Republic of Letters After the Mandela Republic', in *Still Beating the Drum: Critical Perspectives on Lewis Nkosi*, eds Lindy Stiebel and Liz Gunner, Amsterdam-New York: Rodopi: 311–30.
Nora, Pierre, ed ([1984-1992]) *Les Lieux de Mémoire*, 7 vols., transl. Arthur Goldhammer (1996–98), *Realms of Memory*, New York: Columbia University Press.
Nuttall, Sarah and Carli Coetzee, eds (1998) *Negotiating the Past: The Making of Memory in South Africa*, Cape Town: Oxford University Press.
Olney, James (1998), *Memory and Narrative: The Weave of Life-Writing*, London and Chicago: University of Chicago Press.
Parry, Benita ([1987] 2006) 'Problems in Current Theories of Colonial Discourse', in *The Post-Colonial Studies Reader*, 2nd edn, eds Bill Ashcroft, Gareth Griffiths, and Helen Tiffin, London and New York: Routledge: 44–50.
Paton, Alan ([1948] 2000) *Cry the Beloved Country; A Story of Comfort in Desolation*, London: Penguin.
Patt, Lise, ed. (2007) *Searching for Sebald: Photography after W. G. Sebald*, Los Angeles: Institute of Cultural Inquiry.
Pollack, Sydney (1985) *Out of Africa*, film, Universal Pictures.
Punter, David (2000) *Postcolonial Imaginings: Fictions of a New World Order*, Edinburgh: Edinburgh University Press.
Quayson, Ato (1994) 'Realism, Criticism and the Disguises of Both: A Reading of Chinua Achebe's *Things Fall Apart*', *Research in African Literatures*, 25 (4):117–36.
Ranger, Terence ([1983] 1992) 'The Invention of Tradition in Colonial Africa', in *The Invention of Tradition*, eds E. J. Hobsbawm and T. Ranger, Cambridge: Cambridge University Press: 211–62.
———. (1996) '"Great Spaces Washed with Sun": The Matopos and Uluru compared', in *Text, Theory, Space,* eds Kate Darian-Smith, Liz Gunner, and Sarah Nuttall, London and New York: Routledge: 157–71.
Reisz, Edgar (1984, 1992, 2004) scriptwriter and director, *Heimat*, film and TV trilogy: *Eine Deutsche Chronik, Chronik einer Jugend, Chronik einer Zeitenwende*, DVD.
Ritivoi, Andreea Deciu (2002) *Yesterday's Self: Nostalgia and the Immigrant Identity*, Lanham, MD, and Oxford: Rowman and Littlefield.
Rose, Steven (2003), *The Making of Memory: From Molecules to Mind*, rev. edn, London: Vintage.
Rosen, George (1975) 'Nostalgia: A "Forgotten" Psychological Disorder', *Psychological Medicine*, 5: 340–54.

Rossington, Michael and Anne Whitehead, eds (2007) *Theories of Memory: A Reader*, Edinburgh: Edinburgh University Press.
Rousseau, Jean-Jacques ([1782–89] 2000) *Confessions*, transl. Angela Scholar, ed. Patrick Coleman. Oxford: Oxford University Press.
Rousseau, Leon (1999) *The Dark Stream: The Story of Eugène Marais*, Johannesburg: Jonathan Ball.
Rubinstein, Roberta (2001) *Home Matters: Longing and Belonging, Nostalgia and Mourning in Women's Fiction*, New York: Palgrave.
Rushdie, Salman ([1982] 1991) 'Imaginary Homelands', in *Imaginary Homelands*, London: Granta Books: 9–21.
———. (1987) 'A Sad Pastoral: *The Enigma of Arrival* by V. S. Naipaul', *Guardian*, 13 March www.guardian.co.uk/books/1987/mar/13/fiction.vsnaipaul accessed 10 July 2009.
Sacks, Oliver (1986) 'A Matter of Identity', in *The Man Who Mistook His Wife For A Hat*, London: Picador: 103–10.
Sage, Lorna (1983) *Doris Lessing*, London and New York: Methuen.
Sahgal, Nayantarah (1992) 'The Schizophrenic Imagination', in *From Commonwealth to Post-Colonial*, ed. Anna Rutherford, Coventry: Dangaroo Press: 30–36.
Said, Edward W. ([1978] 1995) *Orientalism: Western Conceptions of the Orient*, new edn, with an Afterword.
———. (1994) *Culture and Imperialism*, London: Vintage.
———. (1999) *Out of Place: A Memoir*, London: Granta Books.
Sanders, Mark (2002) *Complicities: The Intellectual and Apartheid*, Durham and London: Duke University Press.
Schipper, Mineke (1987) 'Mother Africa on a Pedestal: The Male Heritage in African Literature and Criticism', in *Women in African Literature Today*, eds Eldred Jones and others, London: James Currey: 35–54.
Schlant, Ernestine (1999) *The Language of Silence: West German Literature and the Holocaust*, London: Routledge.
Schlink, Bernhard ([1997] 2000) *The Reader*, transl. Carol Brown Janeway, London: Phoenix.
Schreiner, Olive ([1883] 1992) *The Story of an African Farm*, ed. J. Bristow, Oxford: World Classics.
Sebald, W. G. ([1982] 2005) 'Between History and Natural History', in *Campo Santo*, London: Hamish Hamilton: 68–101.
———. ([1990] 2002) *Vertigo*, 1990, transl. Michael Hulse, London: Vintage.
———. ([1993] 2002) *The Emigrants*, transl. Michael Hulse, London: Vintage.
———. ([1995] 1999) *The Rings of Saturn*, transl. Michael Hulse, London: The Harvill Press.
———. (2001) *Austerlitz*, transl. Anthea Bell, London: Hamish Hamilton.
———. (2001) 'Recovered Memories' (interview with Maya Jaggi), *Guardian*, 22 September http://www.guardian.co.uk/books/2001/sep/22/artsandhumanities/ accessed 31 July 2009.
———. (2001) 'The Last Word' (interview with Maya Jaggi), *Guardian G2*, 21 December: 4.
Serote, Mongane Wally (2004) *History is the Home Address*, Roggebaai, Cape: Kwela Books.
Skotnes, Pippa (2007) 'The Legacy of Bleek and Lloyd', in *The Archive of Wilhelm Bleek and Lucy Lloyd: Claim to the Country*, ed. Pippa Skotnes, Athens, OH, Auckland Park, South Africa: Ohio University Press and Jacana Media, 2007.
Smith, Kimberly K. (2000) 'Mere Nostalgia: Notes on a Progressive Paratheory', *Rhetoric & Public Affairs*, 3 (4).
Soby, James Thrall (1966) *Giorgio de Chirico*, reprint edn New York: Museum of Modern Art.

Soyinka, Wole ([1978] 2000) *Myth, Literature and the African World*, Cambridge: Cambridge University Press.

———. (2004) *The Climate of Fear: The Reith Lectures 2004*, London: Profile Books.

Sparks, Allister (1990) *The Mind of South Africa*, London, Heinemann.

Spielberg, Steven, director (1987) *Empire of the Sun*, film, Tom Stoppard scriptwriter, film distr. Warner Brothers, DVD.

Starobinski, Jean (1966) 'The Idea of Nostalgia', transl. William S. Kemp, *Diogenes*, 54: 81–103.

Steiner, George ([1959]1979) 'The Hollow Miracle', in *Language and Silence: Essays 1958–1966*, Harmondsworth, Middlesex: Peregrine Books: 136–51.

———. ([1974] 1997) *Nostalgia for the Absolute*, Concord, Ontario: House of Anansi Press.

Steinmetz, George (2007) *The Devil's Handwriting: Precoloniality and the German Colonial State in Qingdao, Samoa, and Southwest Africa*, Chicago and London: University of Chicago Press.

Stephenson, Gregory (1991) *Out of the Night and Into the Dream: A Thematic Study of the Fiction of J. G. Ballard*, New York: Greenwood Press.

Stewart, Susan (1996) *On Longing: Narratives of the Miniature, the Gigantic, the Souvenir, the Collection*, Durham, NC: Duke University Press.

Su, John J. (2005) *Ethics and Nostalgia in the Contemporary Novel*, Cambridge: Cambridge University Press.

Tannock, Stuart (1995) 'Nostalgia Critique', *Cultural Studies*, 9 (3): 453–64.

Tarkovsky Andrey (1987), *Sculpting in Time; Reflections on the Cinema*, transl. Kitty Hunter-Blair, Austin: University of Texas Press.

Terdiman, Richard (1993) *Present Past: Modernity and the Memory Crisis*, Ithaca, NY, and London: Cornell University Press.

Thorpe, Michael (1978) *Doris Lessing's Africa*, London: Evans Brothers Limited.

Thompson, Leonard (2001) *A History of South Africa*, 3rd edn, New Haven and London: Yale University Press.

Thurman, Judith (1982) *Isak Dinesen: The Life of a Storyteller*, New York: St Martin's Press.

Thorpe, Michael (1978) *Doris Lessing's Africa*, London: Evans Brothers Limited.

Todorov, Tzvetan (2005) *Hope and Memory: Reflections on the Twentieth Century*, transl. David Bellos, London: Atlantic Books.

van der Post, Laurens ([1958] 2004) *The Lost World of the Kalahari*, London: Vintage.

Viswanathan, Gauri (1989) *Masks of Conquest: Literary Study and British Rule in India*, New York: Columbia University Press.

Walcott, Derek ([1974] 1998) 'The Muse of History', in *What the Twilight Says: Essays*, London: Faber and Faber: 36–64.

———. (1990) *Collected Poems: 1948–1984*, New York: The Noonday Press.

Walder, Dennis (1993) 'V. S. Naipaul and the Postcolonial Order', in *Recasting the World: Writing after Colonialism*, ed. Jonathan White, Baltimore and London: Johns Hopkins University Press: 111–14.

———. (1998) *Post-colonial Literatures in English: History, Language, Theory*, Oxford: Basil Blackwell.

———. (2003) 'Memory Plays', in *Athol Fugard*, Tavistock, Devon: Northcote House, Writers and Their Work Series: 79–97.

———. (2003) 'Literature, Memory and Nation', in *War, Culture and Memory*, ed Clive Emsley, Milton Keynes: The Open University: 69–102.

Watson, Alan (1994) *The Germans: Who Are They Now?*, London: Mandarin.

Watson, Stephen (1990) 'A Version of Melancholy', in *Selected Essays 1980–1990*, Cape Town: The Carrefour Press.

———. (1991) *Return of the Moon: Versions of the /Xam*, Cape Town: The Carrefour Press.
Watt, Ian (1980) *Conrad in the Nineteenth Century*, London: Chatto & Windus.
Wenzel, Jennifer (2006) 'Remembering the Past's Future: Anti-imperialist Nostalgia and Some Versions of the Third World', *Cultural Critique*, 62 (Winter): 1–32.
Wessels, Michael (2007) 'Antjie Krog, Stephen Watson and the Metaphysics of Presence', *Current Writing*, 19 (2): 24–28.
Whitehead, Anne (2009) *Memory*, London and New York: Routledge.
Wickham, C. J. (1999) *Constructing Heimat in Postwar Germany*, Lewiston, NY: The Edwin Mellen Press.
Wicomb, Zoë (2006) *Playing in the Light*, New York: The New Press.
Wilentz, Gay (1992) *Binding Cultures: Black Women Writers in Africa and the Diaspora*, Bloomington: Indiana University Press.
Williams, Raymond (1975) *The Country and the City*, London: Paladin.
Wilmsen, Edwin (1989) *Land Filled with Flies: A Political Economy of the Kalahari*, Chicago: Chicago University Press.
———. (1995) 'Primitive Politics in Sanctified Landscapes: The Ethnographic Fictions of Laurens van der Post', *Journal of Southern African Studies*, 21: 201–23.
———. (2009) 'To se Ourselves as We Need to See Us: Ethnography's Primitive Turn in the Early Cold War Years', with commentaries and responses, Joost Fontein, ed., *Critical African Studies*, Issue 1, June 2009: 1–76: http://www.criticalafricanstudies.ed.ac.uk/index.php/cas/issue/view/3 accessed 1 November 2009.
Winder, Robert (2005) *Bloody Foreigners: The Story of Immigration to Britain*, London: Abacus.
Winter, Jay ([1995] 2000) *Sites of Memory, Sites of Mourning: The Great War in European Cultural History*, Cambridge: Cambridge University Press.
Wood, Michael (1977) 'You Can't Go Home Again', in *Arts in Society*, ed. Paul Barker, London: Fontana/Collins: 21–24.
Woods, Tim (2007) *African Pasts: Memory and History in African Literatures*, Manchester and New York: Manchester University Press.
Wright (1965) *Preoccupations in Australian Poetry*, Melbourne: Oxford University Press.
Wylie, Dan (2007) '"Now Strangers Walk in that Place": Antjie Krog, Modernity, and the Making of //Kabbo's Story', *Current Writing*, 19 (2): 49–71.
Yelin, Louise (1998) *From the Margins of Empire: Christina Stead, Doris Lessing, Nadine Gordimer*, New York: Cornell University Press.
Young, Robert J. C. (2003) *Postcolonialism: A Very Short Introduction*, Oxford: Oxford University Press.
Zilcosky, John (2004) 'Sebald's Uncanny Travels', in *W. G. Sebald–A Critical Companion*, eds J. J. Long and Anne Whitehead, Seattle: University of Washington Press: 102–20.

Index

A
Achebe, Chinua: *Things Fall Apart*, 116–118; 120–126
Adichie, Chimamanda Ngozi, 116–138; *Purple Hibiscus*, 120–129; *Half of a Yellow Sun*, 129–135

B
Ballard, J. G. (*Empire of the Sun*), 139–162
Benjamin, Walter: on nostalgia, 10–11
Biafran war. *See* Nigeria
Bleek, Wilhelm: and Bushman oral tradition, 55, 63–69
Blixen, Karen: memory and nostalgia in *Out of Africa*, 85–87
Boym, Svetlana (*The Future of Nostalgia*), 7, 9, 11, 78–79
Bushmen, 47–49, 51–56, 59–71; oral tradition of, 61–70

C
Coetzee, J. M. (*In the Heart of the Country*), 56

D
De Chirico, Giorgio (*The Enigma of Arrival*), 36–39
Derrida, Jacques, 26, 28
Dlamini, Jacob (*Native Nostalgia*), 17

E
empire: in J. G. Ballard, 144, 147; German, 94–99; in Edward Said, 96; in W. G. Sebald, 94–115

H
Hall, Stuart, 13, 14, 24, 26, 34
Heimat. See homeland

history: its interpretation and use in J. G. Ballard's *Empire of the Sun*, 141–150, 153–162
homeland (*Heimat*), 48–52, 56; of Bushmen, 70–71; and colonisation, 51–52; and nationalism, 57–61; in W. G. Sebald, 111–113

I
identity: cultural, 24–46; and identification, 34; and memory, 117–118; and the narrative of homeland, 50; national ~ in southern Africa, 57–61; postcolonial, 24–46; and race, 33–34
irony: in J. G. Ballard's *Empire of the Sun*, 144–150

J
Japan: invasion by ~ of China (1937) and Shanghai (1941), 140–162

K
Krog, Antje: and Bushman oral tradition, 68–69
Kundera, Milan: on nostalgia, 9

L
Lessing, Doris: memory and nostalgia in *The Golden Notebook*, 80–82, *The Grass is Singing*, 83–84, *Mara and Dann*, 75–78, *Martha Quest*, 79–80, 'The Old Chief Mshlanga' 87–91; nostalgia for the absolute in, 91–93; remembering Africa in, 72–93

M
memory, 4–7; and Chimamamba Ngozi Adichie's Nigeria, 116–138; and atrocity, 45–46; and St

Augustine, 42–43; of the Bushmen's past, 69–71; and identity, 117–118; and Doris Lessing's Africa, 72–93; and narrative, 35–46; its nature, 42–43; and Romanticism, 43–44; and Jean-Jacques Rousseau, 44

N

Naipaul, V. S., 24–46; *The Enigma of Arrival*, 24–44; and his father, 39; and India, 39–41; and Trinidad, 42

Narayan, R. K. (*The English Teacher*), 25–27

narrative: and nostalgia, 19, 118–119; and writing about Africa, 118–119

Ne'gritude: and women, 120

Nigeria: the Nigeria-Biafra war of 1967–70, 129–135; and religion in the fiction of Achebe and Asichie, 124–129; remembered in the fiction of Achebe and Adichie, 116–138

Nora, Pierre (*Les Lieux de Memoire*), 5

nostalgia, 1–7, 163–167; and Chimamanda Ngozi Adichie's Nigeria, 116–138; and J. G. Ballard's Shanghai, 142–144; and Bushmen, 63–70; creative ~ and the future, 78–79; definitions of, 7–9; the ethics of, 18–19; and history and politics, 9–12; for homeland, 48–54; and immigration, 29; and Doris Lessing's Africa, 72–93; and narrative, 19; postcolonial, 14–15, 16; of Thomas Pringle, 61–62

P

postcolonial: definition of, 3–4; ~ nostalgia, 14–15, 16

Pringle, Thomas: poetry of, 61–62

Proust, Marcel: on nostalgia and memory, 8–9

R

religion. *See* Nigeria

Rhodesia, Southern. *See* Zimbabwe

Ritivoi, Andreea Deciu (*Yesterday's Self*), 7, 29

Rushdie, Salman (*Midnight's Children*), 12

S

Said, Edward, 15; and empire, 96

Sebald, W. G.: *Austerlitz*, 111–113; and Roger Casement, 109–110; and Joseph Conrad's *Heart of Darkness*, 107–110; *The Emigrants*, 101–104; memory of and nostalgia for empire in, 94–115; and the Nazi Reich, 99; *The Rings of Saturn*, 106–110; *Vertigo*, 104–106

South Africa: and nostalgia, 17

V

Van der Post, Laurens (*Lost World of the Kalahari*), 51–54, 56

Z

Zimbabwe: remembered by Doris Lessing, 72–93